WELLINGTON
THE CROSSING OF THE GAVES
AND THE BATTLE OF ORTHEZ

Higher.—THE GAVE DE PAU AT BERENX, LOOKING DOWN STREAM FROM THE ROAD BRIDGE.

Lower.—THE GAVE DE PAU AND THE OLD BRIDGE OF ORTHEZ, LOOKING DOWN STREAM FROM THE NEW BRIDGE.

Frontispiece

WELLINGTON
The CROSSING of the GAVES and the BATTLE of ORTHEZ

BY

Major-General F. C. BEATSON, C.B.

Author of
"With Wellington in the Pyrenees"

The Naval & Military Press Ltd

Published by

The Naval & Military Press Ltd
Unit 5 Riverside, Brambleside
Bellbrook Industrial Estate
Uckfield, East Sussex
TN22 1QQ England

Tel: +44 (0)1825 749494

www.naval-military-press.com
www.nmarchive.com

In reprinting in facsimile from the original, any imperfections are inevitably reproduced and the quality may fall short of modern type and cartographic standards.

CONTENTS

CHAP.		PAGE
	PREFACE	9
I.	INTRODUCTION	15
II.	WELLINGTON'S POSITION: HIS ADVANTAGES AND SOME OF HIS DIFFICULTIES	32
III.	WELLINGTON'S COMMAND OF THE SPANISH ARMIES. THE TREATY OF VALENÇAY	47
IV.	WELLINGTON'S ARMY: ITS PERSONNEL, BASES AND DEPÔTS, SEA AND LAND TRANSPORT, HOSPITALS AND DISTRIBUTION EARLY IN FEBRUARY, 1814	68
V.	THE FRENCH ARMY: SOULT'S DIFFICULTIES AND THE STATE OF PUBLIC FEELING IN THE SOUTHERN DEPARTMENTS OF FRANCE	83
VI.	MOVEMENTS OF THE FRENCH ARMY DURING THE LATTER PART OF DECEMBER, 1813, AND JANUARY, 1814: DEPARTURE OF THE CAVALRY AND TWO INFANTRY DIVISIONS TO JOIN NAPOLEON, AND THE DISTRIBUTION OF SOULT'S FORCES IMMEDIATELY BEFORE THE CAMPAIGN OPENED	91
VII.	WELLINGTON'S PLANS FOR THE CAMPAIGN	112
VIII.	THE OPENING OF THE CAMPAIGN, 10TH TO 14TH FEBRUARY, 1814	125
IX.	15TH FEBRUARY AND THE FIGHT AT GARRIS	135
X.	16TH AND 17TH FEBRUARY, 1814	146
XI.	18TH FEBRUARY TO 22ND FEBRUARY, 1814	155

CONTENTS

CHAP.		PAGE
XII.	23RD FEBRUARY, ARRANGEMENTS FOR THE CROSSING OF THE GAVE D'OLORON. THE CROSSING OF THE ADOUR COMMENCED. 24TH FEBRUARY, THE CROSSINGS OF THE GAVE D'OLORON AND ADOUR	166
XIII.	ALLIED AND FRENCH MOVEMENTS. THE BRIDGE OVER THE ADOUR COMPLETED	182
XIV.	SOME OBSERVATIONS ON THE OPERATIONS UP TO AND INCLUDING 26TH FEBRUARY, 1814	202
XV.	THE BATTLEFIELD OF ORTHEZ, THE ORDERS AND POSITIONS OF THE OPPOSING FORCES	215
XVI.	BATTLE OF ORTHEZ (CONTINUED)	234
XVII.	SOME OBSERVATIONS ON THE BATTLE OF ORTHEZ	254

APPENDICES

A.	ORDER OF BATTLE OF THE ANGLO-PORTUGUESE ARMY AND OF THE SPANISH TROOPS UNDER THE COMMAND OF FIELD-MARSHAL THE MARQUIS OF WELLINGTON	266
B.	ORDER OF BATTLE OF THE ARMY OF THE PYRENEES AFTER THE DEPARTURE OF THE REINFORCEMENTS SENT TO THE GRANDE ARMÉE IN JANUARY, 1814, AND THE INCLUSION OF ABBÉ'S DIVISION IN THE GARRISON OF BAYONNE	275
C.	TREATY OF VALENÇAY	277
D.	ORDER ISSUED BY SOULT ON THE EVENING OF 26TH FEBRUARY FOR THE OCCUPATION OF A POSITION ABOUT ORTHEZ BY THE ARMY OF THE PYRENEES	278
	INDEX	281

LIST OF ILLUSTRATIONS

The Gave de Pau from the Road Bridge	*Frontispiece*
The Gave de Pau from the New Bridge	

To face page

The Harbour of Passages	74
Looking towards Meharin	134
The Field of Garris	136
The River Saison	150
Hastingues and the Gave de Pau	150
Panorama of the Field of Orthez	216
Looking towards the Roman Camp	220
Looking from the Orthez	220
Looking towards the French Position and the Dax Road	234
The Lac Spur	244
Looking towards Sault de Navailles	250

PREFACE

In this book an attempt is made to show how the greatest of modern British Generals planned and carried out the first stages in the execution of the task set him by his Government, namely, to make a further advance into French territory, and thereby render efficient co-operation to the armies of the other Great Powers then about to invade Northern and Eastern France.

The distance between the two spheres of action was too great to permit the hope of active co-operation between the armies under Wellington and those of Austria, Prussia and Russia. This Wellington recognized, though it does not appear to have been so clearly realized at the headquarters of the allied sovereigns. The co-operation had to be indirect and be worked by preventing Napoleon from calling to himself the large force of veteran soldiers he still had in the south, by pushing back those opposed to the allied armies under Wellington, and so bringing under the latter's control a large and wealthy area of Southern France, thereby lessening the Emperor's prestige and imposing on him the loss of considerable resources in men and money, and opening also a field for action against him by the supporters of the Bourbon party.

WELLINGTON, THE CROSSING OF THE GAVES

When considering the shaping of a plan of action political considerations, finance, the forces available and those of the enemy, the nature of the country about to be operated over, its physical features and its communications, the supply of the army, the weather, the character of the opposing commander, his probable object and the moral of his troops, together with local circumstances at the moment which may tend to aid or hamper the enterprise, have all to be considered. It has been felt necessary, therefore, to consider as briefly as possible all or most of these factors as affecting both sides: so that the reader may have sufficient information of what in the circumstances stood for or against the contending leaders.

On a day like this when our thoughts are full of the heroic deeds performed seven years ago by our soldiers, it is perhaps well also not to forget those of our forbears. In February, 1814, that little Peninsular army, the finest of its day, was in the full flower of its moral, its experience, its steadiness, its marksmanship which its opponents could not bear or challenge, full of confidence in itself and in its leader, wayward sometimes and needing to be held with a tight rein, but never dismayed; it was the prototype of that army, small and termed contemptible, which in August, 1914, slipped away over the sea, saved France and Europe, lost itself but never its glory.

Above it stands the figure of its Great Commander, he who, by his genius for war, his

AND THE BATTLE OF ORTHEZ

loyalty, his steadfast confidence, absolute truthfulness, patience and devotion to duty and his country, had led it for five years through good and evil days from the shores of Portugal across Spain and the Pyrenees and over the frontier of France. "With that little army," says Colonel Charras, the French historian of Waterloo, "he did great things, and that army was his work. He will remain one of the grandest military figures of this (the nineteenth) century."

But it may be said, "What is the use of reading or of soldiers studying operations which took place a hundred and eleven years ago. Science and invention have changed the world since then; the lessons they may teach us will be of no use to-day." But is the statement quite true? Let us see what the great master of modern war says. "Generals in Chief must be guided by their own experience or genius. Tactics, evolutions, the art of the engineer and artilleryman may be learnt in treatises, but that of strategy is only to be acquired by experience and by studying the campaigns of all the great captains. Read again and again the campaigns of Hannibal, Cæsar, Gustavus Adolphus, Turenne, Eugène and Frederick. Model yourself upon them. This is the only way of acquiring the secret of the art of war."[1]

And what says his disciple, the great soldier of to-day, Marshal of France and of England? He

[1] "The Military Maxims of Napoleon."

WELLINGTON, THE CROSSING OF THE GAVES
declares that even after the latest campaigns, though war has at its disposal to-day means more powerful, more numerous and more delicate, the same laws as of old must be obeyed. " Forms evolve, directing principles remain unchanged."

A great teacher and writer to whom the British army and empire owe much, the late Lieutenant-Colonel G. F. R. Henderson, often declared that for British officers the campaigns of Wellington have a special and practical value as regards the application of strategical principles, because he considered the British officer will more often than not be called on to campaign under conditions not unlike those in the Peninsula, such as dependence on sea power, association with allies entailing semi-diplomatic functions and always patience and tact, and sometimes having to improvise adminstrative services with scanty means and inexperienced officials.

But for Colonel Henderson's untimely death we should now have a real military life of Wellington. This is not an attempt in any way to fill the gap: but merely to give an example of how that general applied his strategical skill with a highly perfected machine.

To living authors of works quoted I tender my grateful acknowledgments, especially to the historical section of the French War Ministry for permission to quote from the articles on the campaign in the *Revue d'Histoire* in, 1912-13 now published in book form as " L'Evacuation de l'Espagne et

AND THE BATTLE OF ORTHEZ

L'Invasion dans le Midi," and also to their author, Capitaine Vidal de la Blache, and also to the Colonel and officers of the 15th The King's Hussars for permission to make the extracts taken from the diary of Major, afterwards Lieutenant-General Sir J. Thackwell, G.C.B., given in the history of that regiment, and to its editor and publishers.

F. C. BEATSON.

St George's Day, 1925.

CHAPTER I

INTRODUCTION

THE war in the Peninsula had its origin in the national uprising which followed the attempt of Napoleon, then master of much of Europe, to bring Spain also entirely under his sway, and in the determination of Great Britain in 1808 to aid with money, arms and an army a nation which, deserted by its King, weak in everything pertaining to military strength and held down by a French army, had nevertheless risen to regain its freedom.

Though this war was to have considerable influence on the final result of the struggle of the nations against Napoleon's attempted domination of Europe—he said, it will be remembered, " the Spanish ulcer destroyed me "—for several years its only direct effect was in the fact that it retained in the Peninsula a large number of French troops. Wellington in January, 1812, estimated their strength as " nearer 200,000 than 150,000 men." Thus the operations of the allied army under Wellington were but parts of a local struggle, which aimed at the expulsion of the French troops from the Peninsula, and were in no way connected with efforts made against Napoleon by other nations of the Continent.

Indirect effects there were of course, especially

WELLINGTON, THE CROSSING OF THE GAVES

in the example Spain and Portugal were giving to other oppressed nations, and the strengthening of their confidence in themselves as successes in the Peninsula increased.

It was the victory at Vitoria on the 21st June, 1813, which first brought the operations in the Peninsula into direct relations with those of the allied Russian and Prussian armies against Napoleon in Central Europe.

Defeated by Napoleon at Lutzen and Bautzen in May, 1813, the allied armies had retreated into Silesia followed by the French. Both sides now desired a suspension of hostilities. The allied forces were in some confusion, had suffered heavy losses, their reinforcements still distant, and there was friction between the Russian and Prussian commanders. Napoleon stated his reasons as follows: " I decided for it on two grounds: first, because of my want of cavalry, which prevented me from dealing great blows, and secondly, because of a hostile attitude on the part of Austria." [1]

In Austria, nominally the ally of France, a strong party, which clamoured for her entrance into the war on the side of the Allies, had arisen since the French disaster in Russia. But this was not the policy of Prince Metternich, the chancellor of the Empire. He held that for the present it was to Austria's advantage to remain outside and adopt the rôle of mediator between the combatants. She was the power which in reality held the balance between the fairly equal opposing forces, had her own objects to gain, and was determined to throw

---

[1] Napoleon to Clarke (Minister of War), Neumarkt, 2nd June, 1813.

AND THE BATTLE OF ORTHEZ

in her lot with that side which seemed to offer her the better chance of gaining them. To this end Austria commenced to mobilize and concentrate her troops in Bohemia.

The outcome of the negotiations was that on the 1st June an armistice commencing on the 2nd and lasting till the 20th July, with six days of grace, was concluded at Pläswitz. On the 20th June, after Metternich had had an interview with Napoleon at Dresden, the armistice was extended to the 10th August, and a convention agreed to that a congress should assemble at Prague to settle the terms of a general peace.

Probably none of the Powers were really sincere in their desire for it. Napoleon, knowing the hard terms on which alone he was likely to obtain it, certainly was not. With him, as Emperor of the French, it was all or nothing. It was time they all wanted.

On the morning of the 20th June, the day on which the armistice was extended, Napoleon received the first report of the battle of Vitoria. He did all he could to suppress the news; but effective steps had been taken in London to inform the Powers and make it generally known on the Continent.[1] On the 12th July it reached the allied monarchs at Trachenberg, and its effect was immediate and powerful. "The impression on the Allies," says Sir C. Stewart, the British representative at the headquarters of the Prussian army,

[1] Lord Liverpool to Wellington, 3rd July, 1813. Croker to Wellington: "We are despatching your Gazette in French, Dutch and German to all corners of Europe." In the Archives de Guerre in Paris is a copy which a British cruiser obliged French fishermen off the coast at Fécamp to take on 8th July, 1813.

WELLINGTON, THE CROSSING OF THE GAVES

" was strong and universal, and produced ultimately, in my opinion; the recommencement of hostilities." [1]

After many delays the Congress assembled at Prague. It soon became evident that no agreement would be reached. On the 27th July, Austria secretly joined the Grand Alliance; but the Congress was kept in being by both sides as a cover to gain time for completing their arrangements. Napoleon's reply to an ultimatum sent by Metternich on 7th August was not accepted, and on the 12th August Austria declared war against France. On the same day the Russian and Prussian armies commenced to march from Silesia into Bohemia; on the 15th Blücher, with what remained of the army of Silesia, advanced and drove back the French.

On the 19th October, after the three days' battle at Leipsig, Napoleon, with the remnant of an army, was fleeing towards France. Pushing aside on the 30th October the attempt of Wrede's Bavarian corps to block his road, Napoleon and the French army reached Mayence on the 1st and 2nd November. It was indeed but a remnant, for of the 350,000 men with which he had opened the campaign less than 70,000 re-crossed the Rhine. After arranging for the evacuation of the right bank of the river and settling the distribution of his available troops, Napoleon left Mayence on the

[1] Count Nugent to Wellington, Prague, 27th July, 1813: "The action (Vitoria) is acknowledged by everyone to be the most glorious of the whole twenty years' war; and besides its importance relative to Spain, it is far more so by its influence on the state of affairs here. The account of the state of affairs in Spain and your plans, in short everything you desire me to say, had the greatest effect and contributed very much to the decision of the Austrian Government, and the battle of Vitoria, I think, finished the matter."

AND THE BATTLE OF ORTHEZ

7th November and arrived in Paris on the evening of the 9th.

An immediate and energetic pursuit after the battle of Leipsig would probably have annihilated what remained of Napoleon's army. But the Coalition was incapable of swift action. To two corps of the army of Silesia was entrusted the immediate following of the French. These were able to maintain partial contact and to pick up exhausted stragglers and abandoned *matériel*, but were neither strong enough nor sufficiently mobile to seriously delay the retreating French. Reinforcements were sent to the corps blockading St. Cyr's troops in Dresden. Bernadotte, with such of his troops of the army of the north as had taken part in the battle, moved northwards towards Hamburg, and, after a day of rest, the remainder of the allied forces moved towards the Rhine.

On the 4th November Schwartzenberg's advanced guard reached Frankfort, which became the headquarters of the allied sovereigns. During the next few days the main columns of the Allies reached the Rhine and extended along the right bank from Coblentz southwards to Kehl opposite Strasbourg.

Blücher and Gneisenau, his chief of the staff, were urgent in pressing for an immediate entry into France so that Napoleon should have no time to re-organize his troops, raise reinforcements and complete his defensive measures, and the Tsar Alexander supported them. But the other heads of the Alliance, their Ministers and Generals, were against it, and the allied troops went into winter quarters along the Rhine.

WELLINGTON, THE CROSSING OF THE GAVES

An immediate advance having been ruled out, it remained to be decided how and when it should be made later on. But politics came first. The three allied sovereigns, Austria, Prussia and Russia, with their chief Ministers, were present at Schwartzenberg's headquarters at Frankfort, where Great Britain was also represented by Lords Aberdeen and Cathcart and Sir Charles Stewart. Within a few days of their arrival there, it was decided to re-open negotiations with Napoleon, for which the latter had expressed his desire during the battle of Leipsig by means of a captured Austrian general, but to which no reply had then been sent.

On the 9th November a note from the allied Powers was sent to Napoleon by the hands of St. Aignan, the French Minister at Gotha, who had been taken at Leipsig, containing the terms on which they were willing to open negotiations for peace. Briefly the terms were as follow: France to be restricted to her natural limits—the Rhine, the Alps and the Pyrenees. Spain to be restored to its ancient dynasty, and the independence of Italy and Germany under princes of their native families. After some delays and correspondence Napoleon intimated his readiness to treat, and it was finally settled that a congress should assemble at Chatillon-sur-Seine, which was to be considered neutral territory, as both parties agreed that operations were not to be suspended pending the meeting of the Congress or during its session.

Meanwhile, the allied sovereigns on the 1st December published a declaration detailing the principles on which they were prepared to treat with

AND THE BATTLE OF ORTHEZ

Napoleon and the objects for which they contended. They were, it stated, out to obtain a general peace on a solid foundation: that they made war not on France, but on that general preponderance which Napoleon had long exercised beyond its limits, that they desired a peace, which, by a wise division of power and an equilibrium, might in the future preserve their peoples from the calamities, which for twenty years had oppressed Europe, and that they would not lay down their arms till that result was obtained, and the political state of Europe was secured against vain pretensions.

So far the allied communications with Napoleon and their public declarations had shown at least general agreement on policy. When, however, it came to putting that policy into action by military operations, their different aims and objects at once asserted themselves and old jealousies reappeared.

The Emperor of Austria was reluctant to press matters to extremities against his son-in-law if such could possibly be avoided. Things were going well for Austria in Italy, and compensation for the loss of her Belgian possessions might well be obtained there. She had no interest in the complete overthrow of Napoleon, to continue the war meant further losses of men and money with no certainty of success, and, if it was successful, the gains to Prussia and Russia would far exceed those of Austria. Her influence, therefore, was always on the side of moderation and peace.

The Prussian Generals and the nation were all for extreme measures. Napoleon's insults to Berlin must be avenged at Paris; her lost Rhine

WELLINGTON, THE CROSSING OF THE GAVES

provinces must be regained and Napoleon deposed. King Frederick, naturally timid and unenterprising, was by no means warlike. Owing to their sovereign's moderate attitude, his Generals did not have it all their own way.

At the Russian headquarters there were some who held to continue fighting at such a distance from Russia was likely to bring her little real profit. But the Tsar Alexander, a vain and inconsistent visionary, was eager to advance, was full of personal animosity against Napóleon and, like the Prussians, eager to avenge at Paris his entry into Moscow. Moreover, intending to assert extensive claims to Polish territory when the final settlement came to be made, claims which could not be otherwise than detrimental to the interests of both Prussia and Austria, he considered that the larger he figured in the public eye as the destroyer of Napoleon, the greater would his weight be at the final settlement. An idealist, he was constantly proclaiming his high moral attitude. "He spoke of Holy Alliances and universal peace and kept his eye resolutely fixed on Poland."[1]

For twenty long years Great Britain, often unaided, had fought against French revolutionary and Napoleonic supremacy in Europe. "By her exertions," as said Pitt in his last public speech, "she had saved herself," and now, largely by her example, that great confederation he had worked and hoped for had arisen which was to free Europe from Napoleon, the child of the Revolution. Though the fleets of Britain were supreme in all the seas, though Wellington's victories in

[1] *Blackwood's Magazine*, March, 1919.

AND THE BATTLE OF ORTHEZ

Spain had vastly increased the prestige of her army, it was not on account of her fighting strength that in this confederation Britain stood supreme. It was because she was the paymaster and universal provider of the allied armies. Millions in money and more in arms, munitions, equipment and clothing had been poured into the Continent since the spring of 1813. Without them the Governments of Russia, Prussia, Austria and Sweden could not have equipped the armies, huge for those days, arrayed on the Rhine. Holding as she did the power of the purse, the influence of Great Britain over policy was very great.

What, then, was her policy? Simply stated it was to secure for herself and the peoples of Europe security in the future from the aggressive acts of France which, whether under the revolutionary Government or due to the insatiable ambition of her then ruler, aimed at upsetting the political state of Europe and the making of France the arbitress of the Continent.

Such was the policy of Great Britain, who, for twenty long years, had, often single-handed, maintained a contest with France. Such it had been from the beginning of the war. "If France is really desirous of maintaining peace," wrote Lord Grenville to the envoy of the French Republic in 1793, " let her renounce her views of aggression and aggrandizement and confine herself within her own territories without insulting other Governments, disturbing their tranquillity or violating their rights," and such it remained.

When the British Parliament re-assembled in November, 1813, the speech from the throne ended

WELLINGTON, THE CROSSING OF THE GAVES

with a declaration "that no disposition to require from France sacrifices of any description inconsistent with her honour or just pretensions as a nation will ever be on the part of the Prince Regent or his allies an obstacle to the conclusion of peace." The Prime Minister, Lord Liverpool, thus stated the policy of the Cabinet: "It would be the policy of England to give full security not only to her friends but also to her enemies; and that the Cabinet would not countenance any demand from them which they, in their situation, would not be willing to concede."

As regards terms of peace with France, the British Ministers kept an open mind. On one point only they were resolved; namely, that no peace would be a secure one if the port of Antwerp was allowed to remain in the hands of the French, and they made it a *sine quâ non* that Antwerp should be so disposed of that it did not remain under the influence of France.[1]

The Ministry also decided that Lord Castlereagh, the Secretary of State for Foreign Affairs, should proceed to the headquarters of the allied sovereigns in order that he might give "greater unity to our negotiations with the Allies," and "with full powers and enabled still to act as Secretary of State."[2] He arrived at the allied headquarters at Basle in January, 1814.

Owing to the differences in the views and aspirations, hidden or declared, of the members of the Coalition, it is not surprising that, when they proceeded to form a plan of operations, there were

---
[1] Bathurst to Wellington, 31st December, 1813.
[2] Bathurst to Wellington, 31st December, 1813.

AND THE BATTLE OF ORTHEZ

strong differences of opinion. Blücher and Gneisenau, his chief of the staff, held strongly that the advance of the main armies should be made from the middle Rhine directly on Paris,[1] Bernadotte with the army of the north advancing at the same time into Flanders and Holland. For a time this plan was supported by the Tsar Alexander. Austria, on the other hand, having an eye on Italy, and magnifying the difficulties likely to be met with owing to the French frontier fortresses, if Blücher's plan was adopted, desired that Schwartzenberg's army should cross the upper Rhine, occupy Switzerland, co-operate from thence with the Austrian army in Italy, and then cross the Jura and advance on Paris.

The correspondence of Lord Burghersh, who acted as liaison officer between Schwartzenberg and Wellington, gives a graphic picture of the disagreements, hesitations and delays at the allied headquarters. Writing from Frankfort on 24th November, 1813, he reports that: " Schwartzenberg's army of 170,000 men was marching south to occupy Switzerland with a considerable corps, the remainder to protect the movement and be ready to march against the French army wherever it is assembling.''[2] On the 3rd December, 1814, he says: " I am directed to tell you that it is resolved to carry the whole of Prince Schwartzenberg's army into Switzerland and from thence in the latter days

---

[1] This was also Wellington's view. Writing to Bathurst on 10th January, 1814, he says, " They should have operated from Mayence downwards. The revolution in Holland and the advantages acquired in that country would have turned the left of the enemy for them."

[2] Burghersh to Wellington, Frankfort, 24th November, 1813, and 4th December, 1813.

WELLINGTON, THE CROSSING OF THE GAVES

of January next to make a formal entry into France." On the next day, 4th December: "New plans are to-day in agitation. Schwartzenberg desires me to tell you his whole army will be assembled near Basle in the beginning of January, and that he will immediately enter France, first moving on Belfort, next upon Langres and Dijon." On the 5th December: "Don't think me mad for writing such a letter, but I have seen Schwartzenberg, who tells me he is in the greatest trouble, as the Emperor Alexander is opposed to the entry into Switzerland. For the moment, therefore, all plans are at a standstill. Schwartzenberg will write to you as soon as plans are settled. God knows when that will be. The Emperor Alexander three weeks ago was the most anxious to enter Switzerland. The plan was formed on that basis. He has now tacked round, and God knows what will be undertaken." It is small wonder that Wellington, writing to Bathurst on the 10th January, 1814, should say: "In regard to the operations on the Rhine, I confess that I feel no confidence in anything that is doing." Finally it was decided that Schwartzenberg's army, strength about 116,000, should cross the upper Rhine, occupy Switzerland and advance from there by Belfort and Langres on Paris, whilst Blücher with the army of Silesia, 88,000, should cross about Mannheim and advance to the line of the Moselle and then connect the main armies with the allied corps in Holland.

By the 17th December the army of Bohemia was assembled on the frontier of Switzerland, with Schwartzenberg's headquarters at Freiburg; and that

AND THE BATTLE OF ORTHEZ

of Silesia was extended along the right bank of the Rhine from Mannheim to Coblentz.

On the 21st December the Grand Army crossed the Rhine and entered Switzerland. Its left corps moved on Geneva, which was entered on the 30th of December; from there, after occupying the Simplon and Great St. Bernard passes, so as to cut off communication between Napoleon's forces in France and those in Italy, it moved down the Rhone valley, where it remained in observation of Augerau's corps at Lyons. The main body of the Grand Army, less two reserve corps left in Switzerland, entered France in two groups. The centre of four corps by the gap of Belfort, with objectives, Besançon, which was to be blockaded, Langres and Auxerre, and it was followed by a Russian reserve corps. Of the right group, consisting of three corps, two crossed the Rhine near Basle, and moved northwards through Alsace, leaving detachments to blockade Belfort and Brisac —the objectives of these two corps were Nancy and Langres—the third corps crossed below Strasbourg and moved on Nancy.

Beyond a few skirmishes between advanced troops, the march of the Grand Army was practically unopposed. The army of Silesia crossed the Rhine at Mannheim, near Mayence, and at Coblentz on 1st January, 1814. Blücher left part of one corps to observe the large French garrison in Mayence, and with the remainder pushed on towards the Moselle, the French under Marmont retiring without coming into action. After blockading the Moselle fortresses of Metz, Thionville and Luxemburg, Blücher advanced

WELLINGTON, THE CROSSING OF THE GAVES

into Champagne, opened communications with Schwartzenberg, whose advanced troops were now approaching the line Bar-sur-Aube and Joinville on the Marne, and arrived at St. Dizier on the 25th January, by which date the necessary detachments made had reduced his strength to about 30,000 men.

In the north, Bernadotte had been in no hurry to enter French territory, and remained with the main body of his army in Holstein and about the lower Elbe. Three corps only had been moved in succession towards the Rhine. The first, a Prussian corps under Bulow, whose approach towards Holland in November had been the signal for the national rising, had by the end of the year driven the French troops out of Holland with the exception of the garrisons of Bergen-op-Zoom and Bois le Duc. Bulow had then entered Flanders and in conjunction with Graham's British corps invested Antwerp. Meanwhile Saxe Weimar's corps and part of that of Winzingerode had also entered Flanders. The latter, after taking Liege, moved on Namur, which he occupied on the 25th January.

On this date, therefore, the Coalition armies holding a line running from Antwerp by Namur, St. Dizier, Joinville, Bar-sur-Aube, Dijon to near Lyons, were in occupation of almost one-third of France, gained so far with little loss against slight resistance.

On the 25th January Napoleon left Paris for Chalons, and the real campaign was now about to commence.

Meanwhile, Wellington, having repulsed Soult's

AND THE BATTLE OF ORTHEZ

attempts to relieve San Sebastian and taken the fortress at the end of August, 1813, crossed the River Bidassoa on 7th October and established the left wing of his army in French territory, his right, under Hill, extending along the frontier as far as the heights above Roncevaux, with Mina's Spanish troops more to the eastward in the Iraty valley.

Further than this Wellington did not consider it advisable to go until he had obtained possession of the fortress of Pamplona, then invested by a Spanish force under Don Carlos. Pamplona surrendered on the 31st October. He was now ready to attack Soult's strongly entrenched position extending from in front of St. Jean de Luz, by the Rhune Mountain along the heights through which the River Nivelle flows near Amotz to near Espelette. But a heavy fall of snow in the mountains and heavy rain in the foot-hills prevented the movement of Hill's troops and the attack had to be postponed. By the 9th November, however, Hill's troops were assembled in the Baztan valley, being relieved about Roncevaux by Mina's Spaniards, and the battle of the Nivelle was fought on the following day.

Soult's centre and left being driven from their position, he withdrew his right from St. Jean de Luz and his whole army, with the exception of Foy's division, retreated within the protection of the entrenchments thrown up in front of Bayonne covering the roads from the south.

Wellington had intended to cross the Nive immediately after the battle, but such heavy rain set in on the following day and lasted almost without intermission for a week that he felt obliged to

WELLINGTON, THE CROSSING OF THE GAVES

put the British and Portuguese troops under cover in the villages in front of Bayonne, and to send the Spanish troops with the army behind the Bidassoa into cantonments about Irun and in the Baztan valley.

There was a good deal of rain during the rest of November. Writing to Dumouriez on the 22nd Wellington said: " You will have seen the accounts of our recent affairs here. Since then we have been entirely stopped by the rains and absolutely stuck in the mud (*emboubés*). Moreover, the rivers are full of water. It was a comfort to me to be able to put the army into cantonments, the Spaniards excepted; it is in a better state to make a winter campaign than any army I have ever seen."

With the commencement of December better weather set in, and by the 8th Wellington had completed his preparations for the passage of the Nive, and the river was successfully crossed on the following day. Then commenced Soult's attempts to pierce the allied line from the 10th to 13th, finishing on the latter day by Hill's hard fought and brilliant victory about St. Pierre on the right of the Nive.

After this the weather again became bad; the roads were in a dreadful state and the rivers and streams rose high. Though on this coast, directly open to the rain-bearing winds from the Atlantic and where the normal rainfall varies from 40 to 80 inches, heavy rain was only to be expected at this time of year, yet the winter of 1813-14 appears to have been an exceptionally wet one. Larpent's Diary has constant references to the weather. "Still rain, rain, rain" is often repeated, with

AND THE BATTLE OF ORTHEZ

notices of falls of snow and violent gales. When fine days did come—" a bright sky, a smiling sun and smooth bay "—they were evidently highly appreciated.

In such weather and with his communications in such a state Wellington was not going to move. He doubted both the soundness of the plan of campaign adopted by the allied Powers in the north, and their ability to carry it through successfully. Till they advanced he was not going to move. The Emperor Alexander attempted to bring pressure to bear on him through his ambassador in London and the British Government,[1] but he was not to be moved without a positive order, which he knew his Government was not likely to give him. Writing to Lord Bathurst on 21st December, he said : " I beg you will assure the Russian ambassador that there is nothing I can do with the force under my command to forward the general interests that I will not do. . . . In military operations there are some things which cannot be done; one of these things is to move troops in this country during or immediately after a violent fall of rain. I believe I shall lose many more men than I shall ever replace, by putting any troops in camp in this bad weather; but I should be guilty of a useless waste of men if I were to attempt an operation during the violent falls of rain which we have here." Moreover, Wellington was without what would be an absolute necessity when he advanced, namely sufficient cash to be able to supplement his limited food transport capacity by purchases in the country as he went along.

[1] Bathurst to Wellington, 10th December, 1813.

CHAPTER II

WELLINGTON'S POSITION: HIS ADVANTAGES AND SOME OF HIS DIFFICULTIES

AT this time Wellington was in his forty-fifth year, in good health and at the height of his powers and experience. As a Commander in the field his position was a very strong one. Whilst in the previous years of the war there had been not a few, both in and out of Parliament, who hastened to belittle him as a general, and reckoned him dangerous as a man. Now all was different; the campaign of 1813 and the crowning victory of Vitoria had swept away criticisms. When Parliament met in November, 1813, the only fault the opposition could find with the Government as regards the conduct of the war, was that they had insufficiently supported Wellington with men, money and supplies. The whole nation was for him.

To the Government he was more than merely the general whom they trusted. He had become their adviser; and no one can study his despatches and his private letters to Ministers without remarking how much they seemed to rely on his judgment, and not on purely military and Peninsular affairs alone. Doing so, they left him practically a free hand, and he could write as he did in August, 1813: "For my part, I repeat what I told you before,

WELLINGTON

I shall enter France or not (unless I should be ordered) according to what I think best for my own operations, as I have no reliance whatever on what is being done in the north."[1]

With the allied great Powers his reputation was very high, and he was considered as the General most fitted to be pitted against Napoleon. Indeed, in some respects his position as a Commander can be compared to that of Napoleon. As he himself said to Larpent: "He (Wellington) said the other day that he had great advantages as compared with other generals and he had the confidence of all the allied Powers ... he had several advantages as compared with Bonaparte, in regard to freedom of action and power of risking without being constantly called to account. Bonaparte was free from all inquiry, and that he himself was in fact very much so."[2]

Another great asset was his in the thoroughly satisfactory state of the Anglo-Portuguese army. Writing to Lord Bathurst in November, 1813, he says: "The army was never in such health, heart and condition as at present; and it is probably the most complete machine for its numbers now existing in Europe. ... Hitherto these (the troops) have behaved well, and there appears a new spirit among the officers, which I hope will continue, to keep the troops in order."

There is, however, another side to the picture. Outside the burden of the actual command of forces composed of three nations, the greater part of them in actual contact with the enemy;

[1] Wellington to Bathurst, 14th August, 1813. A remarkable letter giving his views on the European situation.
[2] Larpent's Diary, August, 1813.

WELLINGTON, THE CROSSING OF THE GAVES

Wellington had to shoulder the load of not a few serious and troublesome difficulties. Fortunately most of them were solved or modified before the campaign opened; it seems right, if we are to get a true measure of the man, that some of them at any rate should be stated as briefly as possible.

Want of money. Throughout the campaign in the Peninsula, Wellington, as his despatches testify, had often been hampered owing to lack of specie in his military chest. But now, when he was about to open a fresh campaign in the south of France, his need was critical. The course of the campaign was bound to draw the allied army farther and farther away from its sea bases, and it was inevitable, owing to its limited scale of transport and the inferior conditions of most of the roads, that as much of its supply as possible must be obtained from the country it was operating in. On his entering France, Wellington by proclamation had promised the inhabitants that, if they remained at their usual occupations and took no part in military operations, he would shield them from the evils which ordinarily accompany invasion by a hostile army. To keep this promise, to obtain supplies and to ensure their being forthcoming, an ample supply of ready money was essential.

What his financial position was shortly before the campaign opened, is best stated in his own words: "According to the wish by the Government, I am prepared in every respect, excepting with money, to push the enemy to the Garonne during the winter . . . but I cannot move at all. My posts are already so far distant that the

AND THE BATTLE OF ORTHEZ

transport of the army is daily destroyed in supplying the troops; but there is not a shilling in the military chest to pay for anything the country could afford and our credit is gone in this country ... it is incontestable that the army, its departments and the Portuguese and Spanish armies, are at this moment paralysed for want of money."[1]

The pay of the army was six months in arrears. The Spanish muleteers, who provided the transport of the army, had not been settled up with for twenty-six months. The army was in debt in all parts of Spain and was becoming so in France, and, owing to want of credit, prices were rapidly rising. Writing again on the 21st December he said: "We are overwhelmed with debts, and I can scarcely stir out of my house on account of public creditors waiting to demand payment of what is due to them. I draw your lordship's attention to these facts just to show that Great Britain cannot extend her operations by British troops, or even her pecuniary or other assistance, without starving the service here, unless additional means and exertions should be used to procure what is wanted."

The last paragraph conveys a gentle hint to the Government that the lavish issue of subsidies to allied governments in Northern Europe was not quite playing the game with their own army, their Peninsula allies and their own general, whom they were urging to advance.

The Government had, no doubt, great difficulties in providing specie, which was everywhere scarce

[1] Wellington to Bathurst, 8th January, 1814, and 21st December, 1813.

WELLINGTON, THE CROSSING OF THE GAVES

owing largely to its absorption by the then enormous armies of the Coalition. Wellington's letter of the 21st December seems, however, to have convinced the Ministers that something must be done. They came to the wise decision to send Colonel Bunbury, the Under Secretary for War, to Wellington's headquarters " to explain to him more fully than could be done by letters the extreme difficulty the Government had in complying with his urgent and repeated calls for money, provisions and forage. I was likewise to learn the Duke's views and wishes, and to agree with him if possible regarding the extent of the supplies to be forwarded to his army and the places where they should be landed." [1]

Colonel Bunbury arrived at St. Jean de Luz on 23rd January. Meanwhile Wellington's letter of 8th January had arrived in London, and convinced the Government that immediate action was necessary, and on the 20th Bathurst wrote to Wellington that £400,000 in gold was embarked and was being sent to Passages, also that the Admiralty had issued orders that the ships conveying money from Cadiz and Lisbon should proceed at once to the port of destination.[2]

The *Désirée*, with the £400,000, arrived at Passages on the 3rd February. This sum, with £100,000 which had been previously sent in January, Wellington considered would meet his immediate needs. Later on another remittance of £150,000 in dollars was promised by the end of February with the expectation that a further sum

---

[1] " Memoirs of Sir H. Bunbury," by his son.
[2] Bathurst to Wellington, 20th January, 1814.

AND THE BATTLE OF ORTHEZ

of £200,000 in foreign gold would be sent from Holland. Thus happily the financial crisis was ended, and Wellington informed the Government that the *Désirée* had arrived and "I shall begin to move as soon as we can get up the money."

Inadequate co-operation of the navy. A very serious and constant difficulty was the inadequate co-operation of the navy. Dependent as the army was on sea transport for almost everything it required—reinforcements, munitions, money, clothing and most of its food and forage—it was essential that the transports and store ships conveying them through waters infested by both French and American privateers should have adequate protection.

From the opening of the campaign in 1813, when the need was urgent owing to the establishment of a new base at Santander, to the end of the war, the naval force, allotted to the protection of the sea routes along the western and northern coasts of Spain, was insufficient to safeguard the sea traffic and to suppress the coasting trade between Bordeaux and Bayonne. The consequences were serious enough. In 1813 the transports which had been loaded and were ready to sail on 12th May, were still there on 19th June, and the military stores and provisions Wellington expected to find at Santander had not arrived there on 2nd July. Even while the siege of St. Sebastian was going on the navy was unable to prevent almost daily communication between the garrison and Bayonne. In 1814 some British regiments were almost in rags, owing to the capture of ships with clothing, and Wellington felt justified in humiliating

WELLINGTON, THE CROSSING OF THE GAVES

himself by opening negotiations with Soult for the purchase of British soldiers' clothing captured by a privateer and taken to Santona.[1] The result was that when the campaign opened the army was without the services of five battalions, which had to be marched back to St. Jean de Luz to receive their new clothing.

Under agreement with Portugal that Government had to maintain 30,000 men with the allied army. In February, 1814, that number had fallen to about 22,000. At Lisbon there were some 5,000 trained recruits and recovered men ready to embark to join the army—they could not march across Spain owing to difficulties with the Spanish Government—there were, however, insufficient transports and war vessels to protect the convoys, and these men never joined the army.

It has been shown what straits Wellington was in at this time owing to lack of money. His agents at Cadiz and Gibraltar had money obtained by the sale of Treasury bills; it had to come by sea in British warships because of the difficulties and risks of land transport. Owing to the shortage of vessels or faulty arrangements there were constant delays and uncertainties as to its arrival.

From July, 1813, to January, 1814, Wellington's protests were constant and caustic. All, he said, he required from the navy was the guarantee of free and safe communication along the coasts of Spain from Gibraltar to Passages, and the suppression of the enemy's coast traffic on the French Biscay coast. But his protests were unavailing. The Admiralty pleaded insufficient

[1] Larpent's Diary, 28th January, 1814, p. 373.

AND THE BATTLE OF ORTHEZ

means and the dangers in winter of the Biscay coast. No doubt the war with America, the blockade of the French ports and the operations in the Mediterranean were straining their resources, but, with a navy of over 1,000 vessels, of which 644 were in commission, manned by 140,000 seamen and marines, the plea seems inadequate. Dangers there certainly were, but the mercantile marine transports had to, and did, face them despite many losses, and line of battleships, were not required to deal with American schooner and French chasse-marée privateers.

The Admiralty certainly did not rise to the occasion, but the Government was the real culprit in that taking a narrow view of the situation—maybe it was thinking of side-shows, such as the expedition to Holland—they did not oblige the Admiralty to pay attention to Wellington's reiterated demands for the co-operation of an adequate naval force.

The question of the provisional battalions. This was a matter concerning which there had been for a long time a difference of opinion between Wellington and the Duke of York, the Commander-in-Chief.

It arose from the fact that as the war went on Wellington became more and more loath to part with men who had served in one or more campaigns, and had become acclimatized. He stated his view as follows: " I am of opinion, from long experience, that it is better for the service here to have one soldier or officer, whether of cavalry, or infantry, who has served one or two campaigns, than it is to have two or even three who have not. Not only

WELLINGTON, THE CROSSING OF THE GAVES

the new soldiers can perform no service, but by filling the hospitals they are a burthen to us."[1]

At this time the majority of Line infantry regiments had two battalions, a few had more than two, and there were thirty-three single battalion regiments. The British infantry of Wellington's army was largely composed of 1st battalions, but there were also several second battalions and a few single battalion regiments which had been in the army during nearly all the war. When a 1st battalion became depleted in numbers, the usual practice was for its 2nd battalion to be sent out, and when the fit men of the 1st had been transferred to it, the remainder of the 1st were sent to England. With the original 2nd battalions this practice could not be applied, for their 1st battalion was already abroad, or if at home, in such a state, as for instance after the Walcheren expedition, as not to be fit for active service. These 2nd battalions had therefore to depend for their supply of men on depôts at home, which had also to supply drafts for its 1st battalion. In the then state of recruiting the task was more than the depôt could accomplish, and both battalions of the regiment would be generally under strength. The single battalion regiments were in much the same case. It is not surprising, therefore, that the waste so brought down the fighting strength of both classes of regiments that at length they were no longer efficient units, and on the normal procedure would have been sent home.

But, as has been said, Wellington was most

[1] Wellington to Colonel Torrens, Military Secretary, Frenada, 2nd February, 1813.

AND THE BATTLE OF ORTHEZ

anxious to keep those war-tried and acclimatized soldiers, and determined to repeat a temporary expedient he had adopted in June, 1811, when the surviving officers and men of five regiments which had suffered very heavy losses in the battle of Albuera were formed into one battalion under Colonel Colborne. This battalion was partially broken up as reinforcements became available until it eventually consisted of the 2/31st and 2/66th regiments. In December, 1812, the system took a more permanent form by the formation of four provisional battalions under G.O. 17 of 6th December, 1812.

These battalions were as follows:

1st provisional battalion, 2/31st and 2/66th regiments already existing.

2nd provisional battalion, 2nd Queens and 2/53rd regiments commanded by Lieutenant-Colonel Bingham, 53rd.

3rd provisional battalion, 2/24th and 2/58th regiments commanded by Lieutenant-Colonel Kelly, 24th.

4th provisional battalion, 2/30th and 2/44th regiments commanded by Lieutenant-Colonel Hamilton, 30th.

In May, 1813, the 4th provisional battalion was sent to England; the remaining three served as such till the end of the war.

In forming these battalions all the effective privates with a proper proportion of officers and non-commissioned officers were formed into four new companies; all the remainder were sent home, The battalion staffs of the newly formed battalions were those of the battalion to which their commanding officer belonged.

Before the battalions were formed Wellington had informed the Horse Guards of his intention. The proposal, however, did not meet with the approval of the Commander-in-Chief. H.R.H.'s objections were that such an arrangement would interfere with the general adminstration of the army and would also be detrimental to the *esprit de corps* of the units concerned.

To the Commander-in-Chief's objections, Wellington replied as follows from Frenada, 6th December, 1812: " My reason for adopting this arrangement is that I have for the service in this country the whole number of men of which these provisional battalions are composed, all of whom are seasoned to the service and climate. Experience has shown that they could not be replaced by three times their number brought from England or any other part of the world. However, if your R.H. disapproves of the arrangement, it will be easy to break up these battalions and send the officers and men home on receiving your R.H.'s orders to that effect."

The Commander-in-Chief referred the matter to the Secretary at War, who wrote to Wellington on the subject. He replied he was desirous not to reduce his army in old soldiers for the reasons he had already given to the Duke of York. These letters were the beginning of a long correspondence between Wellington and both the War Departments and the Horse Guards, in which Wellington maintained his position; and made it perfectly clear that he maintained and would maintain

AND THE BATTLE OF ORTHEZ

it, because of the advantage to the army he commanded, until he received orders to abandon it. Writing to Colonel Bunbury, Under Secretary at War, in February, 1813, he said: " I wish on all these points the Secretary of State and the Commander-in-Chief would send me positive orders. I only take a limited view of them, one referable to the convenience of the army under my command, and the benefit of the service in the Peninsula. They must necessarily take a larger view, and I can only say that what they order shall be obeyed *coûte que coûte;* but if they leave matters to my judgment, I shall never do anything which in my judgment may be prejudicial to the service here."

The correspondence went on during the whole of 1813, but no positive orders ever came,[1] and the provisional battalions, except the 4th, survived. The question was not finally settled till after Colonel Bunbury's visit to Wellington's headquarters, when Lord Bathurst wrote to Wellington on 16th February, 1814: " Colonel Bunbury, who arrived yesterday, will settle everything as you wish. With respect to the provisional brigades [*sic*] and the German corps—there was a proposal to remove the German Legion troops also from the Peninsula—this is not the moment for making any alteration."

So Wellington kept his 2,000 good soldiers. But the prolonged correspondence shows that the matter was one which had considerably worried him, seeing that the casualties in action from the battle of Vitoria to the end of 1813 had amounted

[1] On the margin of the Duke of York's last letter on the subject, dated 10th January, 1814, Wellington wrote, " This is just the same. No orders."

WELLINGTON, THE CROSSING OF THE GAVES

to about 26,000 officers and men. To a man of such consistent loyalty to his superiors, it must also have been a constant regret that what he considered his duty prevented him from carrying out the wishes of his titular chief. As regards the Duke of York, there is little doubt he should have obtained a Government decision as soon as the matter was raised and given the orders Wellington asked for or else dropped the matter altogether. With regard to the Duke's fears regarding *esprit de corps*, the objection on examination does not seem as strong as might at first appear. The officers and men served in their own companies, which formed a half battalion. One may imagine, for instance, that at first the Queen's half battalion thought none too highly of their 53rd linked half battalion and *vice versâ*; but it may well be that a healthy emulation was thereby encouraged; and all concerned cannot have been unaffected by the high opinion Wellington had, and expressed, of all the provisional battalions. Writing to Lord Bathurst on 11th August, 1813, he said: " I assure you that some of the best battalions in the army are the provisional battalions. I have lately seen two of these engaged, that formed of 2/24th and 2/58th and that formed from the 2nd Queens and 2/53rd. It is impossible for any troops to behave better."

The Santander incident. About the middle of January, 1814, when Wellington was only waiting for money and finer weather to open his campaign, there arose with the local Spanish authorities another of those irritating difficulties he was often troubled with. The official Spaniard, whether from pride, desire not to be hustled, or because he

AND THE BATTLE OF ORTHEZ

knew his attitude would commend itself to his official superiors, was almost invariably hostile to British interests.[1] That Great Britain had freed his country from French domination never seems to have influenced him at all. In this particular case the consequences which might result from the dispute were very serious.

Owing to the difficulties and dangers of navigation and to the fact that Santander was the only good harbour on the eastern portion of the Biscay coast, all vessels with supplies for the army, whether from England or Portugal, went in the first instance to Santander and waited there for orders and for convoy before proceeding to a port nearer to the army. Santander was also the port where all the supplies for the Spanish troops with Wellington were collected.

Ever since the battle of Vitoria, there had been a depôt and a British hospital at Santander, the latter being housed in huts brought from England. The local authorities had for some time been giving trouble, their object being to get the British out of the town. At their desire a local physician was permitted to pay regular visits to the hospital. In January this Spanish doctor asserted he had discovered in the hospital symptoms of a contagious fever. The British medical officers declared there was no epidemical disorder or any contagion whatever in the hospital. Nevertheless the local sanitary committee placed the hospital and all

---

[1] Wellesley to Wellington, 31st January, 1814: "It may be relied on that if the Regency are permanently in their seats all their employés in the difficult provinces, who seem to have been chosen for their dislike of the English, will think they can safely indulge this adverse disposition against us."

WELLINGTON, THE CROSSING OF THE GAVES

persons connected with it in quarantine, and the civil commissioner of the province of Guipuzcoa—notorious in connection with the San Sebastian libels—issued orders to the ports on the coast that all ships coming from Santander were to be placed in quarantine. The effect of this was, as Wellington said, to place the whole northern coast of Spain and the army in quarantine, cutting it off from its sea bases, which meant the stoppage of supplies, munitions and the rejoining of officers and men discharged from that large hospital, with the eventual result, if maintained, of the retreat of the army into Spain.

Wellington was not going to submit to be hampered by any such action. In a vigorous communication addressed to the British Minister at Madrid,[1] he called on him to obtain the orders of the Spanish Government for the immediate cancelling of these edicts, pointing out what the consequences were of the system under which the Spanish provinces were administered. " Duties of the highest description, military operations, political interests and the salvation of the state are made to depend on the caprice of a few ignorant individuals, who have adopted a measure, at least at present, unnecessary and harsh, without adverting to its objects and consequences, and merely with a view to their personal interests and convenience."

Fortunately the prompt intervention of the Minister secured an order from the Spanish Government quashing the instructions issued by the local authorities before real damage was done.

[1] Wellington to Wellesley, 22nd January, 1814.

CHAPTER III

WELLINGTON'S COMMAND OF THE SPANISH ARMIES. THE TREATY OF VALENÇAY

ANOTHER matter which for some time had caused considerable worry, irritation and trouble to Wellington, was the strained relations existing between himself and the Spanish Government, especially as regards his position as Generalissimo of the Spanish military forces. Indeed when the campaign of 1814 opened, he had already tendered his resignation of the command, and was only acting as such until the Cortes, which had re-assembled at Madrid in January, decided whether or no he was to hold command on the conditions he had insisted on when he assumed it in January, 1813.

The story of the intrigues and cabals against him amongst the members of the Regency and the extraordinary Cortes, which then formed the ruling authority in Spain, and was lodged in the far-off city of Cadiz in the extreme south-west corner of Spain, touches our subject only so far as they affected Wellington personally, and the undoubtedly evil effect they had on the efficiency and good order of the Spanish troops serving under him. Had the Spanish Government worked loyally with him, there can be no doubt that instead of the half-starved, unpaid and undisciplined troops now serving with him, he would have had a useful and reliable auxiliary force. A brief account of his relations with the Spanish Government may, however, be useful in enabling the general situation and Wellington's own point of view to be realized.

Wellington had not been long in command of the British army in the Peninsula when his experiences during the Talavera campaign enlightened him regarding the character of the people he had to deal with. He learnt his lesson, which was that in future any concentrated action with a Spanish army was out of the question, and that whatever was to be done must be done by the British army. "I have fished," he said, "in many troubled waters, but in Spanish waters I will never try again."

In 1811, when approached on the subject of the command of the Spanish forces, Wellington intimated to the Secretary of State that he was not anxious to accept the offer, and the British Government refused permission. When, however, he was again approached in the autumn of 1812, he was more inclined to accept. Though at that time unaware of the failure of Napoleon's Russian campaign, it seemed clear that little reinforcement of the French army in Spain would be possible, and he considered that, if he could incorporate into his army for the campaign of the coming spring some of the best of the Spanish troops, he would be able to take the field on more equal terms with the French than had hitherto been possible.[1]

[1] Wellington to Beresford, 10th December, 1812: "It is obvious we cannot save the Peninsula by military efforts unless we can bring forward the Spaniards in some shape or other, and I want to see how far I can venture to go."

AND THE BATTLE OF ORTHEZ

Therefore, with the sanction of the British Government, he decided to accept. But realizing clearly that the Spanish troops must be under his sole control so far as operations were concerned, and that no loophole must be left whereby the Spanish Government could claim any right to interfere with his plans or his conduct of operations, he, after inquiries and personal observations of the Spanish troops, put certain conditions before their Government, on the acceptance of which alone he would consent to assume the command.

The chief of the conditions were:

First, that officers should be promoted, and should be appointed to commands solely on his recommendation.

Secondly, that he should have the power of removing from these commands such officers as he considered necessary.

Thirdly, that the resources of the State, which are applicable to the payment, the equipment and supply of the troops, should be applied in such manner as he might direct.

(It will be remembered that owing to the lack of any real government in Spain at the time, the funds to meet such charges had to be largely met out of the British annual subsidy to Spain.)

Fourthly, in order to enable him to perform his duties, it was necessary that the Chief of the Staff and a limited number of staff officers should be sent to his headquarters, and that the Government should issue orders that all military reports should be sent to him, and he should send his report to the Spanish Minister of War.

WELLINGTON, THE CROSSING OF THE GAVES

Towards the end of December, 1812, Wellington went to Cadiz; after much discussion there with the Regency and with members of the Cortes, the Spanish Government agreed to accept his conditions. He was so informed on the 1st January, 1813, and a decree of the Regency appointing him to the command was issued on the 7th.

But Wellington soon found that, despite of promises and decrees, the Spanish Government did not mean to honour the engagements entered into with him, as early as February, 1813, a Spanish general was removed from his command, without any reference to his immediate commander or to himself, and also that the officers of the army were not being paid owing to the failure of the Government to carry out the arrangements for the purpose concluded with him under the decree of the 7th January.

After Wellington's departure from Cadiz, the political dissensions in the Cortes became more violent than ever. The Regency, to which the Cortes had delegated the executive power, was afraid and suspicious of the Cortes, the Cortes of the Regency, whilst all the different parties in the Cortes, Servilles, Liberales, Americanos, etc., were afraid of each other, and Regency, Cortes and parties were afraid of the newspapers and the populace of Cadiz, because, as Wellington said, "Solano's ghost was staring them in the face."[1] The result was that on 8th March, 1813, the existing Regency was deposed and a new one set up. It was composed of the Cardinal Bourbon, a member

[1] Wellington to Bathurst, 5th September, 1813. Solano was a member of the Cortes, who had been murdered by the mob of Cadiz.

AND THE BATTLE OF ORTHEZ

of the royal family, an old man, infirm and of little authority, P. Agar and G. Ciscar; both the latter, who had been removed from the Regency for incapacity, were anti-British and therefore anti-Wellington. Carvajal, the War Minister, an "idle and incapable man, but well intentioned and friendly to the English,"[1] was removed from his post and replaced by General J. O'Donoju, a man of Irish extraction and hostile to Wellington.

As might be expected, the new Regency made no change in its dealings with its General; indeed matters went from bad to worse. "The Minister is going just as usual. He sends orders to the troops and so do I, and the consequence is neither are obeyed."[2] How galling this must have been to Wellington can well be imagined. His frequent remonstrances had no effect; and matters came to a crisis in July, 1813, when Wellington, then in pursuit of the French army after Vitoria, was informed by the War Minister that General Castaños, Captain General of Gallicia and commanding the 4th Spanish army, and General Giron, his nephew, then commanding that portion of the 4th army then under Wellington's personal command, had been removed from their commands, the order to Castaños being sent to him direct, and that Generals Lacey and Freyre had been appointed to succeed them. The avowed reason for these changes was the wish of the Government to employ Castaños and Giron in other posts; but the real one was purely political, for the Government feared that, if Castaños remained in Gallicia,

[1] Wellesley to Wellington, 25th April, 1813.
[2] Wellesley to Wellington, 31st March, 1813.

he would not take the necessary measures for the abolition of the Inquisition, of which he, the clergy and the people of that Province were declared opponents.

The appointments of Lacey and Freyre, and the sending of orders to Castaños direct were in contravention of the agreement with Wellington. Moreover the Government, to show its malevolence, refused to give effect to his recommendations for the promotion of certain Spanish officers who had done good service during the Vitoria campaign. Wellington was much hurt; he sent a firm but perfectly courteous letter[1] to the War Minister saying that there were limits to forbearance and submission to injury, and that he felt he had been "most unworthily treated in these transactions by the Spanish Government, even as a gentleman."

The reply of the War Minister brought another factor into the case; for he informed Wellington that the Regency did not consider itself bound by the agreement made with its predecessors, and the matter became further involved, when the British Government, on being informed of the incident, ordered Wellington to suspend the operation of the orders for the removal of Castaños and Giron "until the further pleasure of the Spanish Government is signified thereon." Instructions for a note to be presented to that Government were also sent to the British Minister at Cadiz. Unhappily, in wording their instructions to him, the Government made a mistake, perhaps from ignorance of, or not referring to, the exact terms

[1] Wellington to O'Donoju, Huarte, 2nd July, 1813.

AND THE BATTLE OF ORTHEZ

of the agreement, for the removal of the generals was not a breach of it, whilst the nomination of their successors without reference to Wellington was. Sir Henry Wellesley, resenting the form and substance of O'Donoju's letter, immediately took up the right of the Regency to throw over an engagement made by a former Government.

But Wellington was anxious not to proceed to extremities. He wrote to his brother[1] asking him to explain to the Regency and the Minister his exact reasons for the protest he had made, and also to the Minister[2] in conciliatory terms, explaining that his original letter was written on the grounds of the inexpediency of the removal of the Generals at that particular moment, not as a remonstrance against the act as a breach of the engagement with him; nor did he regard the refusal of the Regency to promote the Vitoria officers in the same light. What he did complain of was the appointments of Lacey and Giron without reference to him, and that the Regency should deny it ever intended to adhere to the agreement, when it authorized the former War Minister to inform him on the 28th March that it accepted it; that he hoped the Minister would now explain the intentions of the Government in language which cannot be misunderstood. He added that he desired to serve the Spanish nation, to whom he was indebted, in every possible way, and would continue to do so at the head of the British and Portuguese armies, whatever the decision of the Regency might be,

---
[1] Wellington to Wellesley, 24th July, 1813.
[2] Wellington to O'Donoju, 7th August, 1813.

and that, if he was obliged to resign the command, he would do so at the time and in the manner most convenient to the Government.

He also wrote to his brother advising a more conciliatory attitude towards the Spanish Government.[1] "These fellows," he said, "are sad vagabonds, but we must have patience with them; the state of Europe, of the world, and of Spain in particular, requires that I should not relinquish the command of the Spanish army, if I can avoid it; nor, considering the general prejudice in Spain against foreigners, can I press them too hard against the wall." He recommended also a softening down of the British Government's instructions, when the Minister presented his note to the Government. It was therefore not presented until the 16th August, after the news of the victory at Sorauren had been received at Cadiz.

The "soft answer" had effect. Wellington's letter apparently gave much satisfaction to the Regency; but no definite reply to his demand for a clear answer was sent. He was informed he had the full confidence of the Government, and was to consider himself as exercising the full powers of a Generalissimo, but without the title. General Giron was permitted to return to the 4th Army; but the removal of Castaños was insisted on.

Why the Regency, anxious as they were to get rid of Wellington, came to such a compromise is not quite clear. Probably the members of it knew of the fact that the majority of the Cortes, whatever sentiments individuals might express, was really anxious that Wellington should retain the

[1] Wellington to Wellesley, 9th August, 1813.

AND THE BATTLE OF ORTHEZ

command[1] lest a military dictator should arise and thrust them all out. The fear of such an event was evidently current in Cadiz at the time, for Dr. Curtis, rector of the Irish College at Salamanca, who was then in Cadiz, writing to Wellington on 7th August, urged his retention of the command as an absolute necessity, not only "to vanquish the enemy, but to prevent the Spanish army becoming a dangerous instrument of one or perhaps both of the contending parties in the Cortes, who seem much more intent on each other's destruction than on procuring the welfare of the nation."

Wellington for the moment accepted the situation without further comment. He was well aware of the danger of which Dr. Curtis warned him, and knew also that it was he alone who stood in the way of such an attempt. As, however, he did not receive the definite answer he had asked for regarding the Government's intentions respecting the agreement, he wrote to the War Minister on the 30th August, giving his reasons why he must insist on its terms being adhered to, and that it was necessary the Government should come to an early and final decision on the subject. "Therefore," he said, "in case the Regency should not think it proper to comply with my request, I beg leave hereby to resign the command of the Spanish armies with which the Regency and the Cortes have honoured me."

To this letter Wellington received no answer

[1] Wellesley to Wellington, 24th July, 1813 : " I still believe every individual in the Cortes is anxious you should retain the command; but they will not separate this question from others in which the parties have opposite interests."

WELLINGTON, THE CROSSING OF THE GAVES

until the end of September, when the Minister of War wrote informing him that the Regency had accepted his resignation, and directed it to be laid before the new Cortes which was about to assemble; also that he was to retain the command until further instructions reached him.[1] Wellington replied[2] he would exercise the command as usual, and not announce his resignation until he received these instructions. He also reported the circumstances of his resignation to the Secretary of State.[3]

Meanwhile, the session of the "extraordinary Cortes" having reversed its previous decision that the newly elected Cortes should assemble at Madrid, on the grounds that "the Kingdom was not at present in such a state of security as would justify the removal of the public authority from Cadiz," closed on the 14th September, 1813. Therefore the members of the new Cortes, except some fifty, who went to Madrid and announced their intention of not proceeding to Cadiz, assembled in the atmosphere, pestiferous in all senses of the word, of that city and opened their session on 1st October. It was immediately decided that the assembly should proceed to Madrid as soon as preparations for their reception could be completed, and that in the meantime, also owing to the quarantine due to yellow fever, they should proceed to the Isle of Leon.

On 4th October the question of Wellington's command of the Spanish armies was put before the Cortes. In the meantime the Minister of War had been busy endeavouring to prejudice the issue by

---

[1] O'Donoju to Wellington, 22nd September, 1813.
[2] Wellington to O'Donoju, 5th October, 1813.
[3] Wellington to Bathurst, 5th October, 1813.

AND THE BATTLE OF ORTHEZ

causing to be published all sorts of calumnies against the British troops, especially as regards their conduct at San Sebastian. In one newspaper, the *Duende de los Cafés*, the editor of which held an appointment under the Minister of War, it was more than insinuated that Wellington himself had issued an order for the sacking of that town.[1] When the Cortes came to consider the question it was found that the Regency had laid before it only part of the correspondence relating to Wellington's command, and it demanded the whole of it, which much annoyed the Minister of War. After appointing a committee to consider all the correspondence, which also examined the Minister of War, it was decided to refer the matter back to the Regency and Council of State, requesting them to explain what in their opinion ought to be done,[2] which action of course meant delaying a decision for some considerable time. It was H. Wellesley's opinion that the decision come to by the committee and the Cortes was due to something said by the Minister of War. "There is something unaccountable in the conduct of the committee on this subject. I never saw anyone more determined than Mexia to bring the question to a satisfactory issue, but certainly something passed at the examination of the Minister of War to induce them to pause."[3]

Wellington, who had received from the War Minister a copy of a report made by the civil commissioner of Guipuzcoa, complaining of the

[1] Wellesley to Wellington, 5th October, 1813.
[2] Wellesley to Castlereagh, Cadiz, 11th Octiber, 1813.
[3] Wellesley to Wellington, Cadiz, 19th October, 1813. Signors Vega and Mexia, two of Wellington's stoutest supporters in the Cortes, both died of yellow fever at the end of October.

conduct of Sir T. Graham and the British troops during the storming of San Sebastian, made a vigorous protest concerning it, and the libel in the Duende, to the British Minister. The latter in a note to the Regency demanded satisfaction for both; but he said, "I shall not get it, but am determined to bring the matter to this point, that the British Government shall decide whether they choose to continue their diplomatic relations upon the present footing, under the certainty that no redress is to be obtained through the Regency for the most gross attacks on our honour and good faith."[1] Wellington, still anxious not to let things come to an open rupture, took a calmer view. Writing to Wellesley he said: "The Cortes have acted in respect to the resignation as they have done in every other subject. The delay is a matter of indifference to me, and things may go on as long as they choose to delay .... we ought to keep them at arm's length to take every opportunity of marking our distaste of their infamous system of rule." He recommended his brother, if he found the new Cortes acted on the same system as the former one, to quit them, travel about and amuse himself, leaving a secretary to transact business after referring everything to him.[2] But Wellington was hurt and annoyed. "I do not know," he said, referring to the libel in the Duende, "how long my temper will last. I was never so much disgusted with anything as with this libel."[3]

The Regency having referred the question of Wellington's tenure of command, in accordance

[1] Wellesley to Wellington, Chiclana, 2nd November, 1813.
[2] Wellington to Wellesley, 23rd October, 1813.
[3] Wellington to Wellesley, 11th October, 1813.

AND THE BATTLE OF ORTHEZ

with the resolution of the Cortes, to the Council of State, the latter replied that nothing would cause greater hurt to the Spanish cause than Wellington's resignation of the command. The Regency, however, were in so little hurry to put this opinion before the Cortes, that those members who were on the side of the British, urged on by the British Minister, determined " to bring the question to such a point as should compel the Regency to maintain the engagements entered into with Lord Wellington, until the extent of his powers could be finally settled at Madrid."[1] The debate commenced on the 28th November. It was at first proposed that the report of a committee of the Cortes, which recommended that the powers conferred on Wellington by his agreement, should be exercised by him only with regard to the forces in provinces immediately upon the frontier. The President refused to accept this, and gave his opinion that the Regency should be informed of the dissatisfaction of the assembly at the conduct of the Minister of War throughout the affair. A member then proposed that, as some time must elapse before the question could be settled, the Regency should be directed to express to Wellington the great satisfaction his conduct had afforded to the Cortes, which relied on his patriotism to continue in the same line of patriotism, the Cortes being determined to adhere scrupulously to the conditions under which he held the command. This motion was warmly debated, but the President adjourned the sitting to the following day.

On the 29th the discussion was continued, and

[1] Wellesley to Castlereagh, November, 1813.

WELLINGTON, THE CROSSING OF THE GAVES

eventually the two following questions were put to the House. First, shall Lord Wellington continue in command of the Spanish armies? Second, shall he continue to exercise the command conformably to the conditions under which he now holds it? The first question was carried unanimously: the second by forty-nine votes to forty-four. It was then decided that a message should be sent to the Regency stating that for the present Wellington should continue to exercise the command according to the conditions agreed on by the former Regency; and that the question should be finally settled at Madrid. The session closed the same day, the opening of the next at Madrid being fixed for 15th January, 1814.

When the session of the Cortes opened there, the Servilles (Conservatives) had a majority in the House. Their first movement was to demand the dismissal of the Minister of War, the head and fount of all the intrigues against Wellington. On the 17th January O'Donoju, "that greatest of all blackguards" as Wellington termed him,[1] was removed from his office. Though the Regency promoted him to Lieutenant-General, his removal was a great satisfaction to Wellington.

The Cortes then proceeded to discuss for some time the status of certain elected deputies, and then came the consideration of the treaty of Valençay, and it was not till after this had been decided that the question of Wellington's command was again raised after all the papers on the subject had been again laid before the Cortes for the information of those members who had not been at Cadiz. During

[1] Wellington to Wellesley, 19th November, 1813.

the final discussion the Minister of State declared that everything relating to the command of the Spanish armies had been settled by the Regency to the complete satisfaction of Lord Wellington—an incorrect statement, though it was known that Wellington's attitude towards the Government and Cortes had been considerably modified by their rejection of the treaty.[1] On this declaration the Serviles dropped the matter, as they had raised the question more with the object of making the treatment of Wellington a pretext for the removal of the Regency than of obtaining a proper settlement. Moreover, all knew that the arrival of King Ferdinand would not be much longer delayed.

So little more was said or done, and Wellington continued to exercise the command as before, until at the end of the campaign all the Spanish troops had re-crossed the French frontier, when on 13th June he formally resigned it by a letter to the King of Spain. In another letter written to King Ferdinand several months later, Wellington thus expounded what had been the basis of his actions during the period of this troublesome controversy duty. He says "we groaned over many of the actions of las Cortes. . . . But it was our duty to submit entirely to the authority of las Cortes; if we had committed the grave fault of opposing them, or of encouraging, or even permitting the opposition of others, we would have increased the evils and difficulties of the moment, and have perhaps caused the loss of that best of all causes,

---

[1] Wellington to Wellesley, 26th January, 1814: "Nothing can be more satisfactory than the whole conduct of the Spanish Government regarding the negotiations for peace."

the cause of the whole of Europe, and with it that of Your Majesty's crown." [1]

The Treaty of Valençay.

When Napoleon on 22nd November, 1813, re-crossed the Rhine with the remnant of a broken army, his chief pre-occupation was how to raise a new one with which to meet the vast allied forces which now menaced France. The conscription could be made to procure large numbers; but they would be men, or rather mostly youths, not soldiers. How was he to give them a backbone in the shape of trained and experienced soldiers? At once his thoughts turned again to his armies in Southern France and in Spain, for he had previously considered the matter. Now, however, it was an urgent one, for "the Rhine was much nearer Paris than were the Pyrenees." To obtain the 100,000 veterans with Soult and Suchet, there was for him only one means possible—the conclusion of a peace with Spain.

How was it to be obtained? If it was done at all, it must be done secretly, so that Wellington and the British should have no inkling of what was in hand. On his part Napoleon had some cards in his hand. He had Ferdinand VII, the deposed King, together with his brother, Don Carlos, and his uncle in his power. They were interned in the château of Valençay, a small town some sixty miles south of Orleans. He had also a large number of Spanish prisoners of war; and hundreds of

[1] Wellington to the King of Spain, Paris, 22nd October, 1814.

AND THE BATTLE OF ORTHEZ

Spaniards, refugees with King Joseph, were living on the bounty of the French Government. All the chief civil and military officers who had recent experience of Spain were agreed that the time was propitious for opening negotiations, owing to the growing mistrust in Spain of the British, and the notorious disagreements between the British General, the British Minister and the Spanish Regency and Cortes.

To keep his hostage in his hand, to negotiate direct with the Spanish Regency in far-off Cadiz was impossible, and any attempt to do so would be certain to become known to the British Minister there and to Wellington. Owing to the urgency of the matter, Caulaincourt pressed Napoleon to send the ex-King at once into Spain; but the latter decided to keep his hostage in his hand for the present, and to open negotiations with him. As his intermediary Napoleon chose the Count La Forest, who had been French Ambassador at Madrid during Joseph Bonaparte's régime.

The Commandant of the château having been duly warned, La Forest arrived at Valençay under an assumed name and had an interview with the Spanish Princes on the 18th November. He delivered to Ferdinand a letter from Napoleon in which the latter stated that the condition of affairs in France led him to desire to put an end to the affairs of Spain, "where England foments anarchy, Jacobinism and the destruction of the monarchy and the aristocracy in order to establish a republic." That the destruction of a nation so close a neighbour to France could not be a matter of indifference to him, and that he therefore desired

WELLINGTON, THE CROSSING OF THE GAVES

to remove any pretext for the present English influence and to re-establish the bonds of friendship which had existed between the two nations for so many years.

Ferdinand replied to Napoleon that he could do nothing without the consent of the Cortes and that the interests of his country obliged him to hold the balance equally between France and England. Though the King and his brother had shown during their interviews with La Forest how deeply interested they were in Napoleon's overtures, this was as far as Ferdinand would go at present, being evidently determined not to commit himself till Napoleon showed his hand more clearly.

The next figure to appear on the scene was the Spanish Duque de San Carlos, a refugee courtier. Summoned to Paris, he had an interview with Napoleon on the 19th November, when the latter informed him that he proposed to restore the Bourbon Monarchy in Spain and to release the 100,000 prisoners of war; but required that the properties of the Spanish refugees should be restored to them. He wished, he said, that Spain should be so strong as not to be obliged to cede any of her extra-territorial possessions to the English. To protect himself San Carlos demanded that these terms should be put in writing, which was done.

Armed with these propositions, San Carlos was directed to proceed immediately to Valençay, and it was understood that if they were accepted by Ferdinand the Duque should himself proceed to Madrid with the aid of Marshal Suchet in order to lay the treaty before the Cortes. He arrived

AND THE BATTLE OF ORTHEZ

at Valençay on the 21st November. After considerable discussion and references to Napoleon, a treaty[1] was signed by both parties on 11th December, 1813.

San Carlos left Valençay the same day with the treaty and a letter from Ferdinand accrediting him to the Regency, but he also carried with him a secret instruction reserving to Ferdinand the right to cancel the treaty and also the rights of other Powers with whom the Regency had concluded engagements. Meanwhile Napoleon had sent orders to Suchet to pass San Carlos to the outposts of " the most moderate of Spanish Generals." He arrived at Barcelona on the 14th December, and during the following night was conducted by Suchet's aide-de-camp to the outposts of the 1st Spanish army commanded by Copons. As a precaution, Napoleon caused San Carlos to be followed by other persons under assumed names carrying copies of the treaty, amongst whom was Palafox, the so-called hero of Zaragoza. These were also passed on by Suchet.

Notwithstanding the privacy with which these negotiations had been carried on, the secret leaked out. The fact that they were in progress was known in Paris and also in Bayonne and Toulouse, as well as the names of those concerned therein.

Henry Wellesley, the Minister with the Spanish Regency, arrived in Madrid on the 31st December, 1813. Early in January, he was able to inform Wellington and the British Government of the arrival there of San Carlos and the purpose of his mission, and later of the full terms of the proposed

[1] See Appendix C.

treaty. The news was not altogether a surprise to Wellington; but it added greatly to his embarrassments.

Would the Cortes ratify the treaty? He could not tell. Writing to Bathurst on the 10th January he said: " I have long suspected that Bonaparte would adopt this expedient; and if he had less pride and more common sense, and could have carried his measure into execution as he ought to have done, it would have succeeded. I am not certain that it will succeed now." To his brother he was rather more explicit: " I have long suspected Bonaparte wished to make peace with Ferdinand. I think that by so doing he would succeed in quieting this frontier and perhaps dividing Spain from England. I am absolutely certain that everyone in Spain desires peace, especially those who wish well to the present Government, and the soldiers more than others. Here the soldiers know more or less what has happened, but they have not said a word to me. French people have frequently warned me that the Spaniards were meditating treachery. To-day I learn from the police that several Spaniards have been sent to Bayonne in order that they may circulate reports against us there. It is desirable the decision of the Cortes should be made known as soon as possible."

It was indeed necessary, for till the matter was decided Wellington could not move a step. If the Spanish Government ratified the treaty, it must in the end mean war with Spain; for as matters then stood in Europe and considering the engagements entered into with its allies, it is inconceivable that the British Government would have withdrawn its

AND THE BATTLE OF ORTHEZ

army from the south of France. If Wellington remained there he would have lost all his mule transport, owned and manned entirely by Spaniards; with but one harbour, and that little more than an exposed open roadstead, he could not abandon his depôts and hospitals at ports on the Spanish coast.

Fortunately, the contingency never arose, for on the 2nd February the Spanish Cortes, basing their decision on a decree of 1st January, 1811, which pronounced that every act taken by Ferdinand VII whilst in captivity was null and void—a decree apparently unknown to or forgotten by Napoleon —refused to ratify the treaty, declaring that the Government of Spain had no intention of withdrawing from the common cause of European independence, or of disturbing by withdrawal the plan of the great Powers to assure it.[1]

[1] Chevalier Gennotte to Prince Metternich, 27th February, 1814.

CHAPTER IV

WELLINGTON'S ARMY: ITS PERSONNEL, BASES AND DEPÔTS, SEA AND LAND TRANSPORT, HOSPITALS AND DISTRIBUTION EARLY IN FEBRUARY, 1814

Personnel

IN Appendix A will be found a detailed statement of the organization and strength of the Anglo-Portuguese army.

Of the British contingent of that army it may be said that, with the exception of Lord Aylmer's brigade, the units of which had only recently joined the army, the officers and men were veterans of several campaigns; stout and strong, for the weaker had fallen by the way, they were full of confidence in themselves and their leader: they felt that given reasonable conditions and fair odds, they could beat the French wherever they met them. They had, in short, that *moral* which is the surest guarantee of success. Said Wellington about this time: "The army was never in such heart, health and condition as at present."[1] He welcomed "a new spirit amongst the officers, which I hope will continue, to keep the troops in order."

[1] Wellington to Bathurst, 23rd November, 1813.

WELLINGTON

The spirit and fighting qualities of the Portuguese troops of the army is one of the many examples of that capacity for organizing and leading men of other nations, of which British officers of former times and of to-day have given such signal proofs. Beginning with Marshal Beresford's appointment in 1809 to organize and command the Portuguese army, it went steadily on from bad to good and to better. In 1811, Simmonds, a pretty good judge, wrote: "The Portuguese deserve every praise, they fight like lions."[1] In 1813 the praise of the Portuguese soldiers was in everyone's mouth. Wellington calls them "the fighting cocks of the army"; and Picton, writing to a friend of the conduct of the Portuguese brigade of his division, said "the Portuguese brigade attached to the 3rd division was the admiration of the whole army."[2]

It was a splendid result. "I believe we owe their merits more to the care we have taken of their pockets and bellies than to the instructions we have given them," was Wellington's opinion as to how it had been attained, thanks, largely, to the example and supervision of the British officers.

There were, at this time, serving in Wellington's army, twenty-one line regiments and eleven caçadore (rifle) battalions. Each line regiment had two battalions, each of six companies. The establishment of a line regiment was 1,501, and of a caçadore battalion 590; but, at this time, both were generally much below these figures.[3] The cavalry regiments were all very weak.

[1] Simmonds' Diary, letter of 26th March, 1811.
[2] Picton to Colonel Pleydell, 1st July, 1813.
[3] The Portuguese line battalions averaged about 430 and the caçadore 350 men.

WELLINGTON, THE CROSSING OF THE GAVES

In each Portuguese unit there were four or five British officers; when a British officer commanded it his second-in-command was a Portuguese and *vice versâ*, and the same rule held with brigade commands. With the exception of the 1st, which had no Portuguese, and the Light division, all the remaining divisions had a Portuguese brigade. In the Light division the Portuguese battalions were divided between its two brigades. There was also a Portuguese division of two brigades, and two independent Portuguese brigades.

In November, 1813, Wellington had some trouble with the Portuguese Government regarding their army. With the ostensible reason that the British Government, Parliament and Press had not made as much as they ought to have of the gallantry and good conduct of the Portuguese troops—though behind this was desire of certain Portuguese notabilities to obtain the command of it—the Regency proposed that their troops should be withdrawn from the British divisions and be formed into a separate corps commanded by a Portuguese General, with Portuguese divisional commanders. Though Wellington considered they had something of a grievance in the matter, and wrote accordingly to the Secretary of State,[1] he was not going to have the existing organization of his army broken up at such a time. So, after some correspondence with the British Minister at Lisbon, the question was brought to a finish by the latter informing the Portuguese Government that he would not pay the British subsidy unless the proposal was withdrawn.

[1] Wellington to Bathurst, 6th December, 1813.

AND THE BATTLE OF ORTHEZ

The Spanish Troops

In sharp contrast to the state of the Portuguese army was that of the Spanish troops serving under Wellington. He said he despaired of the Spaniards "owing to their miserable state."[1] It was not of the personnel he despaired, for in physique they were finer men than the Portuguese—writing to Beresford in December, 1812, he said: "In your life you never saw anything so bad as the Gallicians (4th Army), yet they are the finest body of men and the best movers I ever saw"—but of the totally inadequate manner in which the Spanish Government maintained them in the field. "You know quite well," he wrote to General Freyre, "that you have neither money nor magazines, nor anything you ought to have to maintain an army in the field."[2]

The various parties in the Cortes were too busy over their own squabbles to pay attention to their army. The Regency and the Minister of War were intriguing to get Wellington out of the command, and what money the Government had was wasted or misapplied. Wellington thus summed up the situation in a letter to the Spanish War Minister: "More than half Spain has been cleared of the enemy above a year, the most abundant harvest has been reaped in all parts of the country, millions of money spent by the contending armies are circulating everywhere, yet your armies, however weak, are literally starving. Sir, the fact is notorious that there is no real authority in the country to enforce

---
[1] Wellington to Bathurst, 21st November, 1813.
[2] Wellington to Freyre, 24th December, 1813.

the laws and the due payment of the contributions to the Government."[1]

The officers were the weakest part of the Spanish fighting troops. Generally with "no knowledge of their profession, even that lowest part of it acquired at drill, who have no subordination amongst themselves and never obey an order,"[2] it was impossible for their men to have any confidence in them. Spanish pride would not admit of British officers being employed with their troops, and Wellington, from the first, set his face against it, for he knew that if they were employed they would not receive from their Spanish superiors and the Government that support which alone would enable them to render real service to that army and its government.

The very wet and cold weather which set in after the battle of the Nivelle rendered it necessary to get the troops under cover if their health was to be preserved. Even if there had been room in the restricted area occupied by the Anglo-Portuguese army, Wellington considered it out of the question to canton any number of Spanish troops in French territory: with no money, no food and without proper transport they would be sure to loot and ill-treat the inhabitants, which was just what he wanted to avoid. They could not be left in the open in such weather, he was short of money also, and was always averse to feeding the Spaniards,[3] so back into Spain they must go and be put into houses.

[1] Wellington to O'Donoju, 30th August, 1813.
[2] Wellington to Wellesley, 14th May, 1812.
[3] Wellington to Lord Burghersh, 14th January, 1814: "I was obliged to put the Spanish army into cantonments as soon as I passed the Nivelle. It would have been useless to attempt to keep them in the state in which they were, and I should have lost them all."

AND THE BATTLE OF ORTHEZ

Accordingly, the 4th Army moved beyond the Bidassoa into Irun and other villages in the neighbourhood: the Andalusian division into the villages in the Baztan valley. Morillo's division of the 4th Army alone remained on the allied right in the hills in the border-land between France and Spain. The division plundered freely, and it and its commander were a constant source of trouble to Wellington.

Bases and Depôts

The allied army was bound to the sea; and was able to exist and act because of the maritime superiority of Great Britain. For all its numerous requirements it was dependent on England and Portugal. From Spain it drew nothing but cattle.[1] Till after the battle of Vitoria, depôts formed at ports on the coast of Portugal, especially Lisbon and Oporto, had been the source of the supply of its needs.

When, however, the Ebro had been turned, and the fine port of Santander (San Andero) came into allied possession, fresh depôts were formed there and at other ports to the eastward for the supply of the army. Nevertheless, Napier's well-known simile of Portugal being thrown off "as a heavy tender is thrown off from its towing rope," must not be taken literally; for, of the vast stores accumulated at Lisbon and Oporto, by no means all were transported to the Biscay ports even by the end of the war.

[1] Vidal de la Blache, " L'évacuation de l'Espagne," " Les autorités Espagnols n'avait jamais envoyé une charrette, un mulet, un convoi de grains à l'armée anglaise."

WELLINGTON, THE CROSSING OF THE GAVES

As the army advanced, further ports became available: Bilbao, San Sebastian, Passages, Fuenterrabia and St. Jean de Luz. With the exception of Passages, these harbours were shallow and could only be used by quite small vessels. San Sebastian, Fuenterrabia and St. Jean de Luz were very exposed. Santander was the best of all the harbours. Passages, though small with its entrance narrow and intricate between high cliffs, was a good and sheltered harbour; both it and Santander could take vessels of a size up to that of a 74 gunship.

Great Britain was at war with both France and the United States of America, and the narrow seas and the coasts of Portugal and Spain were infested by privateers of both nations. The sea traffic to the army from both England, Ireland and Portugal required naval protection. This protection of the western coasts of Spain and Portugal was in the hands of the Admiral commanding the squadron based on Lisbon, that of the northern coast by a squadron of the Channel fleet under Commodore Sir George Collier, succeeded later by Rear-Admiral Penrose. Ships from the Mediterranean and Portugal went under convoy to Coruña, whence they were taken on by ships of the north coast squadron to Santander, which was the *rendezvous* for all ships from England or elsewhere. The transports and store ships there awaited orders as to the harbour to which they were to proceed and for convoy. To Passages went generally all ships with troops, horses, money, artillery and ordnance stores. Santander was the depôt for the collection of supplies for the Spanish troops and also for hospital ships.

When we think to-day of transports and store

THE HARBOUR OF PASSAGES.

AND THE BATTLE OF ORTHEZ

vessels, we do so in terms of thousands of tons; it is perhaps well to realize what our forefathers had to work with. In the Wellington despatches in the Record Office there is a return of 117 ships, which sailed from Portugal to the north coast of Spain between 1st June and 17th November, 1813, with horses, corn, forage, ordnance and other supplies for the army. Of the two largest, one was a horse transport of 465 tons and a hospital ship of 450, the smallest a vessel of 84 tons, the general average being about 200 tons.

Owing to the constant delays due to lack of convoy and to road transport, Wellington, as a remedy and also as a measure of economy, proposed to the Secretary of State, that a depôt [1] should be formed at Plymouth or Falmouth, whence he could draw direct from England such supplies and stores as the army required, and that "five or six well-found transports or store vessels not drawing more than 12 feet of water should be attached to this depôt, which could be used to send home such sick and wounded as might be necessary to send to England for recovery." Writing later on 25th July to the Prime Minister on the same subject, he said: "I hope I shall be able to have our principal magazines and hospitals in England; and that the expense of the transport of the army be much reduced." [2] The depôt was formed at Plymouth and ready for work early in October, 1813.

Postal communication with England was maintained by packets, which sailed from Falmouth outwards and from Passages or San Sebastian home-

---

[1] Wellington to Bathurst, 9th July, 1813.
[2] Wellington to Liverpool, 25th July, 1813.

wards once every week. These packets were naval cutters, stout armed vessels of the Revenue cutter type of 100 to 150 tons. The time taken on the voyage varied, of course, with the weather and prevailing wind. Taking an average of the outward voyages and receipt of letters as mentioned in Larpent's diary from August, 1813, to February, 1814, the time from Falmouth to Passages or San Sebastian was generally from eight to ten days, and letters from London ten to twelve days.[1] On special occasions despatches and Government letters were sent by ship of war from Plymouth and Passages.

The Land Transport and Supply of the Army

The land transport of the army was performed by pack mules; there were no carriages with it except those of artillery.[2]

The regimental transport of infantry battalions consisted of thirteen mules for the carriage of tents, surgeons' medical panniers, entrenching tools and paymaster's books—cavalry regiments had fourteen mules. The officers had a bât and ration allowance according to rank for the upkeep of animals for the carriage of their kits.

The general transport of the army was under the Commissary-General, Sir J. T. Kennedy, and con-

[1] A very short passage is recorded in the Autobiography of Lord Seaton, when, as Colonel Colborne, he sailed as a passenger in the corvette *Sparrowhawk* from Plymouth in July, 1813, he says: " We ran up the Bay of Biscay in three days, so in about four days I found myself in active service again."
[2] Wellington to Colonel Bunbury, Under-Secretary of State, 19th September, 1813.

AND THE BATTLE OF ORTHEZ

sisted of hired Spanish muleteers and their mules, the number of the latter being from 13,000 to 14,000. These supplied the British divisions, the cavalry and the artillery; the Portuguese troops not incorporated in the divisions had their own transport and commissariat.

These muleteers deserved well of the army. Wellington termed them "the lever of the commissariat." When in 1810 it was proposed to include them in the conscription for the Spanish army, he protested against their being taken, for, he said, "The army will be reduced to the greatest distress if they should leave us," and that he would be entirely crippled without them. In December, 1813, he wrote to the Minister of War: "The greater number of muleteers with this army have been with us from two to five campaigns. They came voluntarily to be hired, and they stay, not because they are well paid, for I am sorry to say the debt to them is very large, but because their accounts are regularly kept, they are worked with regularity, they are well treated and taken care of, justice is done to them, and they know that the debt due to them, however large, will be paid."

The mule transport was organized in what were termed "brigades"—probably of about 150 mules—within which worked smaller bodies and gangs in charge of leaders selected by the muleteers from themselves. There was one muleteer to every three mules, and the rate of pay was one dollar a day for each mule and the same for each man.[1]

For supply purposes there was a Commissary

[1] The cost of land transport for the year 25th December, 1812, to 24th December, 1813, was £1.050,156. "Supplementary Despatches," Vol. XIV.

WELLINGTON, THE CROSSING OF THE GAVES

attached to each division and an assistant Commissary to each brigade and cavalry regiment. When the campaign opened the supply of the army was mainly from depôts formed at Passages and St. Jean de Luz, which were filled up as required from the sea transport. As many of the sailors belonging to St. Jean de Luz remained there on its occupation by the Allies, or escaped back there, these men and their boats were taken into the pay of the Commissariat, and by them supplies brought by sea to Passages were brought round to St. Jean de Luz, a convenient arrangement owing to the shallowness and exposure of the latter harbour. From these, supplies for such divisions as were suitably placed, were sent by boat up the Nivelle to Ascain, and taken on thence by the mules of the divisions.

The greater part of the slaughter cattle for the army came up on the hoof from Spain, being first collected at a depôt at Palencia on the Duero, about thirty miles north of Valladolid. Though depôts of forage and grain were established along the route to the army, the losses in cattle were immense. Larpent says only about two-thirds of the cattle despatched from Palencia reached the army; they were then, probably, in very poor condition.[1] A small weekly supply came from Ireland, and as the country settled down, cattle began to come in for sale by the inhabitants. When the army moved and got beyond the area which had been eaten up by both French and allied armies, supplies came in, in fair quantities, the commissariat now having ready money with which to pay for them.

[1] Larpent's Diary, pp. 378-79.

AND THE BATTLE OF ORTHEZ

Medical

Wellington was fortunate in having an exceptionally able officer and organizer, Inspector-General Dr. McGrigor,[1] at the head of the medical services of his army—a man in whom he had complete confidence and also personal liking.

Though in January, 1814, there were nearly 17,000 British and Portuguese soldiers in hospital, Wellington, on the 14th of the month, wrote to Sir Henry Wellesley: "I can only say that during the five years I have commanded the army, I have never known it so healthy as it is and has been since the month of May last. There is but little sickness, and the men in hospital are generally wounded. We have had nearly 30,000 wounded upon this frontier since June last, besides the sick which there must be amongst so many men kept in a constant state of exertion."

Taking the numbers of " sick present," i.e., the sick not in general hospitals, but under treatment by the regimental medical officers, the percentage for December, 1813, is for British troops 43 per thousand and for Portuguese 39. But for the very sickly state of the battalions of Aylmer's brigade, which had arrived in the country in the previous autumn, and were largely composed of young soldiers, the British percentage would be less, for one battalion of 630 strong had 451 sick

[1] Afterwards Sir James McGrigor, Bart., K.C.B., Director-General of the Army Medical Department.

WELLINGTON, THE CROSSING OF THE GAVES
and another 368. "All the really sick in the army are recruits."[1]

The establishment of general hospitals had followed the advances of the army. The principal ones were at Santander, Bilbao, Vitoria, Cambo on the Nive, Espelette, Passages and Fuenterrabia. For the most part they were housed in portable wooden buildings sent out from England as recommended by Dr. McGrigor in 1812. In a letter to Wellington in January, 1814, he said: "The movable hospitals have been of the greatest service in this country; we have been able by having these buildings to provide accommodation for sick and wounded, and what is of the greatest consequence to separate and class diseases." At all places where general hospitals were established there were also convalescent depôts, where men discharged from the hospitals were re-equipped and kept till fit to march to rejoin the army.

Distribution of the Anglo-Portuguese army at the Beginning of February, 1814

The strengthening by field works of the allied line in front of Bayonne between the Nive and the sea, the reduction in the strength of Soult's army owing to the despatch or reinforcements to Napoleon, and the changes made by Soult in the distribution of his forces, had caused Wellington to make alterations in the cantonments of the army.

At the beginning of February, 1814, the **distribution** was as follows:

[1] Memorandum for Colonel Bunbury, 2nd February, 1814.

AND THE BATTLE OF ORTHEZ

Between the River Nive and the Sea

    1st division—St. Jean de Luz and Ciboure, with one brigade on outpost duty, which was relieved every fourth day.
    Aylmer's brigade—Bidart.
    5th division—Bassussary Plateau.
    Light division—Arcangues.
    4th division—About Arraunts.
    Vandeleur's cavalry brigade did all the cavalry duties between the Nive and the sea.
    Two Spanish divisions—one at Ascain, the other about Ciboure.

East of the Nive

    2nd division—About Mouguerre and Petit Mouguerre.
    Portuguese division—Briscous, Urcuit, Urt, with one brigade on the heights of La Costa.
    These two divisions, under Sir R. Hill, whilst blockading the eastern portion of the entrenched camp of Bayonne between the Nive and the Adour, had their right extended along the left bank of the Adour, watching the river and obstructing its navigation. They were supported by the
    6th division—About Villefranque.
    7th division—Jatxou and Halsou.
    3rd division—Hasparren and Urcuray, in support of the cavalry.
    Morillo's Spanish division—Louhossoa.

Cavalry

    Since the middle of December the brigades of

WELLINGTON, THE CROSSING OF THE GAVES

Light cavalry, Vivian's, Fane's and the Hussar brigade, had been employed watching the country on the right flank of the infantry divisions on the right of the Nive, each brigade holding a section of the line. At the beginning of February these sections were held as follows:[1] Left, Fane's brigade, line of the Joyeuse from its junction with the Adour near Urt to Hasparren. To observe the country between Hasparren and the Adour in the direction of La Bastide, Bidache and Guiche. This section was under Sir R. Hill, and reported to him direct and was to be supported by his infantry.

Centre, Vivian's brigade. Right, Hussar brigade. These two brigades, were under the immediate command of Sir S. Cotton. They were to observe the country beyond Hasparren and towards St. Jean-Pied-de-Port and St. Palais, the right of the Hussars to be in communication with Morillo at Louhossoa. Their immediate support was the 3rd division about Hasparren. Sir S. Cotton was to report direct to general headquarters and also to Beresford and Hill in cases of any important movements of the enemy.

[1] Arrangements for the cavalry, St. Jean de Luz, 18th December, 1813.

CHAPTER V.

THE FRENCH ARMY: SOULT'S DIFFICULTIES AND THE STATE OF PUBLIC FEELING IN THE SOUTHERN DEPARTMENTS OF FRANCE

A DETAILED statement of the organization and strength of the army of the Pyrenees will be found in Appendix B.

In Spain the French armies had lived on the country; their supplies, their transport, sometimes clothing, boots and money had been requisitioned from the area in which the particular army was.[1] After Vitoria these armies escaped into France with only what they stood up in. Their artillery—only the gun teams were saved—their ammunition, their transport, ambulances and what money they had in the military chest, all fell into the victors' hands.

From this arose a problem which up till then had never been contemplated either by the War Ministry or by the Treasury. It had hitherto been Napoleon's successful practice to make war support war: indeed, he made it do more, for much of the heavy contributions he had levied on his enemy

[1] In a very interesting letter to Baron Constant de Rebeque, Wellington in January, 1812, details the origin and practice of the French requisition system, and gives his reasons for thinking that it was even then on the point of breaking down in Spain.

governments and peoples found its way into the French Treasury. Now there was a French army in France without *matériel* of all sorts necessary for service and with its officers and men clamouring for payment of some of the long arrears of pay due to them.

Such was the state of the army when Soult took over command of it in July, 1813. With his undoubted administrative abilities he was just the man for such a crisis. But the one essential means whereby it could be met was wanting. The French Treasury was practically bankrupt, and but little money was forthcoming. It was only by the patriotic conduct of the merchants of Bayonne, who, forming themselves into a committee, advanced money without interest for current expenses, that Soult was able to equip his army with some of its most urgent necessaries.

After taking over the command, Soult, by drastic measures, succeeded to some extent in restoring the discipline of his army. It is, however, undeniable that the defeat at Vitoria, the retreat from Sorauren and the result of the battle of the Nivelle all had a disastrous effect on its *moral*. The attacks of Wellington, whereby he pushed the French from the Bidassoa, the Nivelle and the Nive, weakened the confidence of the army in its Commander, and dissatisfied with his leadership, amongst both officers and men the question whether Soult should not be replaced by Suchet was frequently discussed.[1] To some extent confidence was restored by the fighting before Bayonne

[1] Baltazar to Minister of War, 28th September, 1813. Baltazar was his A.D.C. detached to the army.

AND THE BATTLE OF ORTHEZ

in December;[1] but it does not seem to have stood the test of the campaign we are about to consider. An agent of the sub-Prefect of Orthez writing from Sauveterre on 18th February, says: "Our troops appear too penetrated with the superiority of the enemy, they have no doubt that his plan of invasion will succeed."[2]

Supplies and their transport was one of Soult's greatest difficulties. He had not only to see that his army was fed, but also that the fortress of Bayonne had its required amount of siege supplies. Without money supplies could not be bought, and without a properly organized transport could not be moved. Therefore the system of requisition had eventually to be put in force to the intense irritation of the cultivators, who complained that notwithstanding increased taxation, not only were their crops taken and paid for in almost valueless paper money, but their men and carts were also taken to carry them away. Moreover, faulty arrangements, bribery and peculation prevented all the supplies obtained reaching the army. All the difficulties were also increased, when in December Wellington crossed the Nive and gained possession of the left bank of the Adour, and was thus able to greatly obstruct the navigation of the Adour, which was the main avenue whereby supplies came into Bayonne owing to lack of land transport and the deterioration of the roads due to heavy traffic and the heavy rain.

---

[1] Vidal de la Blache: "The fighting from 10th to 13th December, though moderately planned, restored the confidence of the soldiers, whom the passive defensive had demoralized."

[2] General Dumas, "Neuf mois de Campagnes à la suite du Maréchal Soult," p. 347.

WELLINGTON, THE CROSSING OF THE GAVES

With all that Soult could do, and he was well backed up by the Prefects of the neighbouring Departments, the army continued to exist, as regards food, in a precarious position from day to day. Without pay and short of food, the soldiers sought to obtain their necessities by pillage, though Soult took the severest measures to stop this—he had an officer, a member of the Legion of Honour, tried by court martial and shot for encouraging his men to plunder houses—even this example he feared would not stop it.[1] Desertion increased, especially amongst the conscripts, and with scanty rations came increased sickness.

The medical services of the army were in a chaotic state, and the condition of the sick and wounded lamentable. Scattered as they were about Bayonne and the other small towns in the district, they were dependent for food and treatment on public charity; for the state could provide no funds even for medicine and necessaries in the hospitals. In Bayonne the hospitals were soon filled, and the overflow had to be taken into private houses. The sight and cries of disabled soldiers imploring charity in the public streets went far to increase that dissatisfaction with the Imperial Government which had sprung up in the south. The men discharged from hospital rarely rejoined the army;[2] they either went off to their homes or else concealed themselves in the large towns such as Bordeaux.

Writing to Count Daru, Ministre Directeur de l'administration de la guerre, on 28th December,

---

[1] Soult to Guerre, Bayonne, 16th December, 1813.
[2] " L'Invasion dans le Midi," p. 86.

AND THE BATTLE OF ORTHEZ

1813, Soult thus states his difficulties and his wants: "The army is in the most deplorable state as regards supplies. There is in Bayonne only bread enough for to-morrow, the issue for the following day will not be a full one, and I fear I shall be obliged to draw on the siege stores for the third day.... All the transport of the army is employed in the carrying of supplies, and the Bayonne committee are also using such vehicles as they can obtain; yet I see myself on the point of being entirely without bread, vegetables, brandy and forage. Meat is issued daily, and it comes in.... Everyone complains of the want of money and means for the various services, for allowances and for pay. We want money for the hospitals, notwithstanding the credits the Commissary General has received, we want it equally for artillery and engineer services and for the staff. This obliges us to make requisitions on the inhabitants which exasperates them. My anxiety is extreme. I beg you to take the necessary measures to extract the army from the precarious position in which it has been during the last six months."

By the end of November, 1813, the defeat of Napoleon at Leipsig and the retreat of the remnant of his army across the Rhine, had become known throughout the south of France. The effect was even greater than that produced by the retreat from Moscow.

Though the war with Spain had gone on for so many years, it had had little direct effect on the majority of the population of those Departments adjacent to the frontier. But now war had been

WELLINGTON, THE CROSSING OF THE GAVES

brought to their very doors. Both the enemy and the French army were in their country. Harassed by forced requisitions for food and transport for the army and to form magazines, exasperated by the severity of the conscription and higher taxes, without reliable news of what was happening and dependent on perpetually circulating rumours, the population of the south was in a restless and often disaffected state. Though longing for peace, they were too much under the spell of the Emperor's power to give any public expression to their feelings. There had always been adherents of the former régime in the south, and naturally such were not slow to take advantage of such opportunities as offered to sow the seeds of opposition to the existing Government in such likely soil. Moreover, the French army, with weakened discipline and accustomed for so many years in Spain to live on the country, was in no mood to change its methods; nor, indeed, had its Chief the necessary financial resources to pay and feed it.

An important point in the local political situation was the increasing confidence of the population in the allied Commander and his army. Before that army entered France, what Wellington feared most was lest the inhabitants of that part of the country, whose "warlike disposition" he knew, should be excited into a guerilla warfare against him, owing to personal ill-treatment and damage to their property by the allied army. Everything, he said later, depended on "our moderation and justice, and upon the good conduct and discipline of our troops." What he required of the

AND THE BATTLE OF ORTHEZ

inhabitants was that "they should remain at their homes and take no part in the war."[1]

Despite incidents after the battle of the Nivelle, which were partly the cause of nearly all the Spanish troops being sent back across the frontier, everything had gone well. The only black spot was in the hill country of the upper Nive, where, owing to no other troops being available, Wellington had been obliged to employ Morillo's and Mina's Spaniards; notwithstanding his remonstrances to these Generals, and the stern measures taken, he could never entirely put a stop to outrages there.

Writing to Dumouriez in November, 1813, Wellington was able to say: " The country is not against us, and the country people do not make war on us. They live quite contentedly with our soldiers in their houses, and their property is respected." Thomas Atkins, gentleman, was playing the game, inventing a language, looking after the children and acting housemaid, as he always does in such circumstances, and so did the Portuguese troops. Those few who did not soon found themselves in the hands of the Provost Marshal and a court martial.

There was no dragooning and no forced requisitions. It was a cardinal feature of Wellington's policy that there should be as little disturbance of the existing system of local government as possible. Those of the magistrates, mayors and local officials who consented to retain their offices were continued in them, provided they pledged themselves to break off all relations with the

[1] Proclamation issued 1st November, 1813.

WELLINGTON, THE CROSSING OF THE GAVES

French Government. Those who refused were dismissed, and the communities concerned were called upon to elect other representatives, who, if approved, were duly confirmed in their offices.

Now Wellington was reaping the fruits of his wise policy, indeed greater than he perhaps expected, for the original design to prevent hostility had brought forth both confidence and goodwill. "It is a curious circumstance," he wrote on 1st January, 1814, "we are the protectors of the property of the inhabitants against the plunder of their own armies; and their cattle, poultry, etc., are driven into our lines for protection."

The fact of the peace and protection afforded to the people of the occupied zone, as well as the opportunities afforded them for the disposal of their produce—which they were quick to make use of at no small profit to themselves—soon became known far beyond its boundaries, and all French administrative effort was unable to modify the effect. The Commandant of the gendarmerie of the Landes reported as follows in November: "I cannot describe the state of apathy of all the inhabitants. If I dare say so, they appear to await the arrival of the enemy with impatience." Vidal de la Blache says: "The growing influence of the English was detaching from the Empire, not only the inhabitants of the occupied country, but also those who awaited their arrival."

CHAPTER VI

MOVEMENTS OF THE FRENCH ARMY DURING THE LATTER PART OF DECEMBER, 1813, AND JANUARY, 1814: DEPARTURE OF THE CAVALRY AND TWO INFANTRY DIVISIONS TO JOIN NAPOLEON, AND THE DISTRIBUTION OF SOULT'S FORCES IMMEDIATELY BEFORE THE CAMPAIGN OPENED

SOULT recognized that the trial of strength in the engagements fought outside Bayonne, commencing with the crossing of the Nive by the allied army on the 9th December and ending with Hill's hard-fought and brilliant action on the 13th, was decisive.

He could no longer hope to make any impression by direct frontal attacks on the allied line. If he kept his army in and about the fortress, starvation stared him in the face, for, now that the Allies held the left bank of the Adour, they had it in their power to stop the water traffic on the river, upon which Soult now mainly relied for food and other supplies for his army, owing to the almost complete collapse of his land transport, due to the breaking up of the roads during the continuous wet weather, their inefficient repair and the heavy traffic during the last six months. Moreover, undue concentration about Bayonne left open to the enemy the districts of Béarn and the Soule for such forage and supplies as they could obtain there, as well as the possibility

WELLINGTON, THE CROSSING OF THE GAVES

of an attempt to pass the Adour within the section they controlled. Soult, therefore, was obliged to spread out his army to guard the river, cover the country and maintain connection with his extreme left on the upper Nive and with St. Jean Pied-de-Port.

Thus were fulfilled the expectations Wellington had when he planned his operation for the crossing of the Nive.[1]

After these events Soult's first steps were to arrange for such protection as was possible for the water traffic on the Adour and also for the maintenance of his connection with Paris's force and St. Jean Pied-de-Port. On the 14th December Foy's division was detached to watch the right bank of the river as far as the mouth of the Bidouze, and a flotilla of gunboats, each armed with a pivot gun and manned by naval ratings from Rochefort, was organized for the protection of the water convoys. On the 16th December Darricau's division with a brigade of light infantry, which had formed part of the broken-up reserve division, was placed under the orders of Lieutenant-General Clausel, who was instructed to place his force about Bidache, and Came on the Bidouze, pushing forward advanced guards to hold Bardos and La Bastide-

---

[1] Wellington to Bathurst, 14th December, 1813 : " It appeared to me, therefore, that the best mode of obliging the enemy either to abandon the position altogether, or at least so to weaken his force in it so as to offer a more favourable opportunity of attacking it, was to pass the Nive and place our right upon the Adour; by which operation the enemy, already distressed for provisions, would lose the communications afforded by that river and would become still more distressed. The passage of the Nive was likewise calculated to give us other advantages; to open to us a communication with the interior of France for intelligence, etc., and enable us to draw some supplies from the country."

AND THE BATTLE OF ORTHEZ

Clairence.[1] Soult also ordered that cuttings should be made in the embankments on the right bank of the Adour and the sluices destroyed so as to flood the meadows. " Pour ôter à l'ennemi l'idée de jeter des ponts sur l'Adour.[2]

Meanwhile the Allies, whose posts extended all along the left bank of the Adour above Bayonne, had on the 16th December driven across the river three companies which Foy had put over to occupy Urt, and later pushed the French off some of the islands in the river which they occupied. The maintenance of the river convoys became more and more difficult, until at length they could only pass " by stealth at night."[3] With such a restricted service the supply of the army at Bayonne was bound to become daily more precarious. Moreover the army cooped up in and about the fortress was of little use. If Soult was to be ready to meet his enemy, who, sooner or later, was bound to advance, his army must be so placed that it had space and opportunity for manœuvre. The existing limited deployment of the French army was good enough as a framework, but it had no strength against a resolute advance.

For such reasons Soult determined to move from Bayonne all but four of his divisions and to place his headquarters at Peyrehorade. In his general order for this movement, dated 20th December, the following were the chief points: General headquarters to Peyrehorade. Foy's division to guard the Adour from Bayonne to

---

[1] Soult to Guerre, Bayonne, 16th and 21st December, 1813.
[2] Soult to Thouvenot, Governor of Bayonne, 16th December, 1813.
[3] Soult to Guerre, 21st December, 1813.

WELLINGTON, THE CROSSING OF THE GAVES

Pitres. Darmagnac's from Pitres inclusive to Porte-de-Lanne. These two divisions to be under the command of D'Erlon with headquarters at Biaudos. Boyer's division to Port-de-Lanne and to be under the direct command of the Commander-in-Chief. The four divisions remaining at Bayonne, Abbé, Taupin, Leval, Maransin, to be under the command of Reille, and to be employed in the defence of the entrenched camps on the Spanish front and on that of Mousserolles, i.e., those to the west and east of the Nive. The Chief Engineer to establish a bridge of boats at Porte-de-Lanne. The Commissary-General to organize transport service from Porte-de-Lanne to Bayonne and to open a depôt at Peyrehorade for the supply of Foy's, Darmagnac's and Boyer's divisions. Thus had proceeded the partial withdrawal of the French field army from Bayonne. For the present Soult did not carry it further. At this time he appears to have been obsessed with the idea that Wellington was about to cross the Adour above and near to Bayonne; and that this would be combined with an assault on the entrenched camp. To meet such an attempt, Soult designed to use Reille's four divisions in a manner which well illustrates one of his weaknesses as a general: the attempt to secure himself at all points, rather than to be ready to take risks in order to meet the enemy where danger threatens most with every available man and gun.

Writing to Reille on the 23rd December, he says: "Yesterday I warned you that the enemy was about to cross the Adour, and directed you, if an attempt was made, to leave three battalions to reinforce the garrison of Bayonne. . . . These

AND THE BATTLE OF ORTHEZ

dispositions completed (details connected with the défence of Bayonne), you will move your four divisions as rapidly as possible to the point attacked, reinforce the other divisions, which will be in action, and drive the enemy over to the left bank again. But your movement should be successive so that whilst the head of your column is in action the rear of it may be in a position to give assistance to the troops in the entrenched camp in the event of their being hard pressed by the enemy when he perceives your movement." [1] Instructions which could not fail to hamper a commander and perhaps render his intervention indecisive.

Soult himself returned in a hurry to Bayonne on the 24th December, bringing with him Boyer's division, which he placed on the plateau of Arrance on the right bank of the Adour about a mile and a half to the east of the town. Clausel was also instructed to press the allied right about Hasparren and to be ready to attack there if the enemy attempted to cross the Adour.

As we know, Wellington had at the moment no intention of crossing anywhere. The continued activity of the British on the left bank of the Adour between Bayonne and Urt, which had caused Soult's fears, had, as its object the better hindrance of the water convoys and especially the expulsion of the French from such islands in the river as they still held.

About this time General Count Harispe[2] arrived

[1] Reille was again reminded of these instructions by Soult on 2nd January, 1814.
[2] Harispe was a Basque by birth, a distinguished soldier, and a large landed proprietor in the Baïgorry valley, where he had much influence. He had been Marshal Suchet's Chief of the Staff in Spain for some years.

WELLINGTON, THE CROSSING OF THE GAVES

at Bayonne, and Soult determined to reconstitute the broken up 8th division under Harispe's command. As finally constituted it was made up of Dature's brigade, Paris's brigade and that of Baurot, together with the national guards of the Basses Pyrénées, then with the army.

On 29th December Soult left Bayonne, returned to Peyrehorade, and reported to the Minister of War[1] that he had directed Clausel to concentrate Darricau's and Harispe's divisions and the two cavalry divisions, each on its outpost line, so as to be ready for any eventuality, and also that he might inspect them, which he proposed to do next day. Also, that he had ordered Taupin's division to move to Peyrehorade and reinforce Clausel. "If," he said, "by these demonstrations I can gain eight more days, I will reinforce this line by three other divisions, because by that time the works of the entrenched camp will be sufficiently advanced to be left to themselves and I shall complete the garrison to 12,000 men. From that moment Bayonne will play its own rôle, and it will be no longer necessary for any part of the army to remain covering it."

On the 31st December, more confident perhaps as the result of his inspections, Soult announced to the Minister[2] that he only awaited the arrival of Treilhard's cavalry division to drive the enemy from the right bank of the Joyeuse " in order to see from a closer position what is passing within his lines." A few days later he proceeds[3] to outline what his future line of action would probably be.

[1] Soult to Guerre, Peyrehorade, 29th December, 1813.
[2] Soult to Guerre, St. Martin, 31st December, 1813.
[3] Soult to Guerre, Bardos, 2nd January, 1814.

AND THE BATTLE OF ORTHEZ

"I have made my dispositions to defend *de vive force* the crossing of the Adour should the enemy attempt it. If he should succeed in forcing a passage, I shall leave a garrison of 12,000 men in Bayonne and transfer the zone of operations to the district between the Nive and the Adour, basing my right on Dax, which I have had put in a state of defence,[1] and my left on the mountains of Baygoura in order to attack the enemy's rear as soon as I shall have the necessary means."

On 2nd January, 1814, the left wing of the French army was distributed as follows: Main body, divisions of Darricau and Taupin, about Bidache and Came, a bridge over the Bidouze having been established at the latter place. Dature's brigade of Harispe's division about Ayherre. Their outposts on the line. Bardos-Serrade, La Bastide-Clairence, Pessarou and the Château de Belsuncia. Treilhard's cavalry division, which found the cavalry of the outposts, about La Chapelle and Pessarou. The remainder of Harispe's division with P. Soult's cavalry division prolonged the line to the south, and occupied Helette and Irissary, on the main road from Bayonne to St. Jean Pied-de-Port.

On the 3rd Soult ordered Clausel to move forward with Darricau and Taupin's divisions and occupy La Bastide-Clairence and the heights on the left bank of the Joyeuse; he was also to press all the enemy's posts along the rest of the line. Clausel advanced with Darricau's division, and occupied La Bastide and the heights of La Costa, turning the

[1] The repairs to the defences at Dax were never completed.

WELLINGTON, THE CROSSING OF THE GAVES

right flank of Buchan's brigade of the Portuguese division and obliging it to retire towards Briscous. One brigade of Taupin's division was in support on the heights of La Chapelle to the east of the village, the other brigade was to the north of it about Bardos watching the Bayonne-Bidache road and towards Urt. Dature's brigade of Harispe's division moved to north-west of Ayherre and Paris' to the north of Helette, facing towards Graciette and Mendionde. Between these two brigades, P. Soult's cavalry division with one infantry battalion advanced to near Bonloc. These advances obliged the British cavalry pickets between the Bidouze and the Joyeuse to retire behind the latter river, and the 3rd division post at Bonloc was attacked.

This move by the French was quite unexpected at allied headquarters. On the morning of the 3rd, Wellington "ordered out his hounds and went off early himself. In the middle of the day, however, the signal was made that the French were in motion.[1] Lord March and Campbell went off to Lord Wellington."[2]

On receipt of the news Wellington immediately ordered the divisions of the right wing and of the

[1] Batty, "Campaign of the Western Pyrenees," "To guard against surprise and to give timely notice to the troops in their cantonments of any attack made by the enemy, telegraphic signal stations were formed at the churches of Guethary, Arcangues and Vieux Moguerre. These communicated with a signal station on a high sand-hill on the north side of St. Jean de Luz, near the entrance to the town. By an ingenious combination of flags and banners suspended from high signal posts, it was found that notice could be almost instantaneously given at headquarters of whatever movement the enemy might undertake. The telegraphic sentences were so arranged that each separate signal would at once explain the nature of the communication it was meant to convey."
[2] Larpent's Diary.

AND THE BATTLE OF ORTHEZ

centre to be concentrated and ready to move, and a succession of reliefs took place along the investment line. The 1st division moved up from St. Jean de Luz and took over the whole of the left of the line, relieving the 5th division and Aylmer's brigade, which moving to their right, relieved the Light division about Arcangues; the latter relieved the 4th at Arraunts, which moved to Ustaritz and later across the Nive. The 6th division was assembled and ready to move by the Bayonne-St. Jean Pied-de-Port road towards Hasparren; the 7th from about Cambo moved towards Urcuray, as did also Morillo's Spanish division from Itsatsou to support the right of the 7th. The cavalry brigades of Fane, Vivian and the Hussars concentrated towards Hasparren under Sir S. Cotton.

Wellington at first was not inclined to take Soult's move very seriously. Writing to Hill at 4.40 p.m. on 3rd January from Ustaritz, he said: "The enemy have not shown many men on our right, so it is probable the whole business is a reconnaissance probably to cover the attack I expected to be made on Mina; but I have not yet heard from that quarter." Having the next day made a personal reconnaissance of the enemy's position, and an ample force, some 25,000 men, being available, he determined to attack on the 5th, for the French in such force on his right flank were too close to be comfortable. Owing, however, to the weather, and the rise in the many streams intersecting the country between the Nive and the Joyeuse, he was obliged to postpone the attack till the 6th.

WELLINGTON, THE CROSSING OF THE GAVES

Accordingly on that day the allied troops advanced, the 3rd division, with Fane's cavalry brigade from Hasparren against the French left, the 4th division against the centre and Buchan's brigade of the Portuguese division against their right, the 6th division being in reserve; whilst in front of Hasparren, Cotton with the 7th division, the Hussar and Vivian's cavalry brigades, observed the French about Ayherre and Bonloc. To cover their right Morillo moved to Urcuray.

Soult's object being, as we have seen, to gain time, he had no intention of fighting a general action against such odds in his present position. He had instructed Clausel that, if his position on the La Costa heights was attacked, such resistance only was to be made as would enable the force holding it to make good its retreat across the Joyeuse; if pressed afterwards, he was to retire, taking up successive positions, towards the Bidouze.

Accordingly, when about 3 p.m. the leading allied troops assailed the heights, the French withdrew by echelons across the river, and the allied advance stopped. Soult anticipated it would be renewed the next day, but Wellington had no intention to go farther, and ordered the return of the troops to their former cantonments, " as the weather has again rendered all operations impossible and the roads are in such a state that it has become scarcely practicable to support the troops at the distance they are from the sea coast."[1] But it can be fairly said that these were not the only reasons; he had his own plans of action ready when circumstances permitted him to

[1] Wellington to Bathurst, 9th January, 1814.

AND THE BATTLE OF ORTHEZ

advance, but was not going to do so till he knew how the Spanish Cortes received the Valençay treaty and until a sufficient supply of money[1] reached him.

Soult must have been astonished at the success gained with such little loss; and, gaining confidence, had already begun to talk of assuming the offensive and recovering the ground already lost.[2] He directed Clausel to remain on the right bank of the Joyeuse, and reinforced him with Foy's division, which was distributed between Bidache, Came, Bardos and Hastingues. Dature's brigade was sent from Ayherre to rejoin Harispe at Helette, and this latter proceeded to operate against Mina, whose troops were driven from Bidarray on the upper Nive and from the Baïgorry valley into the Baztan. Wellington was against reprisals. "It does not appear to me," he wrote to Bathurst, "that the French position at these places will at all affect the positions of the rest of the army, and I think it better to leave them there than to continue a contest with the peasantry."[3]

Soult's manœuvre was completely justified by its results. Anxious lest Wellington should make a move, whilst a considerable part of his force was still tied to Bayonne, Soult wished to immobilize him for a time. His particular fear was lest Wellington, by a crossing above Bayonne, should cut

---

[1] Wellington to Bathurst, 8th January, 1814: "I cannot move at all, my posts are already so far distant that the transport of the army is daily destroyed in supplying the troops; but there is not in the military chest a shilling to pay for anything the country could afford and our credit is already gone."

[2] Soult to Guerre, Peyreborade, 8th January, 1814.

[3] Wellington to Bathurst, 18th January, 1814.

WELLINGTON, THE CROSSING OF THE GAVES

his army in two. "The front is strong, try the flanks" is a safe maxim of war, and the menace to Wellington's right was sufficient to cause him to concentrate at once a force sufficient to deal with the threat, but which left him with a remainder insufficient either to make an attempt on the entrenched camp or a crossing of the river. And the point must be noted that, having regard to relative strength, the threat must be sufficiently powerful, or it will fail to produce the desired effect. The fact that Soult was at this time tied to Bayonne by his own persistent mistake in piling up entrenchments beyond the capacity of the normal garrison of the place to man, does not of course affect the argument.

Now, however, there came a change in the general situation, the effects of which can hardly have been a surprise to Soult. The Allies in the north had moved earlier than Napoleon expected. Schwartzenberg's army had crossed the Rhine on 21st December, Switzerland was invaded and Geneva had capitulated to his left column on the 30th, the main column was in the early days of January well on its way to Langres, whilst Blücher, having crossed the Rhine on the 1st January, was marching towards the Saare, and Bulow had entered Holland. The weak opposing French forces were everywhere in retreat.

More and more soldiers was Napoleon's urgent need. The conscription, despite its partial failure, would give him men, but not trained soldiers. Where could he find them? If he withdrew his armies from Spain and from Bayonne, he could count on at least 100,000 of such troops, as Welling-

AND THE BATTLE OF ORTHEZ

ton said, "the Allies have not yet had to deal with,"[1] and this, as has been already stated, was his purpose in negotiating the treaty of Valençay.

On the 25th December he was so confident that the treaty would be ratified by the Spanish Government that he wrote, "I have arranged matters with the Spaniards, which will render available my armies of Aragon, of Catalonia and of Bayonne. I have still there nearly 200,000 men (a highly exaggerated estimate). Do not print this, it is for yourself alone."[2]

But it was just that treaty he so confidently reckoned on which was going to prevent his getting such reinforcements as might have turned the day for him later on. As has been already stated, the treaty was signed at Valençay on 11th December by the French and Spanish plenipotentiaries, and the latter, the Duke de San Carlos, left with it the same day. He arrived at Barcelona on the 14th, and on the following evening was conducted to the headquarters of General Copons, commanding the 1st Spanish army, from whence he proceeded to Madrid. Other messengers, also carrying copies of the treaty, followed him. For a month and a half Madrid remained silent; but on the 2nd February, 1814, the Cortes refused to ratify the treaty, declaring their intention "not to dissociate themselves from the common cause of the independence of Europe, and not to embarrass by withdrawing from the Alliance, the plans of the Great Powers to ensure it."[3]

[1] Wellington to Bathhurst, St. Jean de Luz, 21st December, 1813.
[2] Napoleon to Duc de Lodi, 25th December, 1813, C.N. 21039.
[3] Gennotte, Austrian representative to Metternich, 27th February, 1814.

WELLINGTON, THE CROSSING OF THE GAVES

As long as negotiations were in progress it was evidently necessary for their success that Napoleon should maintain in the south a sufficient force to contain Wellington and impose on the Spanish Government. Therefore, whilst any hope of success remained, Napoleon, the Emperor, would not put into execution his military intention of calling to his Grande Armée all his troops in the south. He, as General, the apostle of concentration of force, would not, as Emperor, treaty or no treaty, put his doctrine in force, and, in spite of urgent danger, kept up the pretence of showing front in all directions; and at a moment "when a thousand motives should have led him to think first of defending his capital, left his best troops at places of secondary importance, where the greatest successes could not possibly have any influence upon the results of the main campaign." [1]

The allied advance compelled him to adopt half measures, and on the 10th of January he called on both Soult and Suchet to send him reinforcements. On that day he dictated an order to the Minister of War as follows: "A special courier must be sent immediately to the Duke of Dalmatia with instructions to him to put in march at once on Orleans half his cavalry and half his horse artillery in organized batteries. The half of the cavalry, composed of good and intact regiments to be taken from those now the nearest to Paris, is to set off at once whatever the state of affairs may be. It will only be necessary to conceal the march from the enemy as much as possible." [2]

[1] Koch, "Memoirs pour suivi à la histoire de la Campaign de 1814."
[2] Napoleon to Guerre, Paris, 10th January, 1814.

AND THE BATTLE OF ORTHEZ

The order having been despatched, the Minister of War wrote the same day to Soult telling him to hold an infantry division, 10,000 strong, ready to be despatched *en poste* to Paris as soon as he received confirmation of the withdrawal of the Spanish troops into Spain.

Napoleon impatiently awaited news of the despatch of these troops, and on the 14th January he ordered Berthier to send one of his staff to Soult to repeat the order and hurry matters on.[1] The letter carried by this officer repeated the order sent by the Minister, and continued: "Hurry on the march of these troops, our needs are great and heavy. Send me a copy of their 'routes' so that I may know where to find them each day and be able if necessary to accelerate their march. The enemy has passed the Vosges, he is on the Moselle and has parties on the Saône. . . . There is news from Spain that the treaty has been received with enthusiasm by the Spaniards, and that in consequence their troops are leaving Lord Wellington. As soon as you have positive news to that effect, make all arrangements for putting your whole army in full march in the direction of Paris. The Emperor awaits with impatience more detailed news from Spain, and with equal impatience confirmation of your movement towards the Loire."

The Minister of War's letter reached Soult on the 14th of January, and he immediately sent the necessary orders to Treilhard's cavalry division, which had been withdrawn behind the line for supply reasons, and was then about St. Sever, Aire and Plaisance. The division, accompanied by two

[1] The Major-General to Soult, Paris, 14th January, 1814.

WELLINGTON, THE CROSSING OF THE GAVES

horse artillery batteries, commenced its march on the 16th. It was followed from Tarbes a few days later by Sparre's brigade of P. Soult's division, also with two batteries.

For the infantry he was required to hold in readiness, Soult selected Boyer's and Leval's divisions, certain changes in their organization being made. On the 19th Soult received instructions from the Minister to despatch them immediately towards Paris. The divisions marched the next day from Bayonne to Peyrehorade so as to conceal their real destinations from the Allies, and thence were despatched *en poste* [1]—Boyer's division by Orthez, Pau, Auch, Limoges and Orleans, and Leval's by St. Sever, Mont de Marsan, Bordeaux, Orleans. Each division was accompanied by a field battery. The total strength sent was: cavalry and horse artillery 3,420 and 24 guns, infantry and field artillery 11,015 and 16 guns.

Similar demands had been made on Suchet's armies of Aragon and Catalonia, and by the end of the month 8,000 infantry, 2,000 cavalry and 12 guns were *en route* for Lyons.

On the departure of these troops, Soult was left with approximately 47,600 troops of all arms,[2] exclusive of the garrisons of the fortified places found by his army, and of unarmed and unequipped conscripts. The strength of the normal garrison

---

[1] *En poste* consisted of vehicles drawn by oxen which travelled night and day. The divisions reached Nogent on the 7th and 9th February.

[2] This total is based on the States for 15th and 16th January, 1814. Captain V. de la Blache gives the strength of the six divisions forming Soult's field army as 32,234 foot soldiers on 15th January, but, unless there is some error in the strength of the divisions given, which compare fairly accurately with those in state for 16th, the total strength is 34,234, not 32,234.

AND THE BATTLE OF ORTHEZ

of Bayonne had hitherto been from 8,000 to 9,000 men, but, with the considerable additions continually being made to the defences by Soult's orders, it was doubtful if this number any longer sufficed to render the place secure.

As has been previously stated, Soult had already determined at the end of December to increase the garrison to at least 12,000 men. This he could do only at the expense of a reduction of his field army. Nevertheless, he now determined to add Abbé's (3rd) division to the garrison, bringing its strength up to about 14,300 men, on the departure of the two divisions for Paris.

As there would then be two divisional generals in the fortress, he decided to place Reille in chief command of Bayonne.[1] The effect of this would be that General Thouvenot, who held his position of Governor of Bayonne by letters patent from the Emperor, to whom he was solely and personally responsible for the safety of the fortress, would be superseded by another officer not appointed by Napoleon, an "act derogatory to the imperial authority and contrary to an inviolable principle of military law."[3]

Both Reille and Thouvenot protested; but Soult would not give way, except to refer the question to the Minister of War. The latter put the matter before the Emperor, who, engaged with more serious and pressing matters, gave no orders, and it dragged on for over a month without any decision being given. On the 18th February Reille took matters into his own hands, and left Bayonne for Dax

---
[1] Soult to Clarke, 29th December, 1813.
[2] Soult to Reille and Thouvenot, 16th January, 1814.
[3] Clark to Soult, Paris, 19th and 23rd February, 1814.

WELLINGTON, THE CROSSING OF THE GAVES

after placing Abbé's division under Thouvenot's command.

Soult was much annoyed, but could take no action, for the Minister's decision, when it arrived, completely exonerated Reille and Thouvenot, and plainly informed Soult that his proposed action was quite irregular and in excess of his authority.

In fact at this time Soult appears to have been in a very unsettled state of mind. He was about to lose a considerable portion of his fighting troops. The Spanish troops with Wellington maintained their positions, and there were no indications that their Government had favourably received the Valençay treaty; indeed, the time which had elapsed since San Carlos' arrival at Madrid and the absence of any news, foreshadowed failure. With a diminished army he remained confronted by Wellington, whom he expected to shortly advance, and the prospect did not please him.

When writing to the War Minister on the 16th January intimating his intention of placing Reille in command at Bayonne as soon as the troops destined for Paris had departed, he said: " The rest of the army will make head against the enemy to the best of its power." On the following day, however, after reporting Reille's objection, he proceeded as follows: " This disposition (Reille's command) will naturally not be put into operation until the place is seriously menaced with investment, which event appears to me possible only when the army of Spain, weakened by detachments, is no longer in a position to successfully oppose the enemy, which, however, will be the case on the very day when I am able to despatch the 10,000 men I

AND THE BATTLE OF ORTHEZ

have been ordered to hold in readiness. Then, it will be useless to maintain with the army such a numerous staff as it possesses at present, and I propose to modify its organization by suppressing the headquarter staff, leaving only one Lieutenant-General to command the remaining troops exclusive of the garrison of Bayonne. Clausel appears to me very suitable to command this corps. He belongs to these parts, speaks the language of the inhabitants and has besides all the knowledge and activity necessary. Reille can then march with the troops destined for Paris. From that moment my presence here is unnecessary, and as I may be useful elsewhere, I beg you to ask His Majesty for my recall. I am the more insistent on the proposal because, should circumstances, in spite of any refusal of the Spaniards to fall in with the arrangements made with Prince Ferdinand, become so pressing that the Emperor is obliged to withdraw from the army of Spain the two corps of 10,000 men each, and the rest of the cavalry and almost all the artillery mentioned in your despatch of 10th instant, the system of war on this frontier should certainly be changed. Partisan warfare should be substituted for that waged by the shadow of an army without body and without worth, which, if it is obliged to wage fresh combats, will probably be lost." [1]

French writers[2] have not hesitated to hint or to say that the inclusion of Abbé's division in the garrison of Bayonne and the attempt to force Reille into the command of the fortress, and the wish to be recalled by the Emperor, were all part of a

[1] Soult to Clarke, Bayonne, 17th January, 1814.
[2] Vidal de la Blache, " L'Invasion dans le Midi," " Soult travailait de ses propres mains à la disolution de son armée."

WELLINGTON, THE CROSSING OF THE GAVES

scheme worked by Soult for personal reasons. What was at the back of it? Looking at all the circumstances, it seems hardly unfair to say it was fear of Wellington. Pitted against him with an inferior army, Soult, a proud ambitious man, cannot but have felt he had only a losing game to play and that loss of reputation was almost inevitable.

Already Wellington had won the first rubber in the game of the coming campaign.

On the allied side, except for raids and counter-raids by Mina, Morillo and Harispe in the upper Nive valleys, there had been no general movement by the main allied army since its return to cantonments on the 7th January. But all along the front held the troops had been busily employed in strengthening it by redoubts and trenches and improving the communications.

The distribution of the French army immediately before the opening of the campaign was as follows:

Adour Section, under Lieutenant-General Count d'Erlon.

2nd division, Darmagnac.
5th division, Rouget.
} On the right bank of the Adour from Bayonne to its junction with the gave de Pau.

Centre Section — Lieutenant-General Baron Clausel.

4th division, Taupin.
6th division, Villatte.
} Behind the Joyeuse stream about La Bastide-Clairence and Ayherre.

1st division, Foy—About Bidache, Came and Bardos in support of 4th and 6th divisions and showing a front towards Urt.

AND THE BATTLE OF ORTHEZ

Left Section—General Harispe.

8th division—About Helette and Irrissary.

Paris's brigade of this division was on the march to relieve Jaca then invested by part of Mina's Spanish division.

The two cavalry brigades under General P. Soult remaining with the army were distributed along the front held.

CHAPTER VII

WELLINGTON'S PLAN FOR THE CAMPAIGN

WAR has its political side as well as that which is purely military, and this is a fact which a British Commander especially has always to bear in mind. In a previous chapter an attempt has been made to state as briefly as possible the then existing political situation in Europe, how it was influencing the current military operations, and on what an unstable foundation the Grand Alliance was based.

Though beset by some difficulties, Wellington at this period was in an exceptionally favourable position. He was not only the acknowledged first soldier of his country, and indeed of the Alliance, but he was also the trusted adviser of his Government on many of those points where politics and war met. He had, so far as the conduct of his own operation was concerned, practically a free hand. His influence over his army was immense.[1] He knew what he and it could do, and what could not be done. Against such visionary schemes as had been broached at the allied headquarters in the north, he set his face. "Is it possible," he said, "that any man can hope that the operations of

[1] Larpent's Diary, p. 227: "He said the other day that he had now great advantages over every other general. He could do what others dare not attempt, and he had got the confidence of all the three allied powers; and it is the same, he said, with the troops."

WELLINGTON

Prince Schwartzenberg, even when joined by Bellegarde's Italian army, can connect with mine from here?"[1] What he was prepared to do, he thus announces to the Secretary at War: "According to the wish expressed by Government, I am prepared in every respect, excepting with money, to push the enemy to the Garonne during the winter; and I am convinced that the greatest advantage to the cause would result from such an operation."[2]

It has been said that much is likely to be gained in a professional study of military history if the student of any campaign be accustomed as a first step "to ask himself the large question on which the opening of all campaigns depends. Why did the General, in the first instance, choose the particular course of action which he followed?"[3] The advice is eminently sensible and useful, and the means of obtaining the information required to answer the question is generally obtainable.

It would seem well, therefore, to consider why Wellington opened his 1814 campaign as he did. The dispositions of the allied army and of the French at the beginning of February have already been given. As stated, Wellington's intention was to advance into France at least as far as the River Garonne, which, rising in the Eastern Pyrenees, flows by Toulouse, Agen, Langon and the important city and port of Bordeaux, below which, after its junction with the Dordogne, it becomes the great sea inlet, the Gironde.

[1] Wellington to Bathurst, 10th January, 1814.
[2] Wellington to Bathurst, 5th January, 1814.
[3] Professor Spencer Wilkinson, R.U.S. Institution, March, 1897.

WELLINGTON, THE CROSSING OF THE GAVES

What possible lines of advance were open to him?

(*a*) On his left was the sea. To move his army, or any considerable part of it, by sea to a point on the coast to the north of Bayonne may, under the then circumstances, be considered as impossible. The necessary transport could not have been made available without much delay, there were no harbours between Bayonne and the Gironde, nearly 150 miles to the north, to land in boats on that dangerous coast in winter was out of the question and the naval force in those waters was insufficient even for its current duties. Moreover, all communication with Spain would have been at the mercy of Soult. Though Wellington appears never to have considered such a movement, information appears to have reached Soult that it was contemplated.

(*b*) In front of the allied army was the Adour, a large river, 200 to 300 yards wide, tidal as far as Peyrehorade, 24 miles from the sea, and on its left bank, some three miles from its mouth, the fortress of Bayonne, its strongly entrenched camp and the citadel on high ground on the right bank commanding the town and the entrenchments beyond it. To obtain possession of Bayonne, and thereby freedom of movement beyond it, would require a formal siege; and, as the strongest part of the defences, the citadel, was on the right bank of the Adour, this would also entail a crossing of the river. All this would require time; heavy losses would be inevitable both in the siege operations and in the attempts to prevent them, which Soult with his field army would be sure to make. The

AND THE BATTLE OF ORTHEZ

result might be to leave the allied army so crippled as to be unable to make any further advance for a considerable time, if at all. To set his army down to siege operations at such a time as this was not to be thought of. To do so would also be entirely contrary to what the policy of his Government required, namely, "that active and efficient co-operation with the allied armies acting on the northern and eastern frontiers of France which the then state of the war rendered it essential he should endeavour to afford them."[1] These considerations, and especially the latter, decided Wellington not to open his campaign by the siege of Bayonne.

(c) On the allied right flank lay the northern foot-hills of the Pyrenees, ridges of gradually decreasing height running for the most part nearly perpendicularly to the main chain, and separated by comparatively narrow valleys in which flow the rivers and streams, at this time deep and swift owing to the heavy rains, whose sources are in the mountains, and which, under the general designation of gave, are mostly known as that of the chief place or town through which they flow. The majority of the population inhabit the valleys and in them ran the main lines of communication. The ridges forming the divides are generally well wooded with a good deal of open heather-land, and cultivation around the scattered villages and farms. The soil is a stiff red clay. The cross communications and those between the villages on the high ground were then probably little more

[1] Memo by Sir George Murray, Q.M.G., " Supplementary Despatches," Vol. VIII.

than tracks. Jones thus describes them, "the other roads are of the very worst description of cross-country communication and become quite impracticable in winter."[1] Vivian, whose cavalry brigade watched part of the allied right flank during the winter of 1813-14, writing to his wife in December, says, "You can have no conception of the sort of lanes—I can't call them roads—we have here, up and down stiff hills, knee deep in mud. From head to foot we are covered, and being without baggage, you may imagine we are pretty figures."[2]

To move to the right, eastwards, was a possibility. It entailed dividing the army, for a portion of it of sufficient strength must be left to blockade Bayonne and cover the communication with the sea bases. If the main body of the army advanced over a difficult country across which the communications were so inferior, it would be hardly possible for it, at that season of the year, to rely on maintaining sure and regular communication with the bases on the sea coast. For this reason Wellington at first decided against it as his principal manœuvre. What then did he propose to do? It had long been apparent to Wellington that in order to advance farther into France he must gain possession of the high roads leading into and beyond Bayonne into the interior of France, because it was only by the possession of these that the supply of the allied army could be guaranteed.

Two good roads lead into Bayonne from the

[1] General Sir J. Jones, R.E., "An Account of the War in Portugal, Spain and South of France."
[2] "Memoir of first Lord Vivian," by Hon. C. Vivian.

AND THE BATTLE OF ORTHEZ

south. They are the "great road" from Spain into France by Irun and St. Jean de Luz—this was entirely in possession of the Allies; the other is the road from St. Jean Pied-de-Port to Bayonne, only partially held. These two roads meet at Bayonne, and as one crossed the Adour by "a beautifully constructed wooden bridge,"[1] about 280 yards long, then the only permanent one was over the river between the sea and Dax.

From Bayonne two main roads lead northwards to Bordeaux. The direct road, called that of the Grandes Landes, through a country thus described by Dumouriez to Wellington,[2] "dans un pays aride, désert sans ressources, obligé de porter tout avec vous," also liable at this time of year to be in places covered by water;[3] and that of the Petites Landes, which, branching off from the former at St. Geours, 15 miles from Bayonne, passes by Dax, Mont de Marsan, Roquefort, Captieux and Langon on the Garonne to Bordeaux, the distances being by the Grandes Landes route 110 miles, and by the Petites 142 miles.

From Bayonne to the eastward there was the main Pau-Toulouse road, which follows the right banks of the Adour and the gave de Pau as far as that place, and thence by Tarbes and St. Gaudens to Toulouse. From this road two others run northwards towards Bordeaux and the interior of France. The first from Orthez, being the continuation of the St. Jean Pied-de-Port-St.

[1] Batty, pp. 141 and 173.
[2] Dumouriez to Wellington, 16th December, 1813.
[3] Soult to Guerre, 19th January, 1814: "Je ne fais pas prendre à ces divisions la route des Landes sur Bordeaux, parceque les Landes sont couvertes d'eau et que les communications sont presque interceptées."

WELLINGTON, THE CROSSING OF THE GAVES

Palais-Orthez road, by Sault de Navailles and St. Sever on the Adour to Mont de Marsan, where it joins the Petites Landes route; the second from Pau, by Aire to Roquefort, thence by the Petites Landes to Bordeaux or by Marmade and Bergerac to Limoges and Orleans. From Aire there is a main road to Agen on the Garonne and thence to Limoges.

The Department of the Landes is a flat sandy plain, for the most part covered with pine forests.[1] There is little cultivation, except round the villages which house the scanty population;[2] these are placed generally on or near the streams, which flow through the district. There are also many lakes, ponds and swamps. The shepherding of flocks of sheep and the extraction of turpentine from the fir trees were the principal occupations of the inhabitants.

To obtain possession of these roads was Wellington's primary object; and the question at once arises: How was it to be done? Three steps were evidently necessary:

(a) To cross the Adour.
(b) To blockade Bayonne on all sides.
(c) To take all possible steps to prevent the enemy's field army from interfering with the crossing of the river.

As regards (a) where was the crossing to be

---

[1] In the Place at Arcachon is a bust of M. Brémontier, 1738-1809, Inspecteur Général des Ponts et Chaussées. "Il arreta l'envahissment des sables en fixant les dunes par des semis de pins." A good account of the district is given by Batty, whose battalion marched through it in May, 1814, *en route* to Bordeaux for embarkation.

[2] A French writer of the latter part of the eighteenth century says, " Les paysans landais sont peu civilisés."

AND THE BATTLE OF ORTHEZ

made, above or below Bayonne? If above the town, there was little chance of making it a surprise.[1] The right bank up to the town was held by the French, their gun-boats patrolled the river, and the rising ground north of it gave command of view. Such roads as existed on the left bank were unsuitable for heavy traffic and much of the low ground on this bank near the river was under water as the French had broken down the sluices in the protecting dykes especially at those points where they considered attempts to cross most likely. Moreover, a crossing above Bayonne necessitated the line of communication crossing the Nive also, with the possibility of interruption owing to bad weather or the action of the Bayonne garrison.

If below the town, a surprise might be possible. The great bend made by the river in its course from Bayonne to the sea, as well as the large pine wood, called the Bois de Bayonne, growing then almost up to the left bank, and covering the space between the sand hills on the coast and the right of the French entrenched camp, would screen an assemblage of troops from observers in Bayonne and would give them a covered approach to the river from a point on the great road near the village of Anglet. The width and depth of the river here, the strong tides, rising about 19 feet at the springs, the swift ebb current, some seven miles an hour, would require, for the construction of the kind of bridge necessary for the main communication of an army, something larger and more stable than the ordinary army pontoons. This might

[1] " Surprise is the greatest of all foes," Colonel Henderson.

WELLINGTON, THE CROSSING OF THE GAVES

possibly induce the enemy to consider any attempt to throw a bridge here as improbable.

Yet it was in this section of the river that Wellington decided to place his bridge. The decision to do so appears to have been come to some time previously, for the Q.M.G. in the instruction to Sir John Hope, in connection with the passage of the Nive, directs him to push back the enemy's advanced posts beyond Anglet in order to reconnoitre the right flank of the French entrenchments, and adds "the same operation may possibly afford an opportunity of reconnoitring the country to the left of the great road towards the mouth of the Adour with a view to ascertain the practicability of a bridge being eventually thrown over there in some future operation of the army."[1] Wellington also hoped that out of the operation he might eventually secure the Adour as a port; but the then navigation difficulties and the fact that the fortress held out till the end of the war, rendered this impracticable.

(*b*) The blockade of Bayonne.

The exact strength of the garrison was not known at allied headquarters; it was estimated at from 10,000 to 12,000 men. In reality the strength in February, 1814, was 13,660, of whom 11,200 were fit for duty under arms. The action about St. Pierre on the 13th December had demonstrated the advantage the French had in their short interior communications, and the disadvantage to the Allies owing to their line being intersected by the River Nive, and their longer and poor communications, liable also to interruptions at the Nive boat

[1] Q.M.G. to Sir J. Hope, 8th December, 1813.

AND THE BATTLE OF ORTHEZ

bridges. For safety, a three to one superiority was considered necessary, and about this figure was what Hope's corps eventually numbered. During the opening phase of the campaign the strength about Bayonne was considerably greater. Later on, when Anglo-Portuguese divisions were withdrawn, their places were taken by a reduced number of Spanish divisions.

(c) Measures to be taken to prevent the French field army from interfering with the passage of the Adour.

The French army was spread over a front of some thirty miles, extending from near Bayonne along the right bank of the Adour as far as its junction with gave de Pau, thence along the Joyeuse stream with its left towards the upper Nive about Helette and Irissary. Beyond Irissary was the citadel and entrenched camp of St. Jean Pied-de-Port, held by a garrison of about 2,500 men.

Dividing this line into sections it was held as follows:

Adour section, 2 divisions.
Joyeuse section, 3 divisions and 1 cavalry brigade.
About Helette, etc., 1 division and 1 cavalry brigade.

Wellington's object was to draw away from the neighbourhood of Bayonne as large a portion as possible of Soult's army. How was this to be done? Manifestly a strong threat of attack or an attack on some part of the French line would be necessary.

Taking the French dispositions as they were,

WELLINGTON, THE CROSSING OF THE GAVES

the question may perhaps be first discussed by considering what courses would be open to Soult when threatened or attacked. His line, being such an extended one in proportion to his strength, was strong nowhere, and an attack could only be met by at least some degree of concentration. This could be effected either by

(*a*) Concentration to the front for attack.
(*b*) Concentration on the line held.
(*c*) Concentration by retreat on to a given line.

Soult was hardly likely to adopt (*a*). The Allies were too close and already more concentrated than he was. If he tried it, he was likely to find the experiment even more unsatisfactory than that on the 6th January, when he pushed forward two divisions beyond La Bastide-Clairence and found himself confronted by Wellington with 24,000 men and only saved himself by precipitate retreat, and the fact that Wellington was not then prepared for any further advance. Much the same reasoning applies to a concentration on the line held, which, especially in the centre, was not one adapted to defence, the Joyeuse stream being no obstacle, being fordable, as Vivian says, " in 10,000 places," [1] except near its junction with the Adour where it is influenced by the tide.

To adopt (*c*) would be the safer plan; and this was what Wellington wanted him to do.

Now on what point of the French line should the allied attack be made? The farther from Bayonne the French strength could be drawn the less chance had Soult of successfully interfering

[1] Vivian to " John," Hasparren, 10th January, 1814.

AND THE BATTLE OF ORTHEZ

with the allied crossing above that fortress. Therefore, other factors being equal, the French left was manifestly the point to be attacked. To attack here had also other advantages. The left was numerically the weakest part of Soult's front, and the one which must therefore be immediately reinforced; if driven back here, he would lose direct communication with St. Jean Pied-de-Port and the Allies gain complete possession of a good road. Moreover, an advance by the allied right was the correct strategical move, for it would threaten the French communications,[1] which ran not due north to Bordeaux, but north eastwards and eastwards towards the Garonne. As we shall see later, the threat by the change in position of the right of the allied army, even before the operation commenced, was sufficient to cause Soult to retire and to order the evacuation of certain of his supply depôts.

These, then, were Wellington's intentions when he opened the campaign. Later on he thus expressed them in his despatch to the Secretary of State:[2] "The sense which I had of the difficulties attending the movements of the army by its right, across so many roads as have been lately passed in its progress, induced me to determine to pass the Adour below the town of Bayonne, notwithstanding the difficulties which opposed this operation. I was the more inclined to adopt this plan, as whatever might be the mode in which I should eventually move upon the enemy, it was obvious that I could depend upon no communication with Spain, the

---

[1] "The force which first threatens the enemy's communications compels the enemy to conform to its movements," Henderson.
[2] Wellington to Bathurst, St. Sever, 1st March, 1814.

WELLINGTON, THE CROSSING OF THE GAVES

seaports of that kingdom and St. Jean de Luz, except that alone which is practicable in winter, viz., the high roads leading to and from Bayonne. I likewise hoped that the establishment of a bridge below Bayonne would give me the use of the Adour as a harbour.

"The movements of the right of the army, which I detailed in my last despatch, were intended to divert the enemy's attention from the preparations at St. Jean de Luz and Passages for the passage of the Adour below Bayonne, and to induce the enemy to move his force to his left, in which objects they succeeded completely."

CHAPTER VIII

THE OPENING OF THE CAMPAIGN, 10TH TO 14TH FEBRUARY, 1814

WITH the beginning of February came a change in the weather, the prevailing south-west winds veered to north, north-east and east, and the ground dried rapidly, though it rained again on the 7th, 8th and 9th with a south-westerly wind; on the 10th it went back to the east-south-east and brought the finest day of the whole winter; the 11th, 12th and 13th continued fresh and frosty and the roads were wonderfully improved.[1]

On the 3rd H.M. ship *Désirée* arrived at Passages with £400,000 in gold; and Wellington determined to advance as soon as the money was brought up and there were a few days of dry weather.[2] The change of wind on the 10th brought the prospect of fine weather, and on that day the Quartermaster-General issued the following instruction:

"ST. JEAN DE LUZ,
"10*th February*, 1814.

"To LIEUTENANT-GENERAL SIR ROWLAND HILL, K.B., SIR STAPLETON COTTON and MARSHAL BERESFORD.

[1] Batty, p. 111.
[2] Wellington to Admiral Penrose, 8th February, 1814.

WELLINGTON, THE CROSSING OF THE GAVES

" Movement of a part of the army.

" With a view to the troops under the immediate orders of Lieutenant-General Sir R. Hill becoming disposable, the following arrangements are to take place:

" The 7th division is to move to the neighbourhood of the Adour, and is to be replaced in its present cantonments by either the 2nd division or the Portuguese division, as Sir R. Hill may direct.

" Marshal Beresford will be pleased then to arrange the distribution of the 6th and 7th divisions, with a view to these two divisions having charge of the defence of the position between the rivers Nive and Adour fronting Bayonne, as also with the maintaining the posts in the direction of Urt (now occupied by the troops under Sir R. Hill), and with the obstructing of the navigation of the Adour.

" Lieutenant-General Sir S. Cotton will at the same time relieve the brigade of cavalry (13th and 14th regiments), which is towards Urt, and will canton that brigade[1] in the direction of Hasparren, replacing it by such other body of cavalry as he may judge requisite to do the duties on the left of the line of outposts on the Arran river;[2] the Commanding Officer of which cavalry is to be instructed by Sir S. Cotton to report direct to the General commanding the 7th division.

" Sir R. Hill will retain one of his divisions in

---

[1] This brigade was commanded by Major-General Fane, who took it over on 24th December, 1813, from Colonel Vivian, when the latter was transferred to the brigade formerly commanded by Major-General V. Alten.

[2] Another name for the lower course of the Joyeuse.

AND THE BATTLE OF ORTHEZ

the neighbourhood of the 7th division, but will canton it in the most advantageous manner for moving on Hasparren; that division will do the outpost duties towards La Bastide, connecting its posts on the right with those of the 3rd division and on the left with those of the 7th division.

"The movement for the change of quarters of the 7th division with one of the divisions under Sir R. Hill is to take place on the 12th inst.; as is also the relief of the brigade of cavalry consisting of the 13th and 14th Light Dragoons.

"The General officers who are concerned in the above movements will be so good as to communicate with each other respecting the most convenient mode of carrying them into effect, as also respecting the other details of the arrangement.

"A separate instruction will communicate the arrangements connected with the further destination of the troops under the immediate command of Sir R. Hill.

Memorandum Respecting the Artillery.

"The half brigade of mountain guns which is at Urt is to remain there and be attached to the 7th division. The half brigade of mountain guns now with the 4th division is to join the troops under Sir R. Hill when sent for.

"Lieutenant-Colonel Ross's troop of horse artillery will continue attached to the troops occupying the position fronting Bayonne between the rivers Nive and Adour.

"The brigade of artillery of the 2nd division will move with the troops under Sir R. Hill, and

WELLINGTON, THE CROSSING OF THE GAVES

Captain Bean's troop of horse artillery will join the troops under Sir R. Hill at Urcuray.

"G. MURRAY, Q.M.G."

The further instructions for the movement of Sir R. Hill's corps was issued on the 12th February as follows:

"ST. JEAN DE LUZ,
"12*th February*, 1814.

"To LIEUTENANT-GENERAL SIR ROWLAND HILL, MARSHAL BERESFORD and LIEUTENANT-GENERAL SIR S. COTTON.

"Arrangements for a movement to be made from the right of the army.

"The troops to be employed in this movement will be under the immediate orders of Sir R. Hill, viz.: the 2nd division, the Portuguese division, Major-General Morillo's Spanish division, the 3rd division, the brigade of cavalry, 13th and 14th regiments, Captain Bean's troop of horse artillery, a brigade of mountain guns (4 guns), a detachment of the pontoon train (18 pontoons).

"Sir R. Hill will be so good as to put the above force in motion on the 14th instant, and move forward so as to place the right towards Helette and the left in the neighbourhood of Gréciette and Bonloc.

"Sir R. Hill will retain also some infantry posts upon the heights of La Costa, opposite La Bastide, till the morning of 15th.

"Marshal Beresford will be so good as to give orders to the 7th division to extend itself on the

AND THE BATTLE OF ORTHEZ

14th instant, so as to occupy Briscous, and put itself in communication with the troops on the heights of La Costa, which it will itself occupy at daybreak on the morning of the 15th.

"The Commander of the Forces will be at Hasparren on the 14th instant, and will instruct Sir R. Hill respecting the further movement of the force placed under his immediate orders.

"The remainder of the cavalry on the right bank of the river under the immediate direction of Sir S. Cotton will be moved forward in proportion to the advance of the force under Sir R. Hill, and Sir S. Cotton will cause part of that cavalry to penetrate towards Bidache and Guiche in the event of the enemy reducing his force in that quarter sufficiently to enable the cavalry to make the movement.

"G. MURRAY, Q.M.G."

Morillo's Spanish division about Louhossoa was also ordered to march on Helette on the 14th, and the detachment of Mina's troops in the Baztan valley to move on the same day on Baïgorry and Bidarray.[1]

In accordance with the Q.M.G.'s instruction of the 10th February, the movements therein ordered commenced on the 12th. The 7th division from Jatxou and Halsou relieved the 2nd and Portuguese divisions along the Adour from Lahonce to Urt. On relief the 2nd moved to Urcuray and the Portuguese division concentrated on the Briscous-Hasparren road with outposts on the La Costa

[1] At this time Mina, with the rest of his division, was investing Jaca, which surrendered to him on 17th February.

ridge. Fane's cavalry brigade moved to the neighbourhood of Urcuray, and Vivian's extended its left towards Urt. The 3rd division was already about Hasparren, and the Hussar brigade watched the front to the east and south-east, the 10th Hussars coming on advanced duties on the 12th February.[1]

The French made no movement on this day. Soult, who had been visiting the outpost line, wrote in the evening to the War Minister from Pessarou that the allied army was moving.

"According to the reports received from various agents, I shall probably be attacked to-morrow or afterwards on the whole line. The enemy has brought forward his pontoon train,[2] and it would seem as if he intends to force the passage of the Adour either above or below Bayonne; unfortunately the weather favours an attempt towards the mouth of the Adour. Letters from St. Jean de Luz say that there is movement among the shipping and that large quantities of ropes and cordage are being carried.

"It is also reported that the Spanish troops, quartered on the left bank of the Bidassoa, have been ordered to move forward. I have ordered all to be alert along the whole line. I think that my divisions between the Adour and the Nive will be attacked by the strongest portion of the enemy's forces, as his movements reported to me point in that direction. As I cannot be sure that communication with Bordeaux will remain open, I

---

[1] History of 10th Royal Hussars.
[2] Batty, p. 111: "On the 5th of this month (February) thirty-four pontoon boats passed through St. Jean de Luz on their way to the right wing."

AND THE BATTLE OF ORTHEZ

think it would be well that the courier service should in future be by Toulouse."[1]

Soult's information was good; he had correspondents even in St. Jean de Luz, Wellington's headquarters, and this the latter knew, but his agents had often difficulty in discovering troop movements owing to these being frequently made at night.[2] Though Soult appears to have recognized the possibility of an allied crossing below Bayonne, he left it as such, and evidently expected the attempt, when made, would be above the town, between the Nive and the Adour. He did not even take steps to cancel the order he had given to dismantle the battery near Boucau on the right bank near the mouth of the Adour.[3]

On the following day, however, Soult got a clearer view of the situation and of Wellington's intentions. The tents and numerous fires on the Urcuray heights, the fact that many observers were seen carefully reconnoitring the country in front from the Ursouia mountain (2,230 feet), all went to show that he had in front of him a very considerable force of the enemy. His Intelligence having informed him that Hill was in command, and that his division had been relieved by troops under

[1] Soult to Guerre, Pessarou, 12th February, 1814.
[2] The following is from the French translation from a report written in Basque to M. Labrouche, ex-Mayor of St. Jean de Luz and head of Soult's civil intelligence service, by one of his agents : " St. Jean de Luz, 8th February, 1814, 11 p.m., etc. etc. I will do all that I possibly can to let you know what is going on, but I must tell it is not easy to find out when they are about to do anything. In this respect they are not like us. They move so secretly and quickly that 5,000 or 6,000 men move in the night without our knowing anything about it. They sound no trumpets or beat drums. They move in silence and *sans haro* like a flock of sheep."
[3] Confidential order, 9th February, 1814 : " A guard only to be left and the *matériel* evacuated."

WELLINGTON, THE CROSSING OF THE GAVES

Beresford, he regarded this as " a certain indication of the enemy's plans. General Hill has always been on the right of the British army and he is now resuming that position." His agents also warned him that he would be attacked either on 14th or 15th. Writing to the Minister on the 13th from Pessarou he thus summed up his conclusions: " The enemy's plan appears to be to turn my left with General Hill's corps, whilst that of Marshal Beresford will move on the Bidouze to attack the divisions which I have allotted to the defence of that river." [1]

Having thus appreciated the situation, Soult determined to withdraw his centre and left to the right bank of the Bidouze. He also sent orders to his Commissary-General, M. Faviers, to evacuate the hospitals at Dax, Tartas and Mont de Marsan to Bordeaux, and the depôts of clothing stores and food to the Garonne.[2] Writing to Faviers on the 14th February Soult said: " Press all your evacuations according to the Chief of the Staff's order. I am falling back on the gaves, defending the country step by step; but the other side is too strong for me to stop his advance, therefore the hospitals, clothing and stores in the depôts must be placed in security." Thus the threat against his flank was sufficient to cause Soult to retreat, and the initiative remained with Wellington.

The concentration of Hill's force was com-

---

[1] Soult to Guerre, Orègue, 14th February, 1814.
[2] Faviers to Volland, commissary of 11th military district, 13th February : " Have received an imperative order to have the hospitals at Dax, Tartas, Mont de Marsan, Bazas, evacuated on Bordeaux. Hospital stores and clothing on the ports of the Garonne nearest Mont de Marsan, thence by water to Agen, also all the stores in the depôts by same route."

AND THE BATTLE OF ORTHEZ

pleted on the 13th and the only movement made[1] by the French was the withdrawal of Rouget's division from the St. Pierre front of the Bayonne defences to St. Etienne, north of the town, where it came under D'Erlon's command. On this evening Wellington wrote to Colonel de Lancey, the deputy Q.M.G., detached with Hope's corps, directing him "without making a piece of work of it" to stop entirely all communications between St. Jean de Luz and Bayonne. "No passes to be given and nobody allowed to enter the French posts."[2]

At daybreak on the 14th of February Hill's troops about Urcuray marched towards Helette. Morillo's division having joined the column, and the French pickets on the Joyeuse having been driven in, Hill attacked Harispe's position near the village with the 2nd division and Morillo's Spaniards. After a short sharp fight, the French, greatly outnumbered, retired towards Meharin, where they bivouacked for the night. Hill's corps remained about Helette.[3]

The 3rd division from Hasparren crossed the Joyeuse and took up a position in front of Bonloc, covered by a squadron of the 15th Hussars.[4]

On the rest of the allied front the cavalry were active along the whole line; but the infantry divisions made no forward movement. The

---

[1] Strength, including Morillo's Spaniards, about 22,000 men and 28 guns.
[2] Wellington to Colonel de Lancey.
[3] Woolright, "History of 57th Regiment," and Caddell, "Narrative of Campaigns of 28th Regiment."
[4] Major Thackwell's Diary in "History of 15th Hussars," afterwards Lieutenant-General Sir Joseph Thackwell, G.C.B., K.H., Colonel 16th Lancers.

WELLINGTON, THE CROSSING OF THE GAVES

French divisions of the centre and right remained in their positions of the 13th. In his despatch to the Minister on the 14th Soult reports Hill's attack on Harispe's division, but says he[1] has not yet received any details; that on the rest of the line of the Joyeuse the enemy has confined himself to demonstrations, but he expects that on the morrow the enemy will cross the river, and advance on a level with his right column. That on the following day he would hold the line of the Bidouze, and, if driven from that, the gave d'Oloron, holding the River Saison as long as possible. Also that he had recalled General Paris, who was on his way to relieve Jaca, and who would be that night at Garris and St. Palais to support Harispe. "You know," he added, "what means I have; I shall do all that is possible to stem the torrent and inflict as much damage on the enemy as I can; but it is indeed time I was reinforced. If the enemy succeeds in crossing the Adour I shall concentrate, for I can no longer hope to cover the country by an extended line."

[1] Soult to Guerre, Orègue, 14th February, 1814.

LOOKING TOWARDS MEHARIN FROM NEAR POINT × ON PLAN III.

To face page 134

CHAPTER IX

15TH FEBRUARY AND THE FIGHT AT GARRIS

EARLY on the morning of the 15th February, Harispe, leaving a rear guard to delay the allied advance, retired from Meharin towards Garris.

The high ground, running from west to east between Amendarits and Iholdy, which forms the divide between the streams which flow northwards into the Bidouze and its tributaries, and those flowing southwards into another river Joyeuse, which joins the Bidouze below St. Palais, turns northward about two miles south and a mile to the east of Meharin, where its highest point is about 1,000 feet. Here it throws off two long many headed spurs, one due north and the other in an east by south direction towards St. Palais. About three miles east of Meharin, one of the minor northern spurs from the latter is joined by a narrow col to the lower western slopes of a high ridge, known as the Mountain of Garris, which runs in a south-easterly direction towards the Joyeuse and St. Palais. From its northern end this ridge maintains an average height of about 700 feet for a little over a mile, and then falls gradually to the river. Below the col mentioned rise two streams: one runs northwards in a deep wooded ravine at the foot of the western slopes of the northern part of the ridge and then between it and the southern slopes of one of the spurs thrown out by the main northern one; the other southwards to the Joyeuse. The country here is quite open, covered with heather, stiff grass and short gorse, scattered trees and a good deal of wood in the lower part of the ground and on some of the spurs. The general aspect of this bit of country is probably very much the same as it was in 1814.

It was on this ridge that Harispe took up his position; his right on its northern end and extending thence southwards for about a mile and a half, with his greater strength in the centre about point 682 on plan No. III;[1] Berton's cavalry brigade, which had joined Harispe, was about Beyrie, two and a half miles south-west of St. Palais.

Starting from Helette early on the 15th February, Hill's troops moved by a mountain track towards Meharin, with an advanced guard of the light infantry companies of the 2nd division and some Spaniards. Owing to the nature of the country, the cavalry brigade followed in rear of the infantry,[2] and the artillery were sent round by a road which, passing through Amendarits, joins that from Meharin to Garris a short distance to the east of the former place. Approaching Meharin the advanced guard came into contact with Harispe's rear guard, and a running fight followed all the way to the French position on the Garris ridge, "the enemy being dislodged successively from numerous strong

---

[1] The positions of the opposing forces on plan are taken from the sketch of the action in Wyld's Atlas. Paris's brigade, recalled from its march towards Jaca, arrived at St. Palais on the evening of 14th February. It seems uncertain how much of this brigade joined Harispe on the Garris mountain. Probably part of it remained at St. Palais to hold the town and the bridges.

[2] Barrett, "History of 13th Hussars."

THE FIELD OF GARRIS FROM ABOUT POINT x ON PLAN III. THE WHITE BUILDING IN THE BACKGROUND IS THE CHURCH OF LUXE.

AND THE BATTLE OF ORTHEZ

positions strengthened by abattis which he attempted to hold."[1] Having information that Harispe was holding the ridge, Hill, before approaching it, appears to have deployed his troops into a line of columns and advanced across the open country with the Spanish division on the right, the Portuguese division in the centre and the 2nd on the left.

As the short winter day was drawing to a close the allied troops were halted—the light companies still skirmishing with Harispe's rear guard about the ravine in front of his position—and were preparing to bivouac.

Meanwhile, Wellington, who had arrived on the field from Isturits, and had ordered Hill to send Morillo's division by the long spur which runs eastward towards St. Palais to turn the enemy's left flank and cut off their retreat by the road from Garris to St. Palais, rode up to Pringle's brigade of the 2nd division, which was on the left of the line holding the spur to the north of the existing main road, with Barnes' brigade and the Portuguese brigade of the 2nd division in its rear on the same spur, and Byng's brigade on the lower ground south of the road. The time, all accounts agree, was about an hour before sunset, and may be taken as about 4 p.m. To General Pringle Wellington gave the concise order, "You must take the hill before dark," and sent the same to General Byng and the Portuguese division. "The expression caught the attention of the troops, and it was repeated by Colonel

---

[1] Woolright, "History of 57th Regiment," Major Aubin's account. "The various regiments of the 2nd division had piled arms preparatory to bivouacking for the night, and were watching the skirmishing between their light companies and the enemy's tirailleurs."

WELLINGTON, THE CROSSING OF THE GAVES

O'Callaghan, as he and General Pringle placed themselves at the head of the 39th, which, followed by the 28th, rushed with loud and prolonged shouts into the ravine." [1] It was not the expression only which influenced the troops, but also the fact that the Commander of the Forces himself was present and had given the emphatic order. That Wellington was there and spoke as he did was probably for that very purpose, for, anxious as he was to get possession of the river crossing, he knew that if he appeared himself everyone would consider the matter one of great importance.[2] To the tired and hungry soldiers, moreover, the hill represented food and rest, so with cheers and the bugles sounding the advance they went for it with a will.

The French fire was heavy, but the timber gave cover, and, though General Pringle fell wounded, there was little loss in ascending the hill. As the 39th reached the summit, the French there, probably imagining from the cheers and noise that they were about to be attacked by a much larger force, retreated somewhat toward their centre, and the 39th gaining the summit, swung round to their right, so as to sweep along the ridge. Then came the French charging back with the bayonet, and many fell on both sides; driven off, they twice came back again. Meanwhile, the 28th being now up, checked them by their fire, and the leading troops of Byng's also

---

[1] Napier.

[2] Larpent's Diary of August, 1813: "He (Wellington) said the other day—and it is the same with the troops 'When I come myself, the soldiers think what they have to do the most important, since I am there, and that all depends on their exertions. Of course these are increased in proportion, and they will do for me what, perhaps, no one else can make them do.'" Which after all is only the experience of any Commanding Officer in whom the troops have complete confidence.

AND THE BATTLE OF ORTHEZ

reaching the top, a sharp fight ensued, and the French right was driven off the hill. Then Harispe realizing the strong determined attack, for the leading brigade of the Portuguese division was also moving up, and that if he delayed any longer his retreat would be cut off by Morillo, now broke off the action, and the French retreated on St. Palais, having lost about 500 men, of whom about 200 were made prisoners.

Dr. Henry,[1] the surgeon of the 66th Regiment in Byng's brigade, thus describes its advance: "At the time General Byng's brigade attacked there was hot work going on on our left, where General Pringle's brigade, having crossed the deep ravine, mounted to the top of the position and were there strongly opposed. When Byng's column was ascending the hill it was one blaze of fire from the enemy's skirmishers behind trees and fences on the summit. This was for the greatest part as harmless as fireworks, the balls going over our heads. Our men soon reached the summit, scattering the enemy and taking some 200 prisoners. This was altogether as showy a piece of fighting as ever I witnessed; the brilliant musketry along the hill-side and from the crest of the hill, the cheering of our men as they mounted, and the continual advance of numerous bugles, the roar of our artillery reverberating in long echoes from one side of the ravine to the other; all was martially grand and fine."

It was dark when the fight was over, and the troops bivouacked on the ground.[2] Neither the

[1] Henry, " Events of a Military Life."
[2] Greenhill Gardyne, " Life of a Regiment (92nd) " : " When the combat ceased it was so dark that the men could hardly see each other."

WELLINGTON, THE CROSSING OF THE GAVES

British nor the French cavalry appear to have come into action. When it was over a squadron of 13th Light Dragoons was sent forward and took up outposts beyond the heights captured.

In his despatch Wellington says: "The troops made a most gallant attack on the enemy's position, which was remarkably strong, but which was carried without very considerable loss."[1] He mentions the 39th Regiment for their gallant repulse of the two French counter-attacks; and Morillo's division for their good conduct in the attack at Helette on the 14th, and in driving in the enemy's advanced posts in front of Garris on the 15th.

Meanwhile the 3rd division, which had halted on the evening of the 14th in front of Bonloc, marched on the 15th and bivouacked about St. Martin, a march of about six miles, having in front of it a squadron of the 15th Hussars, which put out pickets on the heights east of the village watching the road to Orègue.

In the memoir of the war accompanying Wyld's Atlas of the Peninsula battles, which memoir was compiled under the superintendence of Sir G. Murray, the Q.M.G., and contains the movement orders, etc., of the later years of the war, there is the following statement: "Sir R. Hill was instructed to move forward the force under his immediate command on the 15th February in two columns. The right column from Helette on St. Palais and the left column by St. Martin towards Garris. The plan of the movement was that the two columns should advance by the two sides of an isolated

[1] Wellington to Bathurst, St. Jean de Luz, 20th February, 1814.

AND THE BATTLE OF ORTHEZ

hill, which the French occupied in the vicinity of Garris, and thus necessitate the abandonment of the position without its being requisite to attack it. But the difficulties of the country and the circuitous route which the left column was consequently obliged to follow, prevented it reaching its destination: and on the approach of night the attack was made by the troops composing the right column."

On the 14th the 3rd division marched from about Hasparren to a little beyond Bonloc, a distance of about four miles. On the 15th the division marched about five and a half miles. On both days along a road which, in whatever state it may then have been, was the main communication between St. Palais, Hasparren and Bayonne. Garris lies seven miles nearly due east of St. Martin, with the exception of the road from St. Esteben by Meharin to St. Palais, the latter part of which was in the area of the right column under Hill's personal command; there was no direct communication between the two places, for the main northern spur already mentioned with its hills, varying in height from 1,000 to 700 feet, and its valleys runs due northwards from the Meharin-Garris road. It was beyond St. Martin that the real difficulties of the country for the 3rd division would commence. Putting aside a march of seven miles across such a country, two routes to Garris were available, both probably then little better than tracks, and parts of them shown on present-day maps as *chemins carrossable irregulièrement entretenus:* the first from St. Martin by Orègue, Arrante and Masparraute to Garris—fifteen miles; the second, which branches off from the first to the

WELLINGTON, THE CROSSING OF THE GAVES south of Orègue, by Amarots and near Beguios to Garris—twelve miles.

The reason stated in the extract given does not seem to quite fit in with facts, because the division halted at St. Martin before "the difficulties of the country and the circuitous route" really commenced. Why did the division end its march at St. Martin? Any reason given must be a conjecture, for there does not appear to be any record except that given in the memoir. The following is put forward as a possible one.

It can hardly be imagined that in a combined movement, such as the 3rd division was engaged in, Picton would have halted after such a short march unless he had received orders to do so. Wellington's headquarters were at Hasparren on the night 14th/15th February. At 12.45 p.m. on the 15th he was on the heights above Isturits, as we know from a message sent from there to Beresford,[1] and there, for probably the first time, saw the country over which the 3rd division would have to move—the maps of those days were very sketchy as regards representation of the features of the ground—for this reason; or else on account of the information which had reached him of the French movements, and in view of his own intentions consequent thereon, which rendered it desirable to maintain a force in the Isturits-St. Martin area, he probably ordered Picton to halt at St. Martin. The latter is perhaps more probable in view of the orders he had already issued to other parts of the army, which will now be given.

[1] Wellington to Beresford, heights above Isturits, a quarter before 1 p.m., 15th February, 1814.

AND THE BATTLE OF ORTHEZ

From Hasparren at 5 a.m. on the 15th, Wellington sent an order to Beresford that the 4th division was to move at once to the La Costa heights in support of the Portuguese brigade of the 7th division, which had occupied them at daybreak in accordance with the movement order of the 12th February. At 12.45 p.m. from the heights above Isturits, he sent the following message to Beresford: "The enemy are retiring in different directions towards the Bidouze, where, it is reported, they propose to stand. I conclude, however, they will fall back upon the gave (d'Oloron). I think we are a little too much extended, and, in case the enemy standing on the Bidouze, I am not so strong for them as I ought to be. I therefore send to La Costa to order that the 4th division and that part of the 7th which is there may cross to the heights of La Bastide (Clairence) in the morning early; and I wish you would order the Light division to move in the morning to the ground on this side of the Moulin d'en bas. I wish you would likewise take your quarters for the moment at La Bastide, and be there in the morning early. I shall be to-night at St. Esteben." And he adds in a postscript: "The order for the 4th division went at 5 a.m. this morning, but there has been no receipt for it." Doubtless some staff officer heard more of this!

On the 15th February Mina's troops from St. Etienne de Baïgorry and Bidarray advanced towards St. Jean Pied-de-Port.

On this day, in accordance with Soult's orders to fall back on the Bidouze, the French made the following movements. Foy's division retired from the heights of Guiche and Bardos, crossed the

WELLINGTON, THE CROSSING OF THE GAVES

Bidouze at Came by a bridge of boats, which was then taken up, and, leaving posts to watch the river about Came and Bidache, bivouacked on the high ground to the south of Peyrehorade.

Taupin's division moved to about Bergouey, and Villatte to Ilharre and Labets. During the night of 15th/16th Harispe's division with Berton's cavalry brigade evacuated St. Palais, destroyed the bridges, and leaving a rear guard to observe the river, moved towards Domezain and Arriverete.[1]

The French retirement was followed up by the British cavalry as far as the River Bidouze.

Excluding the Bayonne and St. Jean Pied-de-Port areas, the two opposing forces on the night of 15th/16th were spread out on a front of about twenty-five miles; with this difference, however—that on this evening Wellington had a mass of three divisions and a cavalry brigade, about 17,000 men, with another division in rear of it, in close contact with the extreme left of the French line, held by one division and a cavalry brigade.

Wellington's view of the situation may be judged from his orders already quoted.[2] The enemy was retiring, he did not expect them to make a stand on the Bidouze, but, if they did, they must be driven from it, for he judged that for his main purpose, the Adour crossing, they were as yet too close to

---

[1] The present Route Nationale from St. Palais to Osserain and Sauveterre did not then exist. On present-day maps Arriverete is shown as Rivareyte; the former spelling is maintained as that given in all contemporary documents.

[2] Wellington to Bathurst, St. Jean de Luz, 20th February, 1814: "Our posts were on the Bidouze river on the evening of the 15th." The Bidouze runs in a narrow valley, which opens out about Bidache, width from 40 to 50 yards with high banks, is fordable in many places as far as Came, above which it becomes tidal and is unfordable.

AND THE BATTLE OF ORTHEZ

Bayonne and must be driven farther eastwards and induced to concentrate more so as to clear from the Adour front the two divisions still there; whilst at the same time the right flank of his corps in front of Bayonne must be sufficiently protected against any emergency which might arise, which was secured by the orders given for the movement of the 4th and Light divisions. He pressed the attack at Garris on the evening of the 15th so as to secure the passage over the river at St. Palais before Soult could reinforce Harispe.

Soult, as we have seen, had already had the need for further concentration pressed on him. Writing to the Minister on the 5th he says: "There is no longer any doubt that the larger part of his force is on his right, and that his plan is to constantly outflank my left. His great numerical superiority allows him to do this. The Bidouze would be a good line to hold, if I could support Harispe at St. Palais and at the same time guard the passage of the Mauleon (River Saison), but I am already more extended than I ought to be, and I must contract my line and seek a better position. For this reason I shall pass[1] to-morrow to the right bank of the gave d'Oloron. I shall base my left on Navarrenx and my right at Peyrehorade, where I have had a bridgehead made. From there the line will be prolonged along the Adour."[2]

[1] "Je passerai demain." Soult never uses the words retreat or retire.
[2] Soult to Guerre, La Bastide de Bearn, 15th February, 1814. Throughout his despatches at this time, and also generally, Soult invokes the allied overpowering strength as a reason for the failure of his plans, etc. As a matter of fact the allied force operating under Wellington's personal command and that commanded by Soult were practically of equal strength.

CHAPTER X

16TH AND 17TH FEBRUARY, 1814

16th February

THE weather continued fine and frosty. The 4th division and a brigade of the 7th crossed the Joyeuse and occupied the heights to the east of La Bastide-Clairence. The Light division crossed the Nive at Ustaritz and marched to "within a league and a half of La Bastide and encamped on a wide healthy plain."[1] Vivian's cavalry brigade covered the front in this direction,[2] with the Hussar brigade on his right. The 3rd division marched from St. Martin to Orègue, having in front of it a squadron of 15th Hussars at Arrante,[3] from which pickets were posted to watch the roads from Bidache and Came.

Morillo's division occupied St. Palais. The

---

[1] Cope, "History of Rifle Brigade."
[2] "Life of Lord Vivian." In a letter to his wife, dated Ayherre, he says, "I have not fired a shot."
[3] "History of 15th Hussars." Thackwell's Diary says "Arriverete." This would seem to be a misprint or mistake, for the Arriverete, which will be frequently mentioned, is on the right bank of the Saison and was on this day occupied by Harispe's division, and from the map there does not appear to be any other village of this name in the area of this day's operations. Arrante is about two miles east of Orègue on the Garris-Bidache road.

WELLINGTON

advanced squadron of the 13th sent on a party under Lieutenant Doherty to reconnoitre the retreating French; passing the Bidouze by a ford, it moved towards Domezain, but had not proceeded far before it came in contact with a party of French cavalry forming, the point of Harispe's rear guard, which the 13th detachment charged and drove back on to its support and then fell back. The French advanced, but now some infantry of the 2nd division came up, and with them Sir William Stewart. Being thus supported, Lieutenant Doherty charged again and broke the French, who retired and did not come on again.[1] Meanwhile, the allied engineers completed the restoration of the broken bridge, and the remainder of the 2nd division crossed and occupied the high ground on the right bank, the remainder of Hill's corps remaining about St. Palais and Garris. The 57th Regiment was sent back to St. Jean de Luz to receive new clothing and as escort to the French prisoners taken the previous day.

Mina's Spaniards invested St. Jean Pied-de-Port.

As the allied movements on this day did not bring them into contact with the French, except in the rear guard action described, Soult was able to hang on to the Bidouze for a day longer than he expected. But Wellington having now brought up his strength to what he considered necessary, was not going to allow him any further respite, and from his headquarters at Isturits issued the following movement order:

---

[1] Hamilton, "History of 14th Hussars." Manuscript diary of an officer of 13th Light Dragoons.

WELLINGTON, THE CROSSING OF THE GAVES
" ISTURITS,
" *February* 16*th*, 1814.

" Movements of the army.

" Lieutenant-General Sir R. Hill will be so good as to put the whole of the troops under his immediate command (except the 3rd division) in motion at eight o'clock to-morrow morning.

" This force will pass the River Bidouze at St. Palais, and will afterwards proceed towards the gave de Mauleon[1] in the direction of Domezain, Sir R. Hill regulating his movements according to the nature of the country, and the situation and amount of force opposed to him by the enemy.

" The 3rd division will move at 7 a.m. to the villages of Masparraute and Somberaute, and throw posts to the Bidouze river.

" Marshal Beresford will be so good as to order the 4th division to move at 7 a.m. towards Bidache, which place its advanced posts should occupy.

" The Light division is to replace the 4th division in the neighbourhood of La Bastide-Clairence.

" The 7th division is to continue in the present position. Sir S. Cotton will be so good as to push forward the advanced posts of the left and centre of the cavalry to the Bidouze river, or beyond if circumstances permit, the posts of the centre of the cavalry keeping up a communication also with the troops beyond St. Palais under Sir R. Hill.

" Headquarters will move to-morrow to Garris.

" G. MURRAY, Q.M.G."

[1] Or Saison.

AND THE BATTLE OF ORTHEZ

On the 16th February Soult in his despatch to the Minister[1] thus summarized the orders he had given for the occupation of the new position to be taken up by his army on the 17th:

"I have ordered D'Erlon to cause Darmagnac's division to cross the Adour and establish itself on the left bank to defend that river, Rouget's division to move from St. Etienne towards Dax.[2] Foy will hold the right bank of the gaves from the junction with the Adour as far as Sorde and will hold the bridgeheads at Hastingues and Peyrehorade. Taupin will prolong the line from Sorde to Sauveterre, where Villatte will be in position. Harispe on the Saison with detachments towards Mauleon.

"The cavalry under General (P.) Soult will have one brigade at Sauveterre, and the other spread along the whole line. General headquarters will be at Orthez, the adminstrative services at St. Sever and the artillery park at Aire.

"Thus the line held by the army will extend from Dax, which I have had put in a state of defence, as far as Navarrenx, which is in a good state of defence. The army will thus have in its front the course of the Adour and that of the gaves. I am about to have several works thrown up in front of Sauveterre.[3]

"The three divisions of the Bayonne flotilla will

---

[1] Soult to Guerre, Sauveterre, 16th February, 1814.

[2] The move of this division towards Dax appears to have been cancelled later, as we shall find it turning up at Porte-de-Lanne a few days later on.

[3] The only work constructed was a trench on the left bank of the gave in front of the bridge. A report from an agent of the Sous Prefet of Orthez, dated 18th February, quoted by General Dumas, says: "No tête de pont or redoubts have been thrown up at Sauveterre."

WELLINGTON, THE CROSSING OF THE GAVES

defend, as far as they can, the River Adour from the Bec-du-Gave (confluence with Adour) as far as Bayonne, and will act so as to prevent any attempt by the enemy to cross. I hope thus to maintain my communication with Bayonne for several days more. The enemy will probably move forward to-morrow."

During the day the French everywhere fell back in accordance with Soult's orders. Darmagnac's division was marching towards Porte-de-Lanne. Foy's division having crossed the Bidouze on the evening of 15th, was in bivouac on the heights south of Hastingues and Peyrehorade. Taupin crossed the gave d'Oloron near Caresse, leaving one brigade there; he moved with the other to Athos, about three miles down-stream from Sauveterre. Villatte's division moved to Sauveterre, Harispe's division retired over the Saison, leaving a rear guard and part of Berton's cavalry brigade on the left of the river to retard Hill's advance. He also posted detachments to guard the fords at Autevielle, Osserain, Tabaille, Gestas and Rivehaute. The wooden bridge at Arriverete was guarded by two battalions of 25th Léger, one of which held a hill on the left bank which commanded the Domezain road immediately in front of the bridge.

17th February

Hill's column moved off at 8 a.m. headed by Fane's cavalry brigade and Bean's troop of horse artillery, the 13th Light Dragoons being the advanced regiment. The 2nd division led the

Higher.—THE RIVER SAISON FROM THE BRIDGE AT ARRIVERETE.

Lower.—HASTINGUES AND THE GAVE DE PAU FROM THE ROAD FROM PEYREHORADE.

AND THE BATTLE OF ORTHEZ

infantry. At a point, probably between Domezain and the Saison, where "the country was clear and open," the French rear guard "was seen in position in considerable strength, especially in cavalry." The main body of Fane's brigade reinforced the 13th, and Bean's guns came into action, to which the enemy replied, "and a smart cannonade ensued." On the approach of the infantry, however, the French retired and crossed the Saison.[1]

The 2nd division approached the river towards 2 p.m. and formed for attack. Notwithstanding the depth of the river the crossing at Osserain was secured, and also that at Espinte; but at Arriverete the bridge was strongly defended by the 25th Léger, who were also attempting to destroy it. The hamlet of Arriverete consists of a few old stone-built houses on the right bank close to the bridge and a few more a little distance along the road to Sauveterre.[2] A ford having been discovered above the bridge on the eastern side of the hill before mentioned and opposite the village of Arrive, the 92nd Highlanders crossed there, and wheeling to left, dashed off to the attack of the 25th at Arriverete, supported by the fire of Bean's guns. On reaching it, a sharp fight followed which ended in the French being driven out with considerable loss and the bridge secured.

In a letter, written some years later, Wellington thus gives his reason for wishing to get speedy possession of this bridge: "Arriverete is a village on the gave de Mauleon, where there is a wooden bridge. We passed the river at other points, but

[1] From General Brotherton's account in Hamilton's "History of 13th Hussars."
[2] One house bears the date 1663.

WELLINGTON, THE CROSSING OF THE GAVES

our communication across it was difficult, and the enemy was in such strength at Sauveterre in the neighbourhood we could not venture to move along it, and I wanted to get possession of the bridge before the enemy could destroy it. The 92nd forded the river and took the bridge in very gallant style." [1]

Having gained all the crossings, Hill's troops passed the river, and in all directions drove the French towards Sauveterre, where Harispe's division crossed the gave d'Oloron, leaving a battalion to hold possession of the small hamlet of Oreyte on the left bank almost immediately in front of the then position of the bridge,[2] the division was then spread along the right bank of the gave from Sauveterre to the village of Laas.

In the evening, the allied outposts held the villages Guinarthe, Parenties and St. Gladie.

The ground running from south-east to north-west, which forms the divide between the upper gave d'Oloron and the Saison, rises to a height of 600 feet about midway on a line from Montfort on the gave d'Oloron and Gestas on the Saison. From here it falls gradually as it approaches the junction of the two rivers, until, on a line which may be said to correspond approximately with that of the road from Arriverete to Monein on the gave d'Oloron, the ground becomes an almost perfectly flat plateau, raised some 100 feet above the waters of the two rivers. This flat is enclosed, highly cultivated and well wooded about the villages, built generally of stone with a sprinkling of modern

---
[1] Wellington to Lord Nidry, 13th April, 1820.
[2] This was also a wooden bridge in two parts joining an island in the river to the left and right banks.

villa residences. From Sauveterre the high road to Oloron follows the left bank of the gave, whilst from Parenties and Arriverete a good road leads to Mauleon along the right bank of the Saison until about three miles from the latter place when it crosses to the left bank. Once the plateau is left, the high ground conceals any movement along this latter road from observation from the ground on the right bank of the gave d'Oloron.

The other divisions of the allied army made the following movements: 3rd division from Orègue and Masparraute bivouacked in the afternoon alongside the road near Garris;[1] 4th division to Bidache; light division to La Bastide-Clairence; Vivian's cavalry brigade watched the lower course of the Bidouze connecting at Came with the left of the Hussar brigade, whose right was in touch with Hill's corps.

On this evening Wellington, whose headquarters were at Garris, wrote to General Freyre,[2] commanding the 4th Spanish army, warning him that he proposed to order the two divisions of his army then about Irun to march immediately; that he would give them rations and would endeavour to give them pay also. He also requested him to obtain as many mules as possible for his divisions, which Wellington would pay for at the same rate as those employed with the British army.

On the 17th, besides the movements of Harispe's division already described, the only other changes in the French dispositions were as follows: Foy's division, the 1st brigade moved to Oeyregave

[1] Journal of a Commissariat Officer (attached to 3rd division).
[2] Wellington to Freyre, Garris, 17th February, 1814.

WELLINGTON, THE CROSSING OF THE GAVES

and Peyrehorade, the 2nd to Hastingues. Darmagnac's division crossed the Adour, the bridge having been re-established on this day, and moved to Porte-de-Lanne. Soult ordered all the bridges over the gave d'Oloron to be destroyed except that at Sauveterre.[1]

Writing to the Minister from Sauveterre, Soult says: " I hope to be able to maintain my position on the gave d'Oloron to-morrow. If I am forced to retire, I shall take up a position at Orthez, where D'Erlon, with Foy and Darmagnac's divisions, which are on the Adour, will join me." [2]

[1] Lapène.
[2] Soult to Guerre, Sauveterre, 17th February, 1814.

CHAPTER XI

18TH FEBRUARY TO 22ND FEBRUARY, 1814

THERE was a change in the weather, a heavy fall of snow at Garris, rain and sleet at St. Jean de Luz and La Bastide.

About midday Hill moved out a force from the outpost line to test the French defence of the Sauveterre bridge and to reconnoitre the left bank of the gave d'Oloron. Driving in the French outposts, artillery was opened on the position they held in front of the bridge, and some of the houses occupied by the French in Oreyte and Monein were seized. The latter replied with fire from a battery of twelve guns at Sauveterre. About 3 p.m. Hill, having gained his object, retired to his former line. He had a horse shot under him during the day.

Morillo's division moved up the Saison, placing detachments to guard all the fords as far as Nabas. The 3rd division marched through Garris and encamped near St. Palais. No movements were made by any other divisions of the army. The 10th Hussars on the left of the Hussar brigade at Came advanced their pickets beyond the Bidouze in the direction of Hastingues and Peyrehorade, the remainder of the cavalry maintained their general positions of the previous day.

WELLINGTON, THE CROSSING OF THE GAVES

On the French side, D'Erlon having arrived at Peyrehorade and examined the ground, ordered Foy to withdraw his division over the gave de Pau at Peyrehorade. One battalion only was left in the fortified post at Hastingues, where there was a bridge of boats, two battalions in that at Oeyregave and one in the Peyrehorade bridge-head. The division occupied Orthevielle and Peyrehorade.

Soult in his report to the Minister, gives an account of Hill's[1] reconnaissance, and states: "D'Erlon yesterday completed his movement to the left bank of the Adour without incident. To-day I have no news from that side or from Bayonne. . . . Since communication with Bayonne has ceased, I can only draw munitions from the rear. I have depôts at Dax and Navarrenx, which I shall probably not be able to remove; those which I have ordered to be established at Toulouse and Bordeaux are not yet formed, so I may be much embarrassed unless you immediately give orders for compliance with the requisitions which General Tirlet (commanding the artillery) is about to submit. I have also ordered the evacuation of the hospitals on the left bank of the Garonne to Toulouse and Bordeaux, and also the depôts of supplies and clothing at Dax and Mont de Marsan."[2]

The general position on the evening of this day was that, whilst the opposing armies stood opposite each other on a front of about twenty-five miles along the gaves d'Oloron and Pau, both

---
[1] Soult to Guerre, Sauveterre, 18th February, 1814.
[2] These orders, as we have seen, were given on the 12th February. It is characteristic of the man that they were only now reported to the Minister.

AND THE BATTLE OF ORTHEZ

were practically concentrated in two groups towards the extremities of this front. On the French right, D'Erlon with the divisions of Foy and Darmagnac about Porte-de-Lanne and Peyrehorade, some twenty-four miles from Bayonne with the River Adour to cross—with Rouget's division somewhere in the air, either between Bayonne and Dax or along the Adour moving towards Porte-de-Lanne—opposed to Marshal Beresford's allied group of the 4th, 7th and Light divisions with Vivian's cavalry brigade about Bidache, La Bastide-Clairence and Urt. On the French left Clausel with Villatte's and Harispe's divisions and Berton's cavalry brigade about Sauveterre with Taupin's division somewhat scattered on their right, faced Hill's corps of four divisions and a cavalry brigade.

This latter group was the master card in Wellington's hand—for the time being Beresford's was a containing, defensive and pivot force—Soult feared it, because, owing to his strategy hitherto, he was not in a position to meet it, and it was full of potential danger to him. If he fought where he was, he might be cut off from the rest of his army, or he might be driven back along the gave on to the gave de Pau with only one bridge left standing at Berenx between Orthez and Peyrehorade, whilst the enemy would almost certainly gain possession of the great road from Bayonne to Pau behind him. If he retired, any mistake might easily lead to equally disastrous results.

Therefore Wellington might feel reasonably assured that whilst, in his present dispositions, his army was well able to meet any action by the enemy, he had also secured the object he had first set out

WELLINGTON, THE CROSSING OF THE GAVES

to gain, namely, " to divert the enemy's attention from the preparations at St. Jean de Luz and Passages for the passage of the Adour below Bayonne and to induce the enemy to move his force to his left,"[1] also that so far his opponent had failed to discover his ultimate object. He, therefore, determined to return to St. Jean de Luz on the 19th and push on the crossing of the Adour.

19*th February*

The weather continued very cold with snow and sleet. Before leaving Garris, Wellington sent the following letter to Hill giving his views as to the measures to be taken during his absence:

"GARRIS,
"19*th February*, 1814, 6 *a.m.*

"MY DEAR HILL,—Churchill has just left me. If you can retake the Red House[2] in the manner you took it yesterday, it is desirable to have it; but I should think the enemy would have covered themselves during the night from the effect of your artillery fire. If you can't take the Red house, you had better hold the village of Arriverete as a *tête de pont*, the village on the right of the same river, where the *barca*[3] was, in the same manner in order to secure those passages, and St. Gloire

---

[1] Wellington to Bathurst, St. Sever, 1st March, 1814.
[2] Commandant Clerc suggests that for the Red House may be read the hamlet of Oreyte, close in front of the bridge of Sauveterre.
[3] The village referred to is probably that of Guinarthe. *Barca* is the Portuguese for ferry.

AND THE BATTLE OF ORTHEZ

(St. Gladie) and Barraute as advanced posts from them.

"Your position in this case would be on the heights on the left of the gave de Mauleon, and it is a very good one. I think you had better leave the 3rd division where they are, those at St. Palais cover you from any movement from Mauleon, and the others your left. However, you will move them if you think proper. I mention this in case the enemy should undertake any enterprise against you, which is not very probable.

"Yours sincerely,
"WELLINGTON.

"P.S.—In the position above mentioned, concealing your troops and not making any movement of large bodies in sight of the enemy, you will be able to reconnoitre all the passages over the river within your reach."

As there are several fords on the gave d'Oloron between Sauveterre and Navarrenx, generally close to the villages along the main road between these two places and Oloron, which follows the left bank of the gave, Hill sent detachments of British and Portuguese infantry to hold these villages from Barraute to Montfort and guard the fords. He also sent Fane's cavalry brigade up the Saison to Nabas[1]—about five miles from Arriverete—to cover the front and right flank of Morillo's division. This move was apparently not made till late in the day, as the 13th Light Dragoons, which were ordered to cover the extreme right, did not arrive

[1] "History of 13th Hussars." The direct road from St. Palais to Navarrenx crossed the Saison at Nabas.

WELLINGTON, THE CROSSING OF THE GAVES

on the ground till after dark, and it was past 8 p.m. before their outposts were placed. This caused "some anxiety as information was received that the enemy, strong in cavalry, were about one and a half leagues distant."

As recommended by Wellington, Hill kept those of his troops not required for the immediate defence of his forward position on the plateau and the gaves, along the Domezain road where they were covered by the high ground on the left bank of the Saison.

In his report on this day's proceedings, Soult says :

"To-day the enemy has prolonged his line as far as Navarrenx. I was at the village of Laas (six miles south-west of Sauveterre) whilst this movement was going on. One may suppose that the enemy's plan is to move on Pau before I can reach that place; however, it is possible he only intends to spread over the country and hold me in check with part of his army, whilst with the remainder he acts against Bayonne.[1] In a few days I shall know for certain what his intentions are.

"I have ordered General P. Soult, with a brigade[2] of Light cavalry and two battalions, to move to the left of Navarrenx and cover the roads to Oloron and to Pau, and maintain communication with Mauleon. If I am again obliged to retreat,

---
[1] When writing this Soult knew that Wellington had left Garris and had gone in the direction of St. Jean de Luz. "Lord Wellington has been met to-day between St. Palais and St. Martin returning towards Ustaritz."

[2] This brigade consisted of two regiments of Vial's brigade, the 5th and 10th Chasseurs. The infantry consisted of the two battalions of 25th Léger.

AND THE BATTLE OF ORTHEZ

I shall concentrate the whole army at Orthez and fall on that corps of the enemy most within my reach."[1]

He also complains of the bad spirit of the national guards of the Basses-Pyrénées, that "eight days ago General Harispe reckoned 3,300 were on service, now there are scarcely 500, the rest having gone to their homes. With them their private affairs and home ties count before anything else, and, moreover, they are seduced by the perfidious conduct of the enemy, who spend large sums of money and hold out hopes to the inhabitants which will certainly never be fulfilled. In several villages the people have cordially welcomed hostile patrols. In the Department of the Landes the spirit is just as bad."

Wellington reached St. Jean de Luz in the afternoon, and immediately proceeded to confer with Admiral Penrose regarding the prospects of the bridge flotilla, which was assembled in the bay, being able to put to sea. Since the 18th these had not been favourable as the wind was inshore.

20th February

Prospects were less favourable the next morning, as the wind had increased in strength almost to a gale. Larpent,[2] under this date, says:

"The first thing I saw this morning in my walk on the wall was Lord Wellington looking at the sea at half-past seven. The wind was strong,

---

[1] Soult to Guerre, Sauveterre, 19th February, 1814.
[2] Larpent's Diary, p. 398.

right into the bay, and not a ship could stir. He soon saw the Admiral come out also to look, and carried him off home. . . .

"Had the gale this morning increased none of the ships in the bay, in my opinion, could have stood it. It was right into the bay against them, and they were anchored within 200, 300 or 400 yards of the shore. The slip of an anchor or the breaking of a cable would have been destruction."

As the weather was "so unfavourable at sea and so uncertain," Wellington determined to push forward his operations on the right,[1] leaving the superintendence of the crossing of the Adour to Sir John Hope and Admiral Penrose, and the following movement order was issued:

"St. Jean de Luz,
"20th February, 1814.

"Movements of the army.

"The 1st division, with Lord Aylmer's brigade, Major-General Bradford's brigade and Major-General Wilson's,[2] will take up the positions in front of Bayonne from the sea to the River Nive, in such manner as Lieutenant-General Sir John Hope shall direct.

"The Spanish division of Don Carlos d'Espagne is placed under Sir J. Hope's orders, and will be in reserve to the troops above mentioned.

"The 5th division will cross to the right bank of the Nive as soon as relieved, and will take up the position between the River Nive and the Adour.

[1] Wellington to Bathurst, St. Sever, 1st March, 1814.
[2] Then commanded by Brigadier-General A. Campbell.

AND THE BATTLE OF ORTHEZ

"Major-General Vandeleur's brigade will continue to do the cavalry duties in front of Bayonne in such manner as Lieutenant-General Sir J. Hope may direct.

"As soon as the 5th division has taken up the position between the Nive and the Adour, Sir H. Clinton will put the 6th division in march to Hasparren, where it will remain till further orders.

"The 7th division will concentrate to-morrow morning at La Bastide-Clairence and adjacents, where it will remain till further orders.

"The Light division will move to-morrow morning from La Bastide-Clairence to St. Martin and adjacents.

"G. MURRAY, Q.M.G."

On the gave d'Oloron the only movements made this day were that a party of Spanish troops from Nabas was sent to occupy the village of Araujuzon on the Oloron road, and the British cavalry outpost line, in front and on the right of the Spanish division, was somewhat drawn back.[1]

Early on the 21st February, Fane's cavalry brigade and the main body of Morillo's division were concentrated to the east of Nabas as a support to a reconnaissance towards Navarrenx by Sir R. Hill, who, taking with him a squadron of the 13th Light Dragoons and 1,400 Spaniards, moved towards the town. "A little skirmishing took place, but, as the orders were not to press the enemy, no casualties occurred. The object being attained the force returned and the squadron rejoined the regiment." A troop of the 13th was detached

[1] "History of 13th Hussars."

WELLINGTON, THE CROSSING OF THE GAVES

to St. Palais, probably for communication duties.

'During the afternoon of the 21st a patrol of three British horsemen, probably of the 13th, entered Mauleon and announced that on the following day a division of from 5,000 to 6,000 allied troops would arrive in the town; the effect of this announcement will be observed later. At Urt on the Adour Beresford, who had been collecting boats and making other preparations as if to throw a bridge there, sent a battalion over the river, withdrew it in the evening, but still continued his preparations to bridge the river.

The 3rd division from St. Palais crossed the Bidouze and encamped by the Domezain road, the 6th division moved to Hasparren and the Light to Isturits and St. Martin. Wellington returned to Garris.

On the part of the French the only movements made were by P. Soult and his cavalry, which, reconnoitring between the gave d'Oloron and the Saison, came in contact with Hill's movement towards Navarrenx; and a reconnoitring patrol to Mauleon came into the town a few minutes after the British patrol had left it.

On the 22nd the 7th division moved to Came, the Light division to St. Palais, and the 6th to St. Martin. On the French side no movements of any importance were made.

Soult himself left Sauveterre about midday for Orthez to inspect positions on the right bank of the gave de Pau.

Writing from there to the Minister, he informs him of the results of P. Soult's reconnaissances on the previous day, which showed that the enemy had concentrated many troops on both banks of the Saison, and that two fresh divisions had joined Hill's corps. The general conclusion he drew from this was that the enemy had determined to continue his movement on the right. "I do not know," he said, "if he intends to force my line on the gave d'Oloron, or to outflank me completely by moving against my communication with Toulouse. This last would be a very bold movement, and might bring him misfortune before it was finished, for I shall not hesitate to manœuvre against him whatever may be the disproportion in the strengths of the forces."[1] He adds: "The result of the arrival of the three British horsemen at Mauleon was that the legion of National guards, who were guarding the town, retired towards Tardets without firing a shot, on the pretext that the place would be compromised if they stayed to defend it. The inhabitants received the three horsemen *avec affection;* instead of arresting them, they were given refreshments. I can give no stronger proof than this of the bad spirit of the people of the Basses-Pyrénées."

On the evening of the 22nd, the wind being favourable, the bridge flotilla and its escort of warships put out to sea[2] from St. Jean de Luz.

[1] Captain Vidal de la Blache's comment on this is : " De la menace Soult ne passait guère aux actes." (" L'Invasion dans le Midi.")

[2] Larpent's Diary, February 22nd, 5 p.m. : " The flotilla has just got out of Socoa Bay preparatory to the operations to-morrow. A beautiful sight, six or seven ships of war and fifty other vessels."

CHAPTER XII

23RD FEBRUARY, ARRANGEMENTS FOR THE CROSSING OF THE GAVE D'OLORON. THE CROSSING OF THE ADOUR COMMENCED. 24TH FEBRUARY, THE CROSSINGS OF THE GAVE D'OLORON AND ADOUR

23rd February

A BEAUTIFUL day, but very cold. The 6th and Light divisions and the section of the pontoon train having joined the concentration on the allied right, Wellington was now ready to advance, and determined to do so on the 24th.

In front of him was the gave d'Oloron, a considerable river but fordable in several places except when in flood. The French held the right bank with two divisions from Sauveterre to about Laas, beyond which a mixed detachment of two cavalry regiments and two battalions under General P. Soult watched the country about and to the south-east of Navarrenx, a fortified town with a garrison of 1,100 men. Below Sauveterre Taupin's division, considerably extended, guarded the course of the river.

The allied troops held or watched the left bank almost as far as Navarrenx.

How, then, did Wellington propose to force a

WELLINGTON

passage across the river? "When an army approaches a river defended by the enemy . . . it will be better, instead of forming a theory of his (the enemy's) doings—which very likely will be false—to follow a sound plan; that is one which will enable the army to cross with least risk, and at the same time with the most effective strategical results, whether by turning the flank, or breaking the front of the defensive line."[1]

The condition "with least risk" can generally only be fulfilled by crossing at an unexpected and therefore undefended or lightly defended point; in other words by a surprise. To effect this it is essential that, whilst the movement towards the chosen point is concealed as much as possible, the enemy's attention must be held by demonstrations against other points, which will also hold him to his present positions and hinder his attempts to detach troops to oppose the crossing at the selected point, when he receives information of it. It is manifest also that, if the general situation permits the crossing to be on or beyond a flank, concentration by the enemy against it will be slower than when the point lies within his defensive line, for he can concentrate twice as fast towards his centre than to a flank; moreover, in certain cases the strategical result may be decisive.

Wellington's general plan was as follows. The main crossing was to be made by a ford near the village of Viellenave,[2] thirteen miles south-east of Sauveterre and about two miles above Navarrenx.

---

[1] Hamley, " Operations of War."
[2] Spelt Villenave in Wellington's orders and despatch, Viellenave pres Navarrenx on modern maps.

WELLINGTON, THE CROSSING OF THE GAVES

To prevent interference with the movement and the passing of information by the garrison of Navarrenx, Morillo's division, the nearest to the town, was to push parties as close up to the town as possible, and to send a battalion to threaten fords near the village of Dognen, two miles upstream. The 3rd division and the Hussar brigade were to hold Villatte's and Harispe's divisions to their present positions by making demonstrations as if desirous of fording the gave at and near Sauveterre; Vivian's brigade was to threaten the fords below that place, whilst the 4th division was to approach the lower course of the river and the 7th to hold Foy in check in front of Peyrehorade.

The plan appears to fulfil the conditions previously mentioned. Morillo's division would be able to get into position and cover the outer flank of the divisions moving towards Viellenave. The movement of the latter for the greater part of the distance would be concealed by the high and generally well-wooded ground forming the divide between the Saison and the gave d'Oloron; whilst, after crossing this, a long narrow ridge lying between the Lausette stream and the gave, which rises to a height of about 400 feet and is quite close to the village of Viellenave, gives cover near the ford. Once across this, the main road from Oloron and Navarrenx to Orthez is within a mile, the distance to the latter place being about eleven miles. It was within possibilities that, if the French about Sauveterre retired on Orthez, their retreat might be cut off.

To carry out the plan the following movement order was published:

AND THE BATTLE OF ORTHEZ
"GARRIS,
"*23rd February*, 1814.

"Movements of the army to take place on 24th February, 1814.

"The Spanish division will move as early as possible towards Navarreins. The main body of the division will halt near the Lausette rivulet, and General Morillo will throw forward parties from thence as close as possible to Navarreins, and will detach one battalion higher up the gave d'Oloron, to threaten the fords at or near the village of Dognen.

"The object of this arrangement is to draw the attention of the garrison of Navarreins as much as possible away from the side of Villenave.

"The nature of the ground between the Lausette and the gave d'Oloron will enable General Morillo to conceal the force, as likewise the movements made, or the situations occupied by his troops.

"Major-General Fane will be so good as to order a detachment of cavalry to act with General Morillo's division.[1]

"The Light division will move at daybreak from Aroüe, and having passed the ford of the gave de Mauleon at Nabas, will direct its march on Villenave.

"The Portuguese division will move at the same time from Gestas upon Villenave.

"Lieutenant-Colonel Ross's troop of horse artillery, the brigade of artillery of the 3rd division, and the pontoon train will move at the same time upon Villenave by the route which is found to be most practicable for carriages.

"The Light division and the Portuguese division

[1] Captain Gubbin's troop, 13th Light Dragoons : "History of 13th Hussars."

will each furnish one battalion to accompany and assist the carriages, particularly those of the pontoon train.

"The 13th and 14th Light Dragoons, and Captain Bean's troop of horse artillery, will move at daybreak from Espinte upon Villenave.

"The 2nd division will move also at the same time towards Villenave, leaving its artillery, however, to act for the present with the 3rd division in the neighbourhood of Osserain.

"The march of the troops moving towards Villenave should be concealed as much as possible from the view of the enemy.

"The 2nd division will detach a battalion to threaten the fords at the village of Barraute.

"The 3rd division will assemble as soon after daybreak as possible in the neighbourhood of Osserain and Arriverete. The Hussar brigade will also assemble in the same neighbourhood. And these troops will make demonstrations as if desirous of fording the gave d'Oloron at and near Sauveterre. And Sir S. Cotton will be so good as to order Colonel Vivian to threaten in like manner the fords of the river below Sauveterre.

"The 6th division will move at daybreak from St. Palais to Gestas, and thence upon Villenave. The artillery of the 7th division will take the route of Domezain, Aroüe and Nabas to Villenave.

"No part of the baggage is to be suffered to cross the gave de Mauleon until special authority is given for that purpose. Sir R. Hill and Sir T. Picton will be so good as to direct guards to be placed at the bridges and fords of the gave de Mauleon to enforce these orders.

AND THE BATTLE OF ORTHEZ

"Sir S. Cotton will be so good as to arrange a communication from the right near Villenave to the 7th division which will be in the neighbourhood of Bidache and Hastingues, and Major-General Fane will order a detachment of cavalry to remain at St. Palais, and a letter party from it to be stationed at St. Martin, to keep up the communication with Hasparren.

"G. MURRAY, Q.M.G."

Meanwhile, on the 23rd, the first operation in connection with the crossing took place, for the French right group to be held there must be threatened. Therefore, Beresford advanced from Came and Bidache; with the 7th division he moved against Foy's advanced posts on the left bank of the gave de Pau at Hastingues and Oeyregave. These he drove off, the garrison of Hastingues escaping across the river in boats with considerable loss; the battalion at Oeyregave retired on the bridge-head at Peyrehorade, which was subsequently evacuated by D'Erlon's order, and the bridge blown up. During these operations the 4th division and Vivian's cavalry brigade covered the right flank towards Sorde and the lower course of the gave d'Oloron.

During the day the divisions of the right group moved to the starting points fixed in the order. The position of the 2nd division is not given in the order. Certainly part of it, probably two brigades, had been about Arriverete and Osserain since the 17th, and had done the fighting and outpost duties from that date. Where the rest of the division was seems uncertain; it was perhaps about Domezain or

WELLINGTON, THE CROSSING OF THE GAVES

beyond it towards Arriverete in support of its advanced portion. In the journal of a commissariat officer, already quoted, there is an entry under date of 23rd February as follows: "The Light division marched past our encampment (3rd division) with their bugles playing (this division was marching from St. Palais to Aroüe) and followed the 2nd division; while we marched over a large heath towards the gave near Sauveterre, and in the evening came to a small branch of that river running through a village (probably Osserain), here the 3rd division halted and the 45th Regiment passed the stream to support the pickets."

Soult's view of the situation was as follows: "All reports received state that it is the enemy's intention to advance by Oloron on Pau and Tarbes with a formidable force of artillery and several pontoon sections. I am really astonished. But, whatever happens, I have made my arrangements to concentrate and accept battle or march against the enemy if a favourable opportunity offers."[1]

In the morning, below Bayonne, the first steps towards the bridging of the Adour were being taken. It was hoped that the bridge flotilla, which had left the bay of St. Jean de Luz the previous evening, would be off the mouth of the Adour on the morning of the 23rd, but a gale which sprang up in the night had scattered it, and there were no signs of it. Nevertheless, Sir John Hope, who during the night of 22nd/23rd had moved the 1st division, which was relieved by Don Carlos's Spanish corps, the 18-pounder brigade and a pontoon section through the Bois de Bayonne towards the mouth of the Adour,

[1] Soult to Guerre, Orthez, 23rd February, 1814.

AND THE BATTLE OF ORTHEZ

determined not to await the arrival of the flotilla, and commenced to put a covering party across the river.

In a report to the Quartermaster-General, he thus describes the operation: "It was at first, I can assure you, a rather nervous operation. The first day (23rd) we missed the surprise by the pontoons sticking in the sand,[1] and we did not get them up till 10 a.m. We had that day only five small boats belonging to the pontoons to work with, and they did not take more than six or eight men at a trip. The rapidity of the tide for the greater part of the day rendered the rafts of no service.[2] All that day we had no prospect of the flotilla getting in for several days. Fortunately we had no opposition, for the guard at the battery ran away without firing a shot, and the guns had been removed. In the evening the eight companies of the 2nd brigade of Guards that had then crossed were attacked by about 1,200 to 1,400 men, and repulsed them immediately, rockets used against them and the gun-boats with effect."[3]

When the crossing commenced the 18-pounder brigade, established about a mile south of the spot selected as the site of the bridge, and the rocket men came into action against a French corvette, which was anchored between Boucau and Bayonne, and several gun-boats near her; whilst the whole of the allied investing line on the left bank made a false

---

[1] Larpent says they had to be carried down by the guardsmen for the last 500 yards, 26 men to a pontoon. Diary, p. 405.

[2] Each of the rafts referred to were formed of three pontoons lashed together and worked on a cable stretched across the river; each carried about 50 men. Owing, as stated by Hope, to the rapidity of the current, it was found they could only be operated during the short period of slack water between the tides.

[3] Hope to Murray, Boucau, 25th February, 1814.

WELLINGTON, THE CROSSING OF THE GAVES

attack on the enemy's entrenched camp which lasted till about 1 p.m.

24th February, 1814

Weather was fine, but cold and a hard frost. Sunrise 6.50 a.m., daybreak about 6.15 a.m. The ford at Viellenave is a long one, oblique to the course of the river, and its approaches are difficult.

Opposite Viellenave, the main line of heights, forming the divide between the gaves d'Oloron and de Pau, lies within about a mile and a half of the right bank of the former; from there it bends in a north-north-westerly direction by Castebon, 730 feet, and Orion, 745 feet, towards Salies, where the Saleys stream cuts through the ridge, and thence goes north-west towards Peyrehorade.

In this section of the area between the rivers, the roads available for movement from one to the other converge either on Berenx or Orthez, at which places were then the only permanent bridges over the gave de Pau. These roads were as follows:

(a) Sauveterre by Salies to Berenx; eleven miles, crosses the divide due north of Sauveterre at a height of about 680 feet, descends into the Saleys valley and thence to Berenx.

(b) Sauveterre to Orthez, twelve miles, ascends the divide north-east of Sauveterre, runs along it below Orion, whence it descends to the Saleys valley and thence an up and down hill road to Orthez.

(c) The main road from Mauleon and Navarrenx to Orthez follows the right bank of gave d'Oloron from Navarrenx to opposite Viellenave, then strikes

AND THE BATTLE OF ORTHEZ

almost due north across the divide at 700 feet, and thence descends into the valley of the Laas stream and onwards to Orthez, ten miles from Viellenave by Loubieng (six miles), Laa and the Magret heights. Besides these there were cross-country tracks connecting the roads, and a minor one from Naap, opposite Montford, which went due north and joined road (*b*) south of Magret.

The Light division was the first to cross the gave d'Oloron, which it probably reached about 11 a.m. Surtees thus describes the crossing: "On the 24th crossed two deep and rapid rivers, first the gave de Mauleon at Nabas, but the gave de Pau was not only deeper and more rapid, but the passage seemed intended to be disputed, since some French cavalry made their appearance as we approached the river. On bringing up some guns to the bank and a few shots being fired from them, and from a company of our 2nd battalion (95th Rifles), they withdrew. We now prepared to go over. Every man was ordered to take off his pouch and buckle it on top of his knapsack, the ford being so deep as to take the men up to and above the middle. We passed through Viellenave and formed in a field beyond the village[1] till the whole division had got over. When joined and formed, we moved to a high and ugly common in rear of the village of Orion, where we bivouacked for the night."[2]

It was some of the riflemen of G. Simmond's company who opened fire on the French cavalry. In his Diary, 24th February, he writes: "Passed the

---

[1] Should be village of Bugnein, as Viellenave is on the left bank.
[2] Surtees, "Twenty-five Years in the Rifle Brigade."

WELLINGTON, THE CROSSING OF THE GAVES

gave de Mauleon by a ford near the village of Nabas. Moved forward to the gave d'Oloron. Found a squadron of French cavalry drawn up on the opposite bank of the river. A neat little cottage had been built upon an eminence on its bank. I entered with some men and commenced firing from the chamber windows to cover the advance through the ford; the river being nearly up to the men's shoulders, compelled them to link together by the arms to enable them to cross. Millar's and Duncan's companies were the first that crossed"—and then goes on to say how the lady of the house, who, in an hysterical state of tears and laughter, would persist in going to the windows, had for her safety to be removed " with little ceremony " by him and one of his men, and shut up in a back room; also how one of his riflemen, " in very pretty style," shot off his horse a bold French chasseur who persisted in approaching the opposite bank.

The route taken by the Light division, by Castebon and thence along the summit of the divide to near Orion, was in accordance with the following memorandum issued by the Quartermaster-General at Viellenave (time not stated):

"VILLENAVE,
"24*th February*, 1814.

" Unless circumstances should occur to render it necessary to take up a more concentrated position, it is intended that the troops shall be placed as follows:

"Major-General Morillo's division investing Navarreins. The right of the other divisions under Sir R. Hill, in the neighbourhood of the village of

AND THE BATTLE OF ORTHEZ

Loubieng, occupying the great road from Navarreins to Orthez. The left of these divisions to be in communication with the troops at Orion.

"The Light division to be in the neighbourhood of Orion.

"The 6th division to be near the Light division.

"The 3rd division, and the Hussar brigade, to be near Sauveterre.

"The above divisions are to take care to be in direct communication with each other, and the general officers commanding divisions are requested to have the roads ascertained by which their divisions might be moved to either flank.

"G. MURRAY, Q.M.G."

The other divisions crossed the ford in accordance with the order of the previous day—the river was swift and deep, the cold intense and the ford a narrow one, the only casualties were two men drowned—with the exception of the 6th division, which, instead of moving to Viellenave, went direct from Gestas to Montford, and crossing near there by a ford unopposed moved to near Orion.

On receiving information of the allied crossing at Viellenave, Soult withdrew Harispe's division from about Sauveterre and posted it on the heights on the right bank of the Saleys stream between Montestrucq and l'hôpital d'Orion, thus covering the Sauveterre-Orthez road. From there he saw the Light division "arriving on the Castebon heights, from thence wheeling to their left and following the crest of the hills, they moved towards Orion. I was then on the heights of Montestrucq with Harispe's division. The orders I despatched as soon as I saw this movement arrived in time to stop the enemy's movement at about a mile from Orion, where Lieutenant-General Clausel had taken up a position with Villatte's division and Berton's light cavalry brigade.[1] General P. Soult was in front of Navarrenx with a brigade of cavalry and the 25th Light infantry. He was attacked by Morillo's Spanish division, a pretty strong corps of cavalry and a battery of artillery. He could not charge, and, finding himself cut off from the army by the enemy's columns which had crossed at Viellenave, he has been obliged to retire on Monein. The enemy's movement in this direction has stopped at the village of Gurs (on right bank of gave d'Oloron, about two miles south of Navarrenx). He has reported to me that the enemy was moving a column from Mauleon on Oloron and its destination Pau. I have sent out reconnoitring parties and I cannot yet be certain if it has taken this direction."[2]

On the morning of the 24th Picton with the 3rd division and Cotton with the Hussar brigade advanced at about 10 a.m. from Osserain and Arriverete against the bridge-head trenches and the houses opposite Sauveterre held by 300 men of Villatte's division, and the fords in the immediate neighbourhood, and a heavy cannonade was opened against the bridge-head position. Picton, not content to abide by his orders and demonstrate only, now ordered the Light companies of Keane's brigade

[1] Surtees, following on the extract already quoted, says: "Before we reached our ground this evening (24th) we observed a short distance to our left a body of about 200 French infantry moving on parallel to us, but apparently making all haste to get away in front of us." Evidently part of Villatte's rearguard.
[2] Soult to Guerre, Orthez, 24th February, 1814.

AND THE BATTLE OF ORTHEZ

to ford the river at Monein[1] and act against the left of Villatte's division. The ascent from the river was by a narrow and steep track; on reaching the top the party was charged by two battalions of the 119th and driven headlong into the river, losing 90 men, killed, prisoners or drowned. That the survivors were able to cross was mainly due to the fire of a battery which arrived in time to cover their retreat through the river. To support the infantry, which were seen to be seriously engaged, Cotton sent a squadron of 7th Hussars across the river by a ford near Barraute; but "the enemy being in force, and the ground such that cavalry could not act, the squadron was recalled."[2]

Vivian thus refers to the incident: "On the 24th at Sauveterre was the 3rd division with Lord Edward Somerset's cavalry brigade with orders to threaten a passage there, but not to cross; somehow or other, either through Sir S. Cotton or Picton, the Light companies of John Keane's brigade passed, and not being supported, were driven back with the loss of 5 officers and 40 men. I only wonder his getting back at all. There were very high words between Picton and Cotton on the disaster happening, and I expect some inquiry. Thank God, John is not blamed; he received positive orders to cross."[3]

[1] Village just above Sauveterre, not the town mentioned on previous page.
[2] "History of 7th Hussars."
[3] "Life of Lord Vivian." Letter to his wife: "Bastide de Béarn, 25th February, 1814. Vivian was not present, but Colonel Keane was an intimate friend and perhaps he got his information from him or some other cavalry officer who was present. Neither he nor Thackwell mention the crossing of the squadron, 7th Hussars. Napier states the crossing of the Light companies was made by Picton's order, and gives the losses as stated above."

WELLINGTON, THE CROSSING OF THE GAVES

Eventually the defenders of the bridge-head were driven out of it and retreated across the river; then Clausel blew up the bridge[1] and, on receipt of the orders sent by Soult as previously mentioned, retired to Orion, where with Harispe's division about Montestrucq on his left, he was in a position to delay the allied advance, and also give Taupin on the lower course of the gave time to retreat. The latter General was ordered to proceed to Orthez, by way of Salies and Berenx, where the bridge over the gave de Pau was to be destroyed, and thence by the Peyrehorade-Orthez road.

On the allied left, the 7th division remained in front of Peyrehorade, whilst the 4th moved towards Sorde and Lerein, and Vivian's cavalry brigade, headquarters at La Bastide de Béarn, threatened all the fords over the gave d'Oloron below Sauveterre. Morillo's division invested Navarrenx.

At Bayonne the passage of the 1st division across the Adour continued, and went on better than on the previous day, as Hope managed to get some more boats and some seamen from Biarritz. It was not till midday that there was any sign of the bridge flotilla. It was then seen making for the mouth of the Adour; ahead of it came Captain O'Reilly, R.N., with some other men-of-war boats; his boat on nearing the beach was upset, but he, though stunned by a violent blow from the overturned boat, was rescued with most of its crew by the soldiers. O'Reilly was followed by Lieutenant Debenham, whose boat got in safely. The tide, however, was now falling and the rest of

[1] Journal of a commissariat officer. "The 3rd division advanced and drove the enemy's pickets over the bridge into the town. The bridge was then blown up in our faces."

AND THE BATTLE OF ORTHEZ

the flotilla sheered off to await the change of the tide. When he had recovered O'Reilly and his men launched their boat and helped to ferry the troops across.

In the afternoon the wind increased and threatened a violent storm, but fell again towards evening and the surf abated. The flotilla headed by men-of-war boats then stood in again and most of it got into the river with, however, considerable losses in men and boats.

By nightfall the whole of the 1st division and Campbell's Portuguese brigade were over the Adour and bivouacked on the sandhills near its mouth.

CHAPTER XIII

ALLIED AND FRENCH MOVEMENTS. THE BRIDGE OVER THE ADOUR COMPLETED

Friday, 25th February, 1814

WEATHER continued fine and cold. " On the 25th the sun rose unobscured by a single cloud; it was a most beautiful morning ";[1] but rain fell in the evening.

During the night 24th/25th Harispe's division retired from about Montestrucq, crossed the gave de Pau by the Orthez bridge and entered the town. At 5 a.m. on 25th Clausel with Villatte's division and Berton's cavalry brigade marched from Orion for Orthez, four and a half miles; he left a rearguard on the Magret heights, which overlook the town, and in the Départ suburb on the left bank of the river. Later this rearguard was withdrawn and the heights and suburb abandoned. When all the troops had crossed, a mine was fired in the large arch of the bridge connecting the central tower on it with left bank.[2] Owing, however, to the solidity of the masonry and the insufficient quantity of powder used, the arch, though damaged, was not broken. The roadway through the base

---
[1] Batty, p. 125.
[2] Surtees mentions hearing the sound of the explosion as the Light division was marching towards Orthez.

of the tower—which is just sufficiently wide to allow one of the country carts to pass—was built up with masonry.[1]

Taupin, who by the evening of 24th had concentrated his division at Salies, marched during the night, crossed the gave at Berenx and blew up the bridge. At daybreak on 25th the four divisions of Foy, Darmagnac, Rouget and Taupin were assembled in proximity to the main road a short distance on the Orthez side of the village of Baigts, and there awaited orders. Detachments of the 15th Chasseurs had been left at the chief crossings on the gave de Pau from Peyrehorade to Baigts, and a battalion of Foy's division remained to guard the broken bridge at Berenx and the adjacent ford. Having received orders, the four divisions commenced at about 10 a.m. to march towards Orthez. Foy's and Darmagnac's divisions halted *en route* to occupy the Castetarbe spur, which, springing from the high ground to the north-east, crosses the main Bayonne road[2] at point 115 on present-day maps—one and a half miles west of Orthez and known as Point du Jour—and fills up the whole space thence to the river. The other two divisions halted near the western exit from Orthez.

The troops under Hill's command did not make an early start on this morning, for it was not till

---

[1] The bridge is stated to have been built in the fourteenth century. It has now only three arches, but originally had five, two of the four connecting the tower with right bank having been demolished when the railway, which runs close to the bank, was constructed.

[2] This refers to the road as then existing. Between Orthez and Ramous the present road follows closely the right bank of the gave de Pau.

WELLINGTON, THE CROSSING OF THE GAVES

midday that the cavalry followed by the Light division appeared on the heights of Magret overlooking the town and the Départ suburb. It may have been that some of the troops did not get as far forward as was expected owing to the time taken to cross at Viellenave. Napier says the crossing was not over till nightfall, and it is probable that some of the baggage train were unable to cross till the morning of the 25th.

Shortly after the arrival of the troops on the heights, Bean's troop came into action against Villatte's division then in process of forming behind the town, but the firing did not last long. A more serious demonstration was made about 2 p.m. when the Portuguese battalions of the Light division moved down into Départ in order to ascertain how the bridge was defended, to prevent the French working at it and, if possible, to effect a lodgement on it. The fighting went on till dark, but the bridge was stoutly defended by the voltigeurs of Villatte's division on the bridge and in the adjacent loopholed houses on the right bank[1] and they were assisted by the fire of a battery in action on a spur close to the west of the town. The allied troops were then withdrawn and the Light division moved down into the low ground behind the heights where they encamped for the night.[2]

Wellington, who was early on the ground, spent most of the day reconnoitring the enemy and the

---

[1] From Orthez to Puyoo the gave de Pau runs between steep rocky banks, is very deep, and its width not generally more than 50 yards.

[2] Moorsom, "History of 52nd Regiment." Sir Harry Smith in his Autobiography says: "Here our division (the Light) had one of the smartest skirmishes in a town I ever saw. The enemy held the bridge with great jealousy."

AND THE BATTLE OF ORTHEZ

ground. In the evening he went to Sauveterre where headquarters were established.

It would seem that on this day he deliberately kept the greater part of his troops concealed from the enemy behind the heights, which were held by outposts during the night, with cavalry pickets in front near the river.

On the 25th Picton re-established the bridge at Sauveterre. The Hussar brigade marched at 9 a.m., crossed the gave d'Oloron by a good ford below the bridge, and went into scattered cantonments beyond the town of Salies[1] The 3rd division followed and occupied the town that night.

The 4th and 7th divisions remained in front of Peyrehorade, the 4th being near Sorde,[2] where Beresford's headquarters were that night. Vivian's brigade crossed the gave d'Oloron and was distributed between the villages of Sorde, Cassaber and Caresse.

As the allied communications with the base and Sir J. Hope which ran through St. Palais might be interfered with from St. Jean Pied-de-Port, though invested by Mina's troops, or by national guards, Wellington issued an order that each of the regiments, which had proceeded to St. Jean de Luz to receive their new clothing, should on their return march to the army, halt at St. Palais till relieved by the next regiment coming up.

At Bayonne, the crossing of the Adour con-

---

[1] Thackwell's Diary.
[2] Sergeant J. S. Cooper, 7th Fusiliers, " Rough Notes of Seven Campaigns ": " On 25th we crossed a branch of the Adour, and slept in a low marshy meadow after standing for hours in the rain."

WELLINGTON, THE CROSSING OF THE GAVES

tinued,[1] and, as by 10 a.m. 5,000 men were across, Hope commenced his preliminary investment of the citadel of Bayonne and other French posts on the right bank, the troops employed being the 1st division, Campbell's Portuguese brigade, two squadrons of cavalry and two horse artillery guns. It was completed by about 3 p.m. The line held ran northwards from in front of Boucau to the Bayonne-Bordeaux road, thence north-eastwards to the Dax road and on to the Adour opposite Vieux Moguerre. This last section could not be held in strength, as only Campbell's Portuguese brigade was available; later on it was, when Bradford's brigade had crossed. Whilst the investment was proceeding the 5th division, Aylmer's brigade and Don Carlos's Spaniards made a feint attack on the entrenched camp. Work on the construction of the bridge of boats went on all day.

Saturday, 26th February.\ The Allied Movements.

Weather fine with frost.

On the morning of 26th the 2nd division, the Portuguese division and Fane's cavalry brigade with Bean's troop of horse artillery moved up and occupied the Magret heights. Wellington arrived early on the ground.

At 9. a.m the 3rd division with its artillery and that of the 2nd division marched from Salies towards Berenx[2]—distant four and a half miles over a hilly road. On its advanced guard arriving near the bridge it was found to have been blown up; search

[1] Hope to Wellington, Boucau, 3 p.m., 25th February, 1814.
[2] Thackwell's Diary.

AND THE BATTLE OF ORTHEZ

was then made for a ford and one discovered below the bridge.[1] Napier states: " Wellington immediately ordered Lord E. Somerset's cavalry and the 3rd division to cross the gave by fords below the broken bridge of Berenx." This is confirmed in a letter written by Major Jenkinson of the Chestnut troop to Colonel Frazer, Commanding the Royal Horse Artillery, in which, he says, " Sir T. Picton having discovered a ford at Berenx, he was desired to cross there."[2] Apparently the circumstances were reported to Wellington, for as Picton was probably unaware of what progress was being made by Beresford's column, and the enemy's infantry (Foy's battalion) on the further side being doubtless seen, it was manifestly risky for the 3rd division to cross alone until assured of effective support. On receipt of Wellington's order the division commenced to cross and was over by 4 p.m.[3]

To turn now to the troops under Beresford. As has been stated, Vivian's cavalry brigade was located on the night of 25th/26th February in the villages of Sorde, Castebar and Caresse; the portion in Sorde apparently consisted of two squadrons of 18th Light Dragoons. These two squadrons, guided by a miller, very early in the morning crossed the gave de Pau by a ford about a mile above its junction with the gave d'Oloron and close to the village of Cauneille. They then advanced

[1] There were two fords below the bridge, one about half a mile from the bridge and the other a mile and a half. The former was probably used by the 3rd division and the latter by the Hussar brigade, as Thackwell says " the brigade crossed by a good ford about a mile below the bridge of Berenx."
[2] Letters of Colonel Sir A. S. Frazer, K.C.B., written during Peninsula and Waterloo campaigns. Major Jenkinson to Lieutenant-Colonel Frazer, Grenade, 4th March, 1814.
[3] Picton to Colonel Pleyden, Cazeres, 4th March, 1814.

WELLINGTON, THE CROSSING OF THE GAVES

along the Orthez road driving back the French cavalry posts, which had been left to watch the fords, as far as Puyoo and Ramous; here the latter formed on their supports and the whole again advancing compelled the British to retire. Meanwhile the remainder of Vivian's brigade, which marched at 8 a.m., reached the river near Lahontan, forded it and gained the main road at Labatut. Here, by Beresford's order, a squadron of 18th Hussars was detached to the north towards Habas and Tilh to watch the Orthez-Dax road which passes through the latter village. The brigade then reinforced the original two squadrons, and advancing drove the French cavalry through Puyoo and Ramous; the latter then retired on to their infantry posted on a wooded hill over which the road passed; leaving a picket in observation, the brigade fell back to Ramous.

The 4th division, from their bivouac in the fields on the left bank of the gave d'Oloron, crossed that river and then moved northwards to the ford near Cauneille where the 18th squadrons had passed, and there forded the gave de Pau. In a letter Major Mill of 40th Regiment,[1] Anson's brigade, thus describes the crossings. ' " The regiment passed the one (gave d'Oloron) soon after dawn and the other at half-past six, when the entire ground was white with frost and the water so intensely cold as almost to deprive me of breath. The stream was up to my hips and up to the middle of the short men, and the breadth of water was such

---

[1] Smythies, " History of 40th Regiment " : The distance to be crossed was increased by the fact that when using the ford an island in the river covered with oziers had to be crossed.

AND THE BATTLE OF ORTHEZ

that it occupied ten minutes for one man to pass over as quickly as possible." The 7th division followed the 4th.[1]

In the absence of the necessary details it is hardly possible to state at what hours the division passed the points on the route already mentioned. Considering the early start it is probable that besides the usual short halts a considerable one, perhaps of an hour, was also made. Assuming this halt and that each division took about two hours to cross the gave de Pau and close up, the advanced guard of the 4th division would reach Baigts about 3 p.m. and the whole division be up at about 3.50 p.m. and the 7th at about 5 p.m. which, as will be seen, corresponds fairly with the times given by Soult in his report to the War Minister.

The order to cross the gave apparently did not reach the Hussar brigade till after noon. Then moving towards the river, the 15th Hussars leading to the left of the 3rd division, the brigade crossed it " at a good ford about a mile below the bridge of Berenx,"[2] where the 15th came in contact with the French infantry, which had opposed Vivian's brigade, and lost one man killed and several wounded. The brigade then drove back the French battalion towards Baigts, time probably towards 2 p.m. when the 4th division advanced guard was

---

[1] Napier states that Beresford's troops crossed partly by a pontoon bridge, partly by a ford. The memorandum by the Q.M.G. on the movements of the allied troops says: " The 4th and 7th divisions having forded the gave de Pau a little above its junction with the gave d'Oloron." Wellington in his despatch says *below* the junction, which seems a mistake, the tide reaching Peyrehorade and the volume of water there increased by that of gave d'Oloron. A detachment of 51st Light Infantry was left at Peyrehorade to hold the town.

[2] Thackwell's Diary.

approaching. As this came up the 15th Chasseurs and the infantry retired through Baigts towards Foy's division on the Castetarbe spur. The Hussar brigade fell back to Puyoo and Bellocq.

Thus " in the nick of time Wellington secured the fords near Berenx by which he wished to secure the concentration of the greater part of his forces on the right bank of the gave." [1] And now a real junction between the two groups of the allied army was established, and a direct line of communication with Bayonne obtained.

Wellington's original intention appears to have been to attack the French on the 26th. Napier says: " Lord Wellington's first design was to pass these (above the town of Orthez) with Hill's corps and the Light division; but, when he heard that Beresford had crossed the gave de Pau, he suddenly changed his design and, as we have seen, passed the 3rd division over and threw his bridge at Berenx." In the letter from Major Jenkinson to Colonel A. Frazer already quoted, he says: " It had been determined that the passage of the gave de Pau should be effected by Marshal Beresford on the morning of the 26th at Peyrehorade with the 3rd (?), 4th and 7th divisions, and at Départ and Biron by Hill's corps and the Light division and the 6th division should push through the town if possible and establish communication between the right and left columns." Major Jenkinson, of course, was not in a position to know details of Wellington's plan; his statement may have been based on preliminary orders given, or on current reports in the army, but it coincides generally with

[1] Vidal de la Blache, " L.'Invasion dans le Midi."

AND THE BATTLE OF ORTHEZ

Napier's account. In his autobiography, Sir Harry Smith also states it was Wellington's intention to fight on the 26th had the 3rd division been able to reach its position in time; he says: "I heard the Duke say, 'Very well, Murray, if the division does not arrive in time we must delay the attack till to-morrow. However, I must have a sleep.' He folded his little white cloak round him and lay down saying, 'Call me in time, Murray.' Murray woke the Duke saying: 'It is too late to-day, my Lord.' 'Very well, my orders for to-morrow hold good.'"[1] It is unfortunate that the point cannot be cleared up, as there appears to be no record of the orders given to Beresford and Picton. The general impression at headquarters appears to have been that Soult had no intention of awaiting an attack, but would again retire as heretofore. The decision to postpone the fight was probably a fortunate one.

During the day some of Hill's Light troops kept up the skirmish in the Départ suburb and on the banks of the river in order to hold the attention of the French.[2] To further this and divert attention from what was going on down the river, Hill was directed to order the Light division to move round to the right, descend into the low ground and cross the river by a ford some little distance above the bridge—probably where the paper works now are. The movement is thus described in Cope's "History of the Rifle Brigade."

"On 26th ordered to fall in about 12 o'clock and ordered to move to the right and cross a ford

[1] G. C. Moore Smith, "Autobiography of Lieutenant-General Sir H. Smith."
[2] Simmonds: "The light troops skirmished with the enemy till dark."

WELLINGTON, THE CROSSING OF THE GAVES
a little above the ruined bridge. The riflemen marched off; and on the way a staff officer overtook them and ordered them to conceal themselves as much as possible behind any irregularities of the ground.

"This they did and crept on, and just as they got to the open ground, they were suddenly countermanded and moved far to the left. The truth is this was a double feint, first, to make the enemy believe our people were going to attempt the ford, and then, lest they should have suspected that any open demonstration to do so was a feint, to make them fancy that by our stealth and getting under cover that it was hoped to conceal the movement from them."

Simmonds says: "I was so impressed with the certainty of an attack being made, that I pulled off my socks and put them into my cap to keep them dry.[1] A large force of the enemy was joined up ready for us and several pieces of cannon. When we were nearly within range an order came to retire, and now a movement was made to the left of Orthez."

This move to the left was made in consequence of Wellington's change of plan. He had now decided to make his main attack by moving eastwards towards the town and the heights above it from about Baigts, and to provide sure communication and speedy concentration across the gave by forming a bridge near Berenx by means of the pontoon detachment with Beresford's column. To this end the 6th and Light divisions were ordered

[1] Simmonds carried his socks in his shako on occasions; but always the little pocket-book, a few inches square, containing his current diary.

AND THE BATTLE OF ORTHEZ

to move that afternoon towards Berenx—distant four to five miles—where they would be in a position to cross early the following morning, and yet not be too distant to support Hill's Corps before Orthez should it be necessary to do so. The Light division moved by the road along the left bank of the river by St. Suzanne and Salles, and " encamped near Salles close to the pontoon bridge," [1] the 6th marching along the high ground which runs parallel to the course of the river, and halted for the night about Berenx.[2]

At Bayonne the construction of the bridge was continued and was completed towards evening. During the day Bradford's Portuguese division was ferried across, and it moved to reinforce the left of the investing line; another squadron of cavalry was also put across. During the day the cavalry already across had reconnoitred to the north and north-east, patrols of the 12th Light Dragoons reaching St. Paul opposite Dax on the Mont de Marsan road, St. Vincent on the Bordeaux road

---

[1] Simmonds' Diary.
[2] In his despatch to the Minister on 26th February, Soult says that " at the same time as the head of Beresford's corps arrived about Baigts, two other British divisions were descending by the route of Salies and the plateau behind St. Suzanne towards the ford at Berenx." Soult at this time was on the Castetarbe spur at Point de Jour, height 380 feet. From the map it would appear that from this point no part of the route from Salies to Berenx would be visible owing to the heights bordering the left bank, and along which the 6th division was moving, which ranges from 450 to 480 feet. Lapène also states that General Foy, when visiting the posts of his division on the right bank of the river about midday, saw large masses of troops moving on the left bank towards Berenx. From the low ground on the right bank below the Castetarbe spur, it would be impossible to see any part of the Salies-Berenx road. It would seem that Salies in Soult's report is a mistake for Salles, a village on left bank near Berenx and on the road from St. Suzanne.

WELLINGTON, THE CROSSING OF THE GAVES

and Peyrehorade where communication with 7th division was established.[1]

In the evening Wellington returned to Sauveterre. From there he wrote to Hope as follows: ".We crossed the gave de Pau this evening without opposition. The enemy's whole force was in front of Orthez, but I understand they commenced to retire at dusk. I send Campbell to bring up headquarters, and I enclose a letter to General Freyre to request him to march, which I beg you to send him if the bridge is ready. I request you also to send with him the Portuguese 9-pounders. I have ordered up boats from Urt to Porte-de-Lanne to form a bridge. Communication is open with Peyrehorade, and it would be desirable to station parties of dragoons at Biaudos and Biarotte (on the road about midway between Bayonne and Peyrehorade) so as to keep the communication. If we cannot use the Adour as a port, we must carry from St. Jean de Luz across the bridge to the embarking place above Bayonne and then use the navigation." [2] The letter to Freyre contained the order to march, and said: " I have ordered the Commissary-General to see that you are provided with everything, and I pray you to keep the strictest discipline, without which we are lost." In an earlier letter to the Commissary-General he was informed that Wellington had ordered the Andalusian reserve, under

---

[1] Hope to Wellington, 27th February.
[2] Wellington to Hope, Sauveterre, 26th February, 1814. Owing to the dangers of the bar, Admiral Penrose recommended no attempt should be made to use the Adour as a harbour. On the 25th Hope was told to direct Colonel de Lancey, the D.Q.M.G., to select a convenient place, above Bayonne, where stores, etc., could be embarked and a road to it from the site of the bridge.

AND THE BATTLE OF ORTHEZ

the Conde de la Bispal,[1] and the 3rd Spanish army under the Prince of Anglona to be in readiness to march, and that they were to be supplied with ten days' biscuits from the magazine near Pamplona.

Murray also wrote to Hill: "I conclude the detachment of pontoons, ordered to join you, will have arrived to-night. If so, Lord Wellington wishes you to endeavour to establish a bridge near Orthez as early as you can in the morning. I beg you will send a report to the left in the morning of the appearance of things in your front. I expect we shall hear from you that the enemy have retreated. If we get into Orthez every exertion should be made to repair the bridge, so that our pontoons may become again disposable for other service for which they will be immediately wanted."[2]

From these letters, it is apparent that at General Headquarters the expectation was that Soult would again retreat and not stand to fight on the morrow.

26th February, 1814. *The French about Orthez*

About midday on the 26th the French army about Orthez was distributed as follows: Foy and Darmagnac's divisions were holding the Castetarbe spur. Foy on the left extending to the gave de Pau and Darmagnac's division prolonging the line

---
[1] Now commanded by General Giron, O'Donnell having gone on sick leave.
[2] Sydney, "Life of Lord Hill," Murray to Hill, Sauveterre, 26th February. No time given, but must have been written in the evening. It would seem the pontoons did not arrive, or at any rate were not used.

WELLINGTON, THE CROSSING OF THE GAVES

along the spur by point 393 to near the Orthez-Dax road. Behind these divisions were those of Taupin and Rouget, on or near the high road towards the western exit from Orthez. Harispe's division was in and about the town, holding the bridge and along the river and in contact with Hill's light troops on the opposite bank and in Départ. Villatte's division was concentrated to the east of the town on the slopes above Souars.

With the exception of the 15th Chasseurs of Vial's brigade, which, as we have seen, had been detailed to guard the fords over the gave de Pau between Peyrehorade and Orthez, a distance of eighteen miles, the remaining six regiments under General P. Soult were this day,[1] to the south-east of Orthez watching the gave from Orthez to Pau, twenty-four miles, and reconnoitring the roads leading from Pau towards Oloron and Mauleon. Thus, except in the neighbourhood of Pau, there was not a single cavalry man south of the gave to gain information of what the enemy was doing; and the greater portion of the force was on the flank where no real danger threatened.

Lapène states that General Foy, who, with his Chief Staff Officer was visiting the posts of his division on the right bank of the river, distinctly saw about midday large masses of troops moving on the left bank towards Berenx, and reported the fact to the Marshal. The latter, being himself out reconnoitring, did not receive the report till about 3 p.m. when he returned to Orthez. Meanwhile, at about the same hour, Colonel Faverot of the 15th Chasseurs arrived at headquarters, and made

[1] Soult's order of 26th February, 1814.

AND THE BATTLE OF ORTHEZ

a verbal report to Soult regarding the crossing of the gave de Pau by Beresford's column and its subsequent progress. Thus it was not till 3 p.m. that Soult knew of Beresford's crossing soon after daybreak, of his close approach to Orthez and that Picton was already crossing near Berenx. He was badly served by his cavalry, and the news was evidently a surprise to him. "In the brutal manner habitual with him"[1] Soult told Colonel Faverot what he thought of him, and sent him back to his regiment. The Marshal himself then proceeded at once to the Castetarbe spur, about Point de Jour, where he arrived probably about 3.45 p.m. From this point there is a good view to the westward, and he saw that "the head of the enemy's column was already at Baigts, and two other strong columns of the enemy were descending, one by the route of Salies and the other by the heights of St. Suzanne towards the ford below Berenx."[2] A little later Soult was joined there by Generals D'Erlon, Clausel, Darmagnac and Harispe, Foy also being present. The latter in a letter stated: "My position was such that from it the enemy could be best observed; a sort of discussion took place. Clausel, whose custom it was always to recommend vigorous and even rash action, stated as his opinion that this was an occasion to give battle. No other General, however, supported him." Soult was undecided, and the opportunity, whatever might have come of it, was lost.

However undecided Soult may have been between the three courses open to him—to fight

---
[1] Vidal de la Blache.
[2] Soult's report on the battle of Orthez, 27th February, 1814.

WELLINGTON, THE CROSSING OF THE GAVES

then, or on the morrow, or to retire during the night—he, at least, realized that he must at once shake out the excessive concentration in which his army then stood about Orthez if he was to forestall the enemy in the occupation of ground highly important to both sides, but essential to him in case of retreat. He at once sent orders to Reille to take command of Taupin's and Rouget's divisions, and move by the Dax road to the plateau on the Orthez side of the village of St. Boes; and to Darmagnac to extend his right to the Dax road.

Soult then returned to Orthez. Taupin and Rouget moved towards St. Boes at 6 p.m., and it was probably this movement which led to Wellington's agents reporting that the French army was retiring.

In the evening the order for the occupation of the position, in which Soult had at length decided to fight, was issued to the Corps Commanders. The following is a summary of it:[1]

Reille, to whose command Paris's brigade[2] and the 21st Chasseurs were provisionally attached, was directed to extend his position as far as St. Boes, to keep patrols out on the Dax road and to keep the most careful watch on the enemy's movements in front of St. Boes and on the slopes descending towards Baigts and Ramous.

D'Erlon, with Foy's and Darmagnac's divisions, was to change position, Foy taking up a line from about the point where the 393 spur springs from the main ridge and thence southwards to the

---

[1] For a full copy of the order see Appendix D.
[2] In the order Paris's brigade was given a divisional status and designated 9th division.

AND THE BATTLE OF ORTHEZ

Orthez-Peyrehorade main road. Posts only were to be left on the Castetarbe spur. Darmagnac to be on Foy's right on the upper part of spur 528. The artillery of both divisions to be on the Dax road near its junction with that leading to Sallespisse. So placed both divisions would be able, if necessary, to support Reille's corps.

Clausel's corps to form the left of the army. Harispe's division to be placed in echelons behind Orthez on the long spur running south from point 572, detachments being left in the town to hold the bridge and in advance of the suburb at the western exit from the town, these detachments to be supported by one battalion. Villatte's division to be moved during the night to a position north of the town and so placed that it could be moved rapidly to join the right of the army. If so moved Paris's brigade was to again come under Clausel's command.

P. Soult, who, with four regiments of cavalry and 25th Light infantry was still on the left of the army between Orthez and Pau, was directed to order the 22nd Chasseurs at Lescar to send constant patrols towards Oloron and Mauleon. This regiment together with national guard legion of the Hautes-Pyrénées was, if necessary, to defend Pau. He was to leave General Berton with the two regiments of his brigade and the infantry battalions to watch and guard the fords over the gave de Pau between Orthez and Lescar; and himself with the two remaining regiments, 5th and 10th Chasseurs, to move over the hills to Sallespisse so as to arrive there at daybreak on the 27th. If Berton was obliged to retire during the

27th, he was to do so towards Sault de Navailles, reporting his movements to Harispe, and offering as much resistance as possible to the enemy's advance.

If the army was compelled to retreat it would do so on Sault de Navailles, Reille to so manœuvre as to have a division at Amou. (On the Luy de Béarn, five miles north-west of Sault de Navailles.)

The reserve artillery to be at Sault de Navailles and the headquarters of the ambulance service at Sallespisse—all the trains of the army to move that night to Sault de Navailles and engineer troops were to be moved to the junction of Dax and Sallespisse roads and were to immediately commence to repair the latter.

In his despatch to the Minister that night[1] Soult reports the information he had received regarding the crossing of the gave by Beresford's column and its advance, as has been already detailed, and the orders he had given. He goes on to say: " It is very probable that there will be a battle to-morrow as the two armies are so close together that it can hardly be avoided. I shall act so that it may be one glorious to the Emperor's Arms. If I am obliged to retreat, I will do so towards Sault de Navailles. I expect, however, that to-morrow columns of the enemy will cross between Orthez and Lescar, because he has been seen reconnoitring the fords, and making demonstrations which leave no doubt on the point. Two regiments of cavalry and two battalions will guard this line. I have left a cavalry regiment and the Legion of the Hautes-Pyrénées to defend Pau,

[1] Soult to Guerre, Orthez, 26th February, 1814.

AND THE BATTLE OF ORTHEZ

and reconnoitre in that direction. Reports received announce that a column is marching on Oloron, but had not arrived there this morning. Enemy's cavalry was at Monein and a heavy cannonade has been heard in the direction of Navarrenx. All the national guards of the Basses-Pyrénées have deserted, either abandoning their arms or taking them with them."

In Soult's order may be read his evident anxiety for the safety of his right, for, if defeated, his retreat on Sault de Navailles would be gravely compromised, and, as before, his fear that the enemy was undertaking a wide turning movement on his left.

CHAPTER XIV

SOME OBSERVATIONS ON THE OPERATIONS UP TO AND INCLUDING 26TH FEBRUARY, 1814

THE 26th February saw the completion of the plan, which was not the least masterly conception of the great allied Commander.

By a surprise the Adour had been crossed below Bayonne, that "stupendous undertaking"—as Napier terms it; the bridge of boats had been completed, by the patient and intense attention to detail of its designers and constructors, by the gallantry of the seamen who brought in the materials, and by their and the soldiers' labour.

During the thirteen days the Joyeuse, the Bidouze, the Saison and the gaves of Oloron and Pau had been crossed with under 400 casualties; the citadel of Bayonne had been invested; direct communication between the three groups of the allied army was opened and possession of the great roads from above the citadel, Wellington's primary object, was secured.

Now the opposing forces stood face to face for the fight, which was to take place to-morrow.

This would seem a convenient opportunity to discuss some of the interesting points connected with the operations up to this date.

It will have been noticed that on more than one occasion Soult, in his despatches to the

WELLINGTON

War Minister, either as a reason for action taken, or to account for an allied success, lays stress on the overwhelming numerical superiority of the latter's forces. It is, of course, a fact that Wellington's total resources in men largely exceeded those of his adversary; but this superiority largely consisted in the 40,000 Spanish troops under his direct command, of whom only about 16,000 were on French territory, 12,000 in the investments of Bayonne and St. Jean Pied-de-Port, and only Morillo's 4,000 in the field army who from the 24th February were employed investing Navarrenx. The point is an important one; several French writers on the campaign give an exaggerated estimate of the allied strength, and, so far as the operations hitherto described in detail are concerned, it is well the reader should have as accurate a detail as is possible of the strength of the French and allied field armies.

When, in January, 1814, the cavalry, infantry and artillery which, at the Emperor's call, left the army of the Pyrenees to join the Grand Army, the strength of the former was reduced to 67,433 of all arms,[1] of whom 19,060 were in the garrisons of Bayonne, St. Jean Pied-de-Port, Navarrenx, etc., leaving 48,373 men available for field operations, this total was further reduced to 43,153 on the 17th January by the inclusion of Abbé's division (5,220) in the Bayonne garrison. This 43,153 was therefore the maximum available for Soult's field army—if we disregard any parties of conscripts

---

[1] Vidal de la Blache, "L'Invasion dans le Midi," p. 203. State of 16th January, 1814—men present and fit for duty only included.

WELLINGTON, THE CROSSING OF THE GAVES

which may have joined him meanwhile—which was made up as follows:

	Strength	
Light cavalry, 2 brigades	2,966	
Infantry, 6 divisions	34,234	
Troops, hors de ligne, i.e., artillery and its train. Engineers, 4 companies; pontoon train, 2 companies; Gendarmerie and 2 battalions; transport train	5,953	45 guns
Total of field army	43,153	

Wellington opened the campaign with about 36,000 men of whom 4,000 were Spaniards. When he determined to push matters on the right, and ordered up the 6th and Light divisions his total force was as follows:[1]

Light cavalry[2]	3,340	
Infantry, 7 divisions, less 5 battalions	34,493	
Artillery, engineers pontoon train and Staff Corps, say	2,000	54 field guns 4 mountain guns
Morillo's division	4,000	
Total	43,833	reduced on 26th February by 370 casualties to 43,453

[1] These figures are exclusive of officers, and are taken from the detailed monthly state showing the strength of each division of the army on the 30th December, 1813—which appears to be the last one in the Record Office—and include non-commissioned officers and rank and file present and fit for duty, the sick and wounded, all on command, and missing still on the strength being deducted. The cavalry figures are from the state of 17th February; those for artillery and engineers from that of 25th, an approximate division being made between the force with Wellington and that with Hope. As the difference between the total infantry (British and Portuguese) present and fit for duty in the states for 30th December and 17th February is only 419, the figures of the former state may be taken as approximately correct.

[2] All the heavy cavalry were still in Spain.

AND THE BATTLE OF ORTHEZ

It will thus be seen that, instead of an overwhelming superiority on the allied side, the fighting portions of the opposing forces were practically of equal strength; and that after the investment of Navarrenx on the 24th February, Wellington's force was numerically inferior to that of Soult by about 3,000 men. The statements of the latter were made to throw dust in the eyes of the War Minister and the Emperor.

Soult from the first spread his field army along the river lines he made believe to defend. Napoleon himself tells us how river lines should be defended. "There is nothing more dangerous," he says, writing to Prince Eugène, "than to attempt seriously to defend a river by lining its bank; the enemy will always gain a passage by surprise. To defend a water course there is no other way than to dispose your troops so as to be ready to fall *en masse* on the enemy before his crossing is completed."[1] Which can only be done by maintaining a close watch on the enemy, and keeping the mass of the defending force concentrated at a carefully selected point.

Soult, with all his experience and ability, probably knew this as well as Napoleon did. He had had one personal experience of Wellington's readiness to effect a surprise at the passage of the Duero at Oporto on the 12th May, 1809, another by the crossing of the Bidassoa on 7th October, 1813, and was within the next few days to have it twice repeated. Despite his brave words to the Minister, he seems from the first to have made up his mind

---

[1] Napoleon to Prince Eugène, 15th March, 1813, "Correspondence de Napoleon, No. 19721."

WELLINGTON, THE CROSSING OF THE GAVES

not to put up any real defence on any of the gaves. His orders to evacuate his depôts to the Garonne and thence eastwards by water, and his private letter to the Commissary-General, M. Favier, of 14th February—" I am approaching the gaves defending the country *pied à pied*, but the enemy is so strong I cannot stop his advance. I beg you send our wives towards Auch (forty miles west of Toulouse), and they ought to be always ready to proceed to Toulouse "—seem to indicate clearly the line he intended the campaign to take, so far as it was in his power to do so.

Why was it that from the first he should take the view that what he terms a *pied à pied* defence of the country, which in plain terms meant a constant retreat before his enemy, was the most suitable plan to adopt? No doubt there are reasons which can be advanced for such an attitude. His small remaining army stood as the only defence of the south of France; its only hope of any substantial support was in what remained of Suchet's army of Aragon and Catalonia; newly raised conscripts were of little use even if they could be clothed and armed. To continually retire meant drawing the enemy daily farther from his bases on the sea and adding to his difficulties, which difficulties might give rise to an opportuny for a counterstroke. It is not easy to give Soult, operating in his own country with many sources of information open to him, credit for an honest belief in his enemy's superiority, an enemy with whom he had been in close contact for many months, even if, as was the fact, that throughout these first operations on every important occasion of contact the allies were

AND THE BATTLE OF ORTHEZ

in superior force. This was due to Wellington's skill, not to his numerical superiority.

But was such a plan of defence a suitable one under the existing circumstances? His Emperor with inferior forces, but with matchless skill, was thrusting right and left in Northern France against his enemies, for France and his Empire was at stake. Who shall say that Soult should not have tried to follow his example? Certainly Napoleon did not. "Cause the War Minister," he wrote to King Joseph at Paris, "to repeat again my order to the Duke of Dalmatia that he is not to surrender country without fighting a battle, even if he has only 20,000 men." It must not be forgotten, moreover, that Soult deliberately reduced his field army by one division when he sent Abbé's division into Bayonne.

The fact seems to be that Soult in those early days was in a confused and uncertain state of mind; he was dominated by Wellington. He early recognized that the object of Hill's force was to menace his left and oblige him either to fight or retreat. He was not strong enough to fight there, so retreat he must; and it was not long before he realized that if this was to continue, he could not maintain his long extended line and that his right was likely to be isolated. Instead, however, of boldly concentrating towards his left and being ready to attack, his best defence against a crossing of the Adour, he adopted half measures, sent Darmagnac's division, the nearest to Bayonne, towards Dax on the 17th February and Rouget's towards Porte-de-Lanne. Thus the defence of the lower Adour was given up just when it was most

WELLINGTON, THE CROSSING OF THE GAVES

necessary; and just when it suited Wellington, who, having established his right between the Saison and the gave d'Oloron, now considered that he had removed the French army sufficiently far from Bayonne to permit him to proceed with the main object of his plan—the crossing of the Adour below that city. Another result of this half-hearted concentration was that from the 17th to the 24th Darmagnac's and Rouget's divisions under D'Erlon remained quite inactive.

It has been said that the allied left on the 15th was in peril of being driven back had Soult concentrated the four divisions on his right about Bidache, and advanced against Beresford. Wellington has admitted that then he was not strong enough there; but the prompt measures he took removed the danger.

It must be remembered also that at this time, owing to a sudden rise in the Adour, communication across the river at Porte-de-Lanne was interrupted, and that the bridge of boats there was not re-established till the 17th, so that Darmagnac and Rouget could not have joined Foy and Taupin till the 18th at the earliest.

To mystify and mislead your enemy is an axiom of war. Soult had a master in the art against him. "No general, not even Napoleon, ever brought about so many startling surprises as Wellington."[1] The passages of the Duero and the Adour are instances quoted by Colonel Henderson. We may perhaps add the crossings of the Bidassoa and that of the gave de Pau at Viellenave. The operations we have been considering may be held to contain

---

[1] Henderson, "Stonewall Jackson," Vol. II, p. 491.

AND THE BATTLE OF ORTHEZ

yet another instance, which, though it led up to no tactical surprise, appears to have had a very considerable influence on the operations so far followed, and also on the battle of Orthez.

This is the story: On the afternoon of 21st February three British cavalry men were seen approaching the little town of Mauleon on the Saison, whence a good road leads to Oloron and Pau. In the town there was a party of the national guards of the Basses-Pyrénées detailed to defend it. Seeing the approach of the enemy's cavalry, and doubtless imagining the small party was the advance of a considerable force, the national guards evacuated the town and retreated southwards towards Tardets, saying they did so in order not to compromise the town by active defence. The British patrol then entered the town and announced, probably to the Mayor or other authority, that on the following day a British division of some five to six thousand men would arrive, and doubtless desired that the local authorities would make the necessary arrangements. The patrol was cordially received, and, after having been given refreshments, departed.

News of the incident reached Soult next day. Already anxious about his left flank and his communications with Toulouse, he may have been the more likely to credit the report, as at this time he was under the impression that the allied troops had been or were about to be withdrawn from the investment of Bayonne, and replaced by a Spanish force. Again on the 23rd similar reports, which doubtless emanated from Wellington's agents, reached him. Writing to the Minister on that date, he says: "All reports state that the enemy's plan is to advance by Oloron on Pau and Tarbes with a formidable artillery and several pontoon sections. I am indeed really astonished." Again on the 24th P. Soult reported that an enemy's column was moving from Mauleon on Oloron with Pau as its objective. On the 25th Soult wrote that all reports received confirm the march of the enemy on Oloron. Thoroughly alarmed, Soult now sent the greater part of his cavalry up the gave in the direction of Lescar and Pau. From his order of the 26th it is clear that on that critical day out of his seven cavalry regiments six were above Orthez in the Pau direction, and one only on the Peyrehorade road, and that except near Pau, there was not one French cavalryman over the gave; and no attempt seems to have been made to find what was happening on the left bank, or to watch Picton and Beresford. Though all the bridges had been broken, except at Orthez, the numerous fords were just as open to the French cavalry as they were to the allied. No force can be safe from surprise; and no cavalry can do its protective work properly unless, once contact has been gained, it keeps the enemy continuously under observation. Remaining as it did on the right bank of the gave, the French cavalry was in no position to do this, or to gain any clue to the further movements of the enemy.

Soult's disposition of his cavalry shows how little he really knew of how his enemy was located. Six regiments far on the flank where no danger threatened; one only on the road which was the direct route whereby Wellington's left wing could join him. From his despatch of 25th February,

AND THE BATTLE OF ORTHEZ

Soult appears to have considered that on that date Wellington had with him about Magret his whole field force, for he says: "All the enemy's army, except that part of it about Bayonne, is in front of me."[1] He had quite lost touch of the allied left under Beresford; closely concentrated about Orthez, and with his cavalry wrongly placed, he was, as General Dumas aptly describes, "being stifled for want of air," that is of information. That he was so may be said to be due, in part at any rate, to that afternoon ride of the three horsemen to Mauleon.

Colonel Faverot of the 15th Chasseurs certainly failed on the 26th in not sending early reports of the allied crossings near Peyrehorade, though he and his regiment put up a good resistance against heavy odds. That he was pitted eventually against two brigades was not his fault but that of Soult. How different the events on that day might have been if there had been a strong French cavalry force towards Peyrehorade and Soult had had early notice of Beresford's movements.

It is only fair to add that towards the end of the day the British cavalry do not seem to have been as enterprising as they might have been. Both brigades retired behind Beresford's infantry when it came up, and no attempt was made to push towards Orthez and gain such information of the French dispositions as was possible. They would have been brought up on approaching the Castetarbe spur, but that would have been something to know, and it had to be done eventually by the infantry after a long march.

Napoleon has said "it is an axiom that the

[1] Soult to Guerre, Orthez, 25th February, 1814.

WELLINGTON, THE CROSSING OF THE GAVES

junction of the different corps of an army should never take place near the enemy."[1] Yet Napoleon himself, and Generals such as Wellington, Lee and Molke have violated this safe rule—Wellington at Vitoria, and here again on the 26th in the march of Beresford's column. Here was an opportunity for the fulfilment of Soult's repeatedly expressed intention of falling on the first allied column which gave him a chance. Learning about 3 p.m. that a strong column was on the march towards Baigts, about an hour later he saw its advance arriving on ground less than two miles in front of his position, on which one division was standing under arms, with another on its right and two more a little over a mile in rear—a great opportunity for an enterprising General.

Why did Wellington give him such a chance? It must be because, greatly daring when circumstances required it, he took no counsel of his fears, knowing so intimately his opponent's character. And he was right; Soult surprised, declined the opening offered him. "He dared not attack, he dared not retreat, because from the 17th to the 26th February he had repeatedly told Clarke that he only awaited the opportunity to attack the enemy, and because the news of the action at Monterrau had just reached the army."[2]

A constant feature of Wellington's leading was the concealment of his troops, except when circumstances required it to be otherwise. We have seen his caution to Hill, when he left him in front of Sauveterre, and himself returned to St. Jean de Luz

---

[1] Yorck, " Napoleon as a General," Vol. I, p. 74.
[2] Vidal de la Blache, " L'Invasion dans le Midi," p. 231.

AND THE BATTLE OF ORTHEZ

on the 19th February; and again in front of Orthez on the 25th, when Soult believed the whole allied force lay hidden behind the heights of Magret. On the 26th he showed a larger number, and made feints to cross in order to concentrate French attention on himself during Beresford's march.

The comparative inaction of Beresford's corps during the 24th and 25th may appear to be without reason; for Foy and the other divisions had marched towards Orthez on the 24th, and it would seem that Beresford might have crossed on the 25th and made good some of the distance towards Baigts. Had he done so, however, it would certainly have become known to Soult, and it was probably to avoid this and also to make sure of Picton's junction that Wellington left him there till the 26th.

It has become the fashion of late amongst writers and critics to decry the staff work of Wellington's army. It is easy to do so, if, instead of bearing in mind the limitations imposed by the conditions of one hundred and ten years ago, we think in terms of 1924. Wellington's opinion of his army that it was "the most complete machine of its numbers now existing in Europe" may have some weight,[1] as well as that of a French writer: "Il (Soult) avait affaire à un adversaire plus tenace, en fait plus énergique et décidé, conduisant une armée mieux organisée, et dont les elements bien reliés, malgré les distances et l'extension des fronts d'opérations, étaient mieux dans la main de leur chef."[2]

---

[1] Wellington to Bathhurst, St. Jean de Luz, 21st November, 1813.
[2] General Dumas, "Neuf mois de campagnes à la suite du Maréchal Soult," p. 388.

WELLINGTON, THE CROSSING OF THE GAVES

Such conditions could not have obtained without the work of a competent staff.

In these operations Wellington completely attained his objects. He did so by forcing his opponent to do as he wished much more by his strategy than by force of arms. This is the measure of his generalship. "It is contrary to the nature of a true General to have his course of action imposed on him by the enemy; and it was Napoleon's instinctive determination to force his opponent to do as he wished more than any other condition that dictated to him his line of action."[1]

[1] Yorck, "Napoleon as a General."

CHAPTER XV

THE BATTLE-FIELD OF ORTHEZ, THE ORDERS AND POSITIONS OF THE OPPOSING FORCES

RUNNING due north from its sources in the main chain of the Pyrenees, the gave de Pau at Lourdes turns north-westwards, and flows by Pau and Orthez to join the Adour near Peyrehorade. About six miles to the east of Pau rises the Luy de Béarn, which also flows north-westwards and falls into the Adour to the south of Dax. The average distance between these two rivers is about eight miles; as, however, the high ground which divides them is generally considerably nearer to the gave de Pau than to the Luy, the valley of the latter on its left bank is the wider.

The divide between the two rivers rising to 900 feet about Lourdes falls gradually as it goes northwards, till about Orthez its height is generally from 550 to 600 feet. Comparatively narrow up to this point, it broadens out into two branches, the main one running west from St. Boes parallel to the gave de Pau, and the other bending north-northwest towards Dax.

On the southern face of the ridge, the almost tropical sun of the summer months and the

WELLINGTON, THE CROSSING OF THE GAVES

prevailing south-westerly wind with its accompanying rain have done their usual erosive work; the upper slopes are generally steeper and the spurs narrower than on the northern side. On the lower slopes of the south side, the soil is rich and highly cultivated; whereas on the north, there stretched between the ridge and the Luy about Sault de Navailles a poor marshy country covered with thorn trees, brushwood and heather, and cut up by muddy streams, ditches and banks.[1]

The plans of the battle-field given in the earlier published accounts of the action are misleading as regards the nature of the country. The then system of the representation of ground led to exaggeration of slopes and confusion of features. In reality, the country between the main ridge and the gave de Pau, over which the greater part of the action was fought, is, for the most part, an open rolling and fairly easy country. The upper slopes, especially at the heads of the valleys formed by the numerous spurs thrown off from the main ridge, are steep, up to 25° in places; they are generally covered with coarse grass, short gorse and some heather above the cultivated area. The bottoms of the valleys are soft and marshy, but probably less so than in 1814, owing to the greater attention now paid to the courses of the streams in them. The soil is a sticky red clay. In places, especially towards Baigts, there is a good deal of wood. All along the lower southern slopes on both sides of the old Orthez-Baigts road the ground is highly cultivated—principal crops, vines, Indian corn,

---

[1] Dumas. It would appear to be more cultivated and considerably improved at the present time.

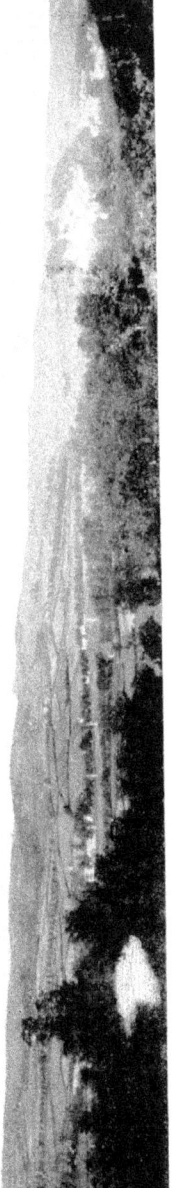
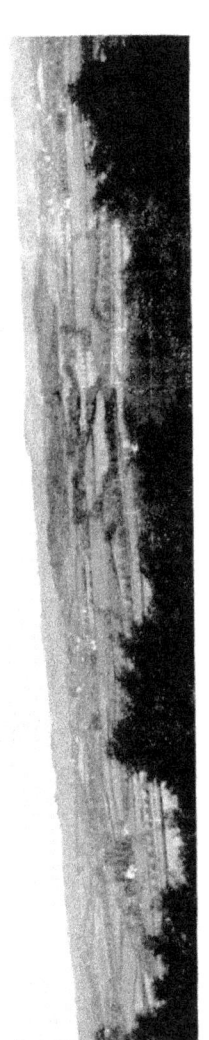

PANORAMA OF THE FIELD OF ORTHEZ FROM THE HEIGHTS OF MAGRET. EASTERN PORTION ABOVE. WESTERN BELOW

AND THE BATTLE OF ORTHEZ

beetroots and hay grass—and is enclosed by banks and growing hedges.¹

It is difficult to say how far the aspect of the country has changed since 1814. Probably there is now more wood than then, and an increased area under cultivation. In summer and autumn it is a beautiful country; the woods, the enclosures, the general greenness of the fields, and the undulating ground give it a very English appearance.

As regards buildings there is probably little change except about Orthez itself—where the extension has been mostly eastwards, the last houses on the west are very old, many of them bearing dates of the eighteenth century—and about St. Boes and about Point de Jour, where there are a number of evidently modern houses of the villa type. The farm-houses scattered about the area are mostly very old.

The present modern road from Orthez to Bayonne skirts the river after leaving the town. The old road runs straight towards Baigts, up and down over the ends of the spurs, over thirty yards wide with a metalled centre; it must have been a fine road in its day.² That from Orthez to Dax leaves the town near its western end, and ascends by an easy gradient a spur running due south from the main ridge, on reaching which it is joined by—

---

¹ Moore Smith, "Autobiography of Sir Harry Smith": "We saw the enemy very strongly posted both as regards elevation and the nature of the ground, which was intersected by long banks and ditches, while the fences of the fields were most admirably adapted for vigorous defence."

² Vivian, in a letter of 26th February, says, "The great road leading from Peyrehorade to Pau is more admirable than any road I ever beheld."

WELLINGTON, THE CROSSING OF THE GAVES

a narrow road from Sallespisse; it then follows the crest of the high ground to St. Boes. Here the main ridge divides, the road to Dax takes the northern branch, and from it leads a narrow road which, following the crest of the western branch, leads by Bellevue to Habas and Pouillon.

That portion of the ridge running westwards from St. Boes maintains on its south side the general character of the main divide; its spurs run southwards towards the gave de Pau, and on these are tracks running down to the main Bayonne road at Baigts and Puyoo. On the northern side the slopes are steep and fall directly into the valley of the Tailland stream which has its source on the slopes below St. Boes church. This branch of the ridge is connected with the northern one at St. Boes by a narrow neck carrying the road with some houses on either side of it; about 800 yards from the Dax road this neck widens out into a rounded plateau, on the eastern slopes of which, slightly below the highest point, stands the church of St. Boes (A.D. 1718) surrounded by its grave-yard and a few houses.

From the neck at about 400 yards from the Dax road a long spur runs in a south-westerly direction. On this spur at 1,000 yards from its origin rises a rounded hillock, about 100 feet higher than the surrounding ground, on which is an ancient entrenchment with steeply scarped sides known as the Roman camp. In 1814 this hillock and the camp was covered with grass, and on it were a few fir trees. From it a good view over most of the field was to be obtained; and on or near it was

AND THE BATTLE OF ORTHEZ

Wellington's position during a considerable part of the 27th February.[1]

The ancient road from Orthez to Sallespisse and Sault de Navailles ascended the spur to the north of the town on which stands the Tour de Moncade, all that remains of the castle built in the eleventh century by Gaston VI Count of Béarn and Foix. From the tower it passes by the convent of the Trinitaires and by points 394 and 572 to join the St. Boes-Sallespisse road at point 585. It is metalled to-day as far as about 394; beyond this point it is a narrow sandy track. It appears uncertain whether the present main road from Orthez to Sallespisse, which lies in the valley between the Moncade spur and that of the Mont de Tury, was in existence in 1814. It is, however, shown in Wyld's Atlas.[2]

Battle of Orthez. Orders and Preliminary Movements

Sunday, 27th February, 1814. Sunrise; 6.44 a.m.; daybreak 6.15 a.m. "A remarkably fine morning announced a glorious day."[3]

According to Soult's order of the previous evening, the French army on the morning of 27th had taken up its position as follows:

Reille's corps, composed of Taupin's and

---

[1] The camp is now cultivated, and is so surrounded by coppice wood that nothing can be seen from it.

[2] From old maps it would also appear that the Orthez-Dax road left that to Bayonne some 500 yards to the westward of its present trace, and that it went up the spur on which the convent of the Bernadines stood, joining the present trace about a mile to the north.

[3] Thackwell's Diary.

WELLINGTON, THE CROSSING OF THE GAVES

Rouget's division and the 15th Chasseurs, opposite the hamlet of St. Boes about point 575, with Paris's brigade in support on right rear about Plassotte. At daybreak Reille advanced Rey's brigade of Taupin's division, the 15th Chasseurs and four guns to the plateau west of the Church of St. Boes; the rest of the division holding the 575 height and extending thence northwards along the Dax road.

Later Soult himself came up, and by his order Rey's brigade was withdrawn nearer the main position and the 15th Chasseurs and the two battalions of the 12th Light only left on the plateau. These took position near the church and the neighbouring houses, with advanced parties on the ridge beyond the plateau. At 7 a.m. a strong reconnaissance was sent out westward along the ridge, but it was recalled before it had obtained any information of the allied movements. The twelve guns with Taupin's division were placed some about point 575 and the remainder along the high ground to the north, with a cavalry detachment watching the Dax beyond the right of the guns and the infantry.

Rouget's division was on Taupin's left on both sides of the Dax road, and held the Luc and Berge spurs, which face the Roman camp hill. On the Dax road near the Luc farm there were sixteen guns, covered from view and fire by a shallow cutting through which the road there passes.

D'Erlon's corps of Foy's and Darmagnac's divisions prolonged the line to the left. On Rouget's left, Darmagnac held the head of the 528 spur, with his left extending along the road as far as its junction with that to Sallespisse. Foy, whose

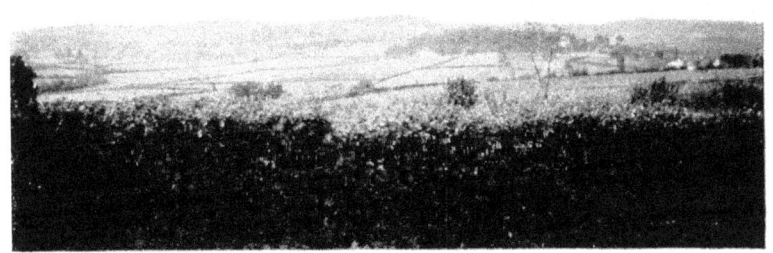

Higher.—LOOKING TOWARDS THE ROMAN CAMP AND ST. BOËS FROM THE POINT DE JOUR.

Lower.—LOOKING FROM THE ORTHEZ—DAX ROAD ABOUT A MILE NORTH OF ORTHEZ, NORTH-EASTWARDS TOWARDS VILLATTE'S POSITION AND THE GROUND OVER WHICH FOY'S DIVISION RETREATED AFTER CROSSING THE ROAD.

AND THE BATTLE OF ORTHEZ

division had moved before daybreak from the Castetarbe spur, where outposts only had been left, prolonged the line to the Orthez-Peyrehorade road. His 1st brigade was massed behind a hillock on the 393 spur about 450 yards to the west of the Dax road, and the 2nd on the spur which crosses the Peyrehorade road about a quarter of a mile from the western exit from Orthez, and on which stood the convent of the Bernadines. Skirmishers in the valleys connected the two brigades.

Clausel's corps held Orthez and the spur to the north of the town. Harispe's division, which formed the extreme left of the line, had a few troops in Orthez, about two battalions, for the defence of the bridge and of the river in the vicinity of the town; the remainder of the division was on the ridge which runs northwards from the town past the Moncade tower and the convent of the Trinitaires.

Villatte's division was moved by Clausel during the night from the Souars spur and placed across the old Orthez-Sallespisse road on the high ground, points 585-572, above the village of Rontum.

So far as can be ascertained no copies exist of the orders issued by Wellington previous to or during the battle of Orthez. Their general purport only can be gathered from his despatch of 1st March, and from a "Memorandum of the movements of the allied troops preparatory to and during the attack upon the enemy at Orthez." Both are similar in wording and in very general terms, and do not mention many details essential to a correct understanding of the various phases of the action.

WELLINGTON, THE CROSSING OF THE GAVES

The Memorandum gives the situation, and the substance of the orders issued as follows:[1]

At daybreak on the morning of the 27th, the 6th and Light divisions, which had remained in a situation whence they could support the troops under Sir R. Hill, should it have become necessary to do so, crossed to the right bank of the gave de Pau at Berenx, and the left of the army then consist of the following troops: The Hussar brigade, with a troop of horse artillery; the 3rd division, with its artillery; the 6th division, with its artillery; the Light division, with a troop of horse artillery; the 4th division, with its artillery; the 7th division, without artillery; a brigade of reserve artillery (that of 2nd division); Colonel Vivian's brigade of cavalry.

The position of the enemy was upon the heights along, which the road runs from Orthez towards Dax, through the village of Thil, the right being opposite the village of St. Boes, the left at Orthez.

Arrangement made for the attack on the 27th February.

The 4th division, the 7th division and Colonel Vivian's brigade of cavalry, and the brigade of artillery of 2nd division, were ordered to move out from the column to the left, under the orders of Marshal Beresford, who was instructed to gain the heights, and direct his attack against the extremity of the enemy's right, which appeared to be the key of his position. The 3rd division and 6th division, and the Hussar brigade were ordered to move

[1] Memorandum by the Quartermaster-General, "Memoir of the War in Spain and France."

AND THE BATTLE OF ORTHEZ

forward, in the first instance, by the great road towards Orthez, and then to direct their attacks against the enemy's position, by moving up the tongues of land which originate from the ridge on which the centre and right of the French army was posted, and which fall towards the great road and the gave.

The Light division, with its artillery, was placed, in the first instance, upon a commanding wooded height crowned by an old entrenchment which is between the great road and the village of St. Boes; it was afterwards moved forward and acted in support of the attack of Marshal Beresford's column immediately on the right of the 4th division.

Lieutenant-General Sir R. Hill had instructions to effect the passage of the gave near Orthez as soon as he could, and to co-operate afterwards according to circumstances, with the left of the army.

Wellington spent the night of 26th/27th at Sauveterre, and arrived at Baigts early on the morning of 27th probably soon after daybreak. Whether on his way from Orthez to Sauveterre on the afternoon of 26th he went by way of Berenx and there saw Beresford is uncertain; no reference to his having done so appears anywhere, and he probably did not do so. From the Magret heights the general run of the main features of the ground held by the French can be made out fairly clearly; but from the distance and intervening features it would not be possible to form any really accurate idea of the local topography about St. Boes and the French right. The Roman camp stands out clearly and that is about all.

WELLINGTON, THE CROSSING OF THE GAVES

On his arrival Wellington no doubt received such information as Beresford and the divisional generals had been able to obtain regarding the ground and the French movements; also, probably later, the report which the Q.M.G. had requested from Hill in his letter of the previous evening. Any personal reconnaissance would hardly be possible till after sunrise, and then only from ground covered by the outposts. It would not be till the troops, covered by their advance guards, had commenced to move towards their assigned positions that any further detailed reconnaissance of the ground and the enemy would be possible to the Commander-in-Chief. He had, of course, such maps of the country as there existed; that of Cassini, published for this area in 1770-78, appears to have been the one generally used by Wellington and his staff,[1] but on this the representation of the ground was very inadequate. It appears reasonable to conclude that the orders setting the troops in motion, and as regards their preliminary actions, were given verbally, except in the case of those to Hill.

From the correspondence quoted in a previous chapter, it seems evident that neither Wellington nor his staff on the previous evening regarded a battle on the next day as a certainty. But we may also be sure that, when on the morning of the 27th Wellington got knowledge of the existing situation, he, despite certain manifest disadvantages in his own position, welcomed the opportunity of getting to grips with an adversary, who had so far skilfully avoided any general action. He certainly

[1] Larpent's Diary.

AND THE BATTLE OF ORTHEZ

lost no time in putting his force in action. Its strength on the right bank was about 28,500 of whom 2,350 were cavalry, 24,870 infantry and thirty-six guns. On the left bank Hill had 800 cavalry, 9,600 infantry, eighteen field and four mountain guns.

In the accounts given of the battle, there are comparatively few references to the times at which the various movements began or were completed—the French documents are more complete in this respect than the British—in several instances it is difficult to reconcile the various times given, and, it is the more so owing to the uncertainty which exists as to the exact routes taken by various divisions. On one point there is unanimity. All accounts agree that the movement of the 6th and Light divisions began at daybreak. The 6th division was the first to cross the pontoon bridge, which had been laid below the broken road bridge at Berenx during the night. If this division commenced to cross at 6.30 a.m. its head would reach the assembly point, about half a mile beyond the eastern exit from Baigts, at about 7.30 a.m. and the whole division up by 8.45 a.m. The bridge would be clear for the Light division, a very weak one under 3,000 men, at about 7.45 a.m., its head would be up about 8.50 a.m. and the whole division about 9.25 a.m.[1]

[1] From Napier's account of the battle, and other writers who have followed it, it would seem as if the troops, after crossing the pontoon bridge, had " to wind up a narrow way hemmed in between high rocks," until they reached the old Bayonne-Orthez main road, a distance of rather over three-quarters of a mile. This is quite an exaggeration. As will be seen from the illustration, the gave here flows between high rocky banks, the top of which may be about 50 feet above the water. After ascending from the water-side by a narrow cart

WELLINGTON, THE CROSSING OF THE GAVES

With regard to the 4th and 7th divisions there is not the same data to go on, for there is no record of when they started, or of the routes taken. In his report to Soult on the action, Reille states that the advanced guard of the 4th division arrived on the crest of the ridge to the west of St. Boes, about points 528 and 558, two miles from Baigts—between 8 and 9 a.m. If we take the mean 8.30 a.m. it may serve as a basis of calculation.

There were three possible routes by which Beresford's corps could reach the ridge to the west of St. Boes unobserved from the main French position.

(*a*) By following the track, which lies in the re-entrant down which flows the little stream, which crosses the main road at Baigts for about a mile, then bending to the right and ascending the Barbaou spur by a track which joins the ridge road at Saubetat (558).

(*b*) By the same route, but, instead of turning to the right, keeping straight up the ravine and ascending to the main ridge about point 528 Brasquet.

(*c*) By the country road which ascends the long spur which runs down to Baigts from point 496, and is then level along the ridge road.

The plan of Orthez in Wyld's Atlas of Peninsular battles shows the 4th division as coming on to the ridge near Saubetat by route (*a*), the 7th, which had no artillery, by route (*b*) and the reserve artillery

<small>track to the top of the right bank, the ground is quite level, and a broad road leads from the stone bridge to the old main road. The writer, walking at an ordinary pace from the waterside, reached the top of the bank in six minutes, the old Orthez road in eighteen minutes, and Baigts village in twenty-six minutes from the starting time.</small>

AND THE BATTLE OF ORTHEZ

and Vivian's brigade by (c). The plan in Moorsom's "History of 52nd Regiment" agrees as regards the 4th division, but shows the 7th as coming up by route (c). The sketch in Napier's history shows Beresford's corps as moving by the valley routes, but puts the 7th division and Vivian's cavalry towards the end of the action on the Dax road. The difference between routes (b) and (c) is not very important so far as distance is concerned, as (c) is only half a mile longer than (a) and (b). What is important is the route of the 4th division, which the French confirm as being route (a);[1] as by it the approximate time at which this division, which led Beresford's corps, started may be calculated. By route (a) the distance from Baigts is just under two miles. The ground traversed is soft and marshy and the ascent to the Barbaou steep; progress must have been slow. If the rate of marching is put at one and a half miles an hour the head of the advanced guard probably commenced to move at 7.10 a.m., reached the ridge at about 8.30 a.m., and the fighting part of the division complete would be up about 10 a.m. If the 7th division moved by route (b) and immediately followed the 4th, it probably started about 8.50 a.m. and would be up complete about 11.10 a.m.[2] Troops moving by routes (a) and (b) would be completely hidden from the main French position,

---

[1] Reille to Soult, "Rapport sur l'affaire du 27 Fevrier. The advanced guard of the division Cole appeared on the crest (528-562) to the west of St. Boes at the exit from the ravine it had followed from Baigts between 8 and 9 a.m."

[2] If 7th division took route (c) and moved independently, the division would have arrived very soon after the 4th. All accounts, however, agree it arrived considerably later than the 4th.

WELLINGTON, THE CROSSING OF THE GAVES

except perhaps their movement from the assembly point; their visibility there depends on whether the country about Baigts was then more or less wooded than at present.

The cavalry, the Hussar brigade about Ramous and Bellocq, and Vivian's brigade about Puyoo, had three miles to cover to reach Baigts; if both brigades started at 7 a.m. and moved at a trot and walk both could easily be up before 8 a.m. and considerably earlier if necessary. In Lieutenant Woodberry's diary (18th Light Dragoons) it is stated "about 9 a.m. the engagement commenced and our brigade (Vivian's) left the great road and occupied (ascended) a hill to the left." The distance to the St. Boes plateau by the spur road is two and a half miles; so, if the brigade only moved at a walk up the long spur and at a trot along the level top, it would be up behind the 4th division by about 9.45 a.m. Gardiner's troop of horse artillery and Maxwell's reserve battery followed the cavalry; but some mishap occurred to the latter, and it did not arrive on the ridge in time to come into action that day.[1]

The Light division—if this division, after a short halt at the assembly point, continued to move on its head,[2] would arrive behind the Roman camp about 10.15 a.m. and the whole division be

---

[1] Major Dyer's report to Beresford.
[2] "Autobiography of Sir Harry Smith," then Brigade-Major of Barnard's brigade of Light division: "As we were moving to the right of the 3rd division (morning, 27th February), Sir T. Picton, who was ever ready to find fault with the Light, rode up to Colonel Barnard saying, 'Who the devil are you?' knowing Barnard intimately, who replied, 'We are the Light division.' 'If you are Light, sir, I wish you would move a little quicker,' said Picton in his most bitter and sarcastic tone."

AND THE BATTLE OF ORTHEZ

up about 11 a.m. Ross's troop followed the division.

Before proceeding to describe the course of the action in such detail as is possible, it appears desirable for a proper understanding of it, to examine the orders already given by Wellington to the different corps of his army on the morning of the 27th, in order to ascertain whether any further information can be extracted from them, not only as regards their execution, but also concerning the ultimate results which he perhaps hoped to obtain.

Beresford was directed to gain the heights about St. Boes, and attack the extremity of the enemy's right, which was regarded as the key of his position. This was evidently to be the main and decisive attack, to be undertaken as soon as the commander on the spot considered he had sufficient strength in hand to carry it out. The orders to the Light division clearly emphasize its rôle; it was to be the link between Beresford's and Picton's corps, and to be the general reserve under the immediate orders of the Commander-in-Chief.

Picton was ordered to move along the great road towards Orthez and then "direct his attack against the heights on 'which the enemy's centre and left stood, by moving up the tongues of land which originate from the ridge on which the centre and right of the French army was posted."[1] It might be inferred from this wording that Picton's attack was to be made simultaneously with that of Beresford. But it appears this was not Wellington's intention, for later on in his despatch, he says, " I

---

[1] Wellington's despatch, 1st March, 1814, and " Memorandum on the Battle of Orthez."

therefore so altered the plan of the action as to order the immediate advance of the 3rd and 6th divisions."[1] From this it may be legitimately inferred that the original orders given to Picton made it clear to him that the rate of advance of his divisions was to be regulated by that of Beresford's corps on his left, and that he was not to press his real attack until a decided impression had been made on the French position about St. Boes. Thus, at first, all that Picton had to do was to so threaten the French centre and left as to hold it to its ground and prevent any assistance being given to the right.

To Hill, on the left bank, the order was sent to cross "the gave as soon as he could and to turn and attack the enemy's left."[2] Both Wellington and Murray had spent a considerable part of the previous day with Hill's corps. Though, as the correspondence written later in the day, and already quoted, shows a battle on the 27th was not regarded by them as inevitable, both had probably discussed with Hill what the action of his corps was to be if a fight took place. Under the circumstances, it was not likely that definite orders were given him. When, therefore, was this order received by Hill? Napier states it was sent when Wellington changed his plan of attack. This can hardly have been so, for, if sent so late, Hill's corps could not have crossed the gave by the time it did. Moreover, there is evidence to show that the order was received considerably earlier. Dr. Henry, surgeon of the 66th Regiment says: "On 27th February we

---

[1] Wellington to Bathurst, St. Sever, 1st March, 1814.
[2] Wellington to Bathurst, St. Sever, 1st March, 1814.

AND THE BATTLE OF ORTHEZ

were early under arms. About 9 a.m. we saw heavy fighting commence two or three miles down the right bank of the river, which continued and increased into the tumult of a general engagement. All this time our corps was looking on most anxiously. At 11 o'clock a panting A.D.C. arrived from Lord Wellington with orders to cross instantly how we could. Immediately all was in motion."[1]

When was the order despatched? It is perhaps possible to give an approximate time. Major Ross Lewin, 32nd Regiment, 66th division, writes:[2] "On the morning of the 27th I saw Lord Wellington for the first time in this campaign. He had been reconnoitring the enemy, and seating himself on the grass in his well-known white cloak, he took out some paper and began to write. As Lord Hill was seen crossing the river above Orthez not long afterwards, we concluded the orders were written for him."[3] The 32nd being in the 6th division, it follows that when the order was written Wellington must have been on the right, probably not far from the main road to Orthez to the east of Baigts. The distance from there to the Magret heights, by way of Baigts and the pontoon bridge, is about seven miles; as the aide-de-camp appears to have travelled at speed, he perhaps covered it in forty-five minutes, if so, the message must have been sent off about 10.15 a.m.

The question may be asked, why did not Hill's

---

[1] Henry, "Events of a Military Life."
[2] Ross Lewin, "With the 32nd in the Peninsula," etc. The original possessor of the white cloak being a trooper of French dragoons.
[3] The actual crossing of the river could not possibly have been seen, but the movement of Hill's troops from the Magret heights would be clearly visible.

WELLINGTON, THE CROSSING OF THE GAVES

corps cross the river earlier? The answer evidently is that he could not safely attempt to cross until the action was well under way, and the French held to their positions by the Allies' advance and attack. Moreover, Hill where he was, and with his repeated attempts to gain possession of the Orthez bridge, was fulfilling another function, holding the French left under Clausel to their positions and preventing Harispe from aiding Foy's left or attacking Picton's right.

The question, however, covers more than this, and might give a clue to the part in the battle Wellington intended Hill's corps to take, and, through that, to what he had in his mind, when giving his preliminary orders regarding the results he hoped to achieve by the action.

Wellington, with a small army and with little hope of reinforcements especially in British troops, was bound to be cautious; but, when occasion required it, he could also be very daring. He must have realized he was breaking a rule of war: Hill's corps, nearly a third of his strength, cut off by a considerable obstacle, could give no direct aid to his main attack; but, with absolute confidence in his army and himself, he took the risk, and it does not seem unreasonable to conjecture that he hoped the French right, which Beresford was ordered to turn and attack, would be driven back on the centre, and that eventually both, under the combined pressure of Beresford, Picton and the Light division, would be obliged to fall back in a south-westerly direction into or past Orthez, that there or thereabouts, Hill, in possession of the gave de Pau valley road, would act as a stop, and a complete

AND THE BATTLE OF ORTHEZ

round up of the French army be effected. If, on the other hand, the turning movement against the French right was unsuccessful, Hill was well placed to block the Pau road, and also, if the French retreated northwards, to intercept them towards the nearest bridge over the Luy de Béarn at Sault de Navailles.

This, of course, can only be a conjecture, but something of the sort seems required, owing to Wellington's statement of his change of plans. To return, however, to the original orders, if the previous discussion of them is in any way correct, they may be epitomized as follows: Beresford to attack, and, if possible, turn the enemy's right about St. Boes. Picton to keep the enemy's centre and left employed, but not to push attack home until success against his right was being obtained, the Light division to be in reserve. Hill to again attack the bridge and its adjacents, the rest of his force to be ready to move immediately orders reached him to ford the river.

CHAPTER XVI

BATTLE OF ORTHEZ (*continued*)

On the allied right, the action commenced about 9 a.m. by the advance of the Light companies of the 3rd and 6th divisions towards the Castetarbe spur and the driving in of the French skirmishers pushed forward from Foy's detachments there. Whilst this was going on, the Light division moved along the main road for about half a mile, then turning to the left took the track which leads directly to the Roman camp, being followed by the 3rd division on the road,[1] and the 6th on its right moving across country between the road and the river.

Meanwhile on the left, the advanced guard of Ross's brigade, which led the 4th division, had reached the ridge to the west of St. Boes, when the advanced parties of the 12th Light fell back on to their main body,[2] which, supported by the 15th Chasseurs, had taken up a position about the

---

[1] Moore Smith, " Autobiography of Sir Harry Smith," then Brigade-Major 1st brigade Light division.

[2] Sergeant Cooper, 7th Fusiliers, relates how " we directly surprised a picket behind a farm-house; they were busy cooking, but their bugler roused them, and they fell back, firing briskly. On the flat below, the contest was sharp between the French skirmishers and ours."

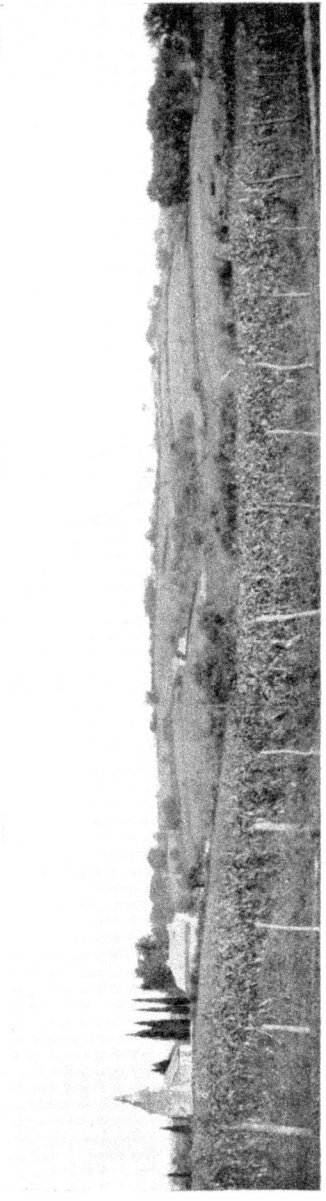

LOOKING TOWARDS THE FRENCH POSITION ABOUT POINT 575 AND THE DAX ROAD FROM THE ST. BOËS PLATEAU

WELLINGTON

church [1] and the neighbouring houses. When the greater part of the division had gained the plateau, Cole sent Ross's brigade against the 12th. After a sharp fight, possession of the church and houses was gained and the 12th fell back on the remainder to its brigade, which was deployed farther back across the neck connecting the St. Boes plateau with the main ridge at point 575.

At about 11 a.m.[2] when the 7th division had come up, Beresford sent forward Cole and the 4th division to the attack of the French main position about 575 and the Dax road held by Taupin's division, whilst the 7th division held the church and the eastern edge of the plateau. With Ross' and Vasconcellos' brigades leading and Anson in support, Cole attempted to force his way across the neck and gain the heights beyond. But struck in front and on his left flank by Taupin's musketry and artillery and on his right by the fire of the battery of sixteen guns on the Dax road, it was more than the "enthusiastic"[3] division could do and back it had to come. Then down from Taupin's heights came his lines at the charge with their flanks covered by skirmishers in the ravines on either side. But they got no farther than the first houses

---

[1] Called by Napier the high church of Baigts. In 1814 the hamlet of St. Boes is stated to have consisted only of the church, the few houses about it and others along the Roman road, and that the rising ground about point 575 was then open and bare of houses, whereas to-day the larger number of houses are about this point and on the Dax road.

[2] Vivian, who was present, says in a letter dated 2nd March, 1814 : " The attack commenced about 11 o'clock." This seems to refer to the main attack, not to the clearing of the plateau, which had probably commenced before his brigade reached the ground.

[3] The nickname given in the army to the 4th division.

WELLINGTON, THE CROSSING OF THE GAVES

on the plateau, when turning on them the 4th drove them back. Again and again for at least three times did the 4th division renew the attack, it was attack and counter-attack. Ross fell severely wounded, and, on the French side, General Bechaud was killed.[1] Despite the bravery and endurance of all ranks the 4th division failed to gain the heights held by Taupin's division.

As has been already stated, Rouget's division was on Taupin's left, its right with artillery on the Lac spur and its left about Berge; the French line was then carried on by Darmagnac's division holding the Lafaurie spur (558 and 528), its left connecting with Foy's division on the Lassoureille spur (393). The main body, Fririon's brigade, of this division was massed behind a sandhill, which rises abruptly from the spur about 200 yards east of point 393; on this hill was the battery of the division. Berlier's brigade carried on the line to the Orthez-Baigts road along the Bernadine's spur. On the whole of this French front advanced detachments, sometimes accompanied by artillery, had been pushed down the spurs, and were in their turn covered by a skirmishing line.

It was against this front that the 3rd and 6th divisions, followed by the Hussar brigade, were now advancing into the positions assigned to them. Brisbane's and Keane's brigades of the 3rd, with two guns, had left the main road and, moving by

[1] On the wall of a house by the roadside, close to where the road to the Roman camp leaves the neck, is a memorial tablet inscribed : " A la memoire de Général de brigade Bechaud, des officiers, sous officiers et soldats tués à la defense de St. Boes, bataille de Orthez, 27 Fevrier, 1814, à nous le souvenir, à eux l'immortalité. Souvenir Nationale Française."

AND THE BATTLE OF ORTHEZ

the track which leads up the spur towards point 528, "were posted in a ravine under cover of a little hill ready to attack as soon as circumstances should require."[1] The 6th division, moving between the high road and the river, gained the Castetarbe spur a little before 11 a.m.,[2] and then joined the 3rd brigade of Picton's division. Here its artillery came into action against Foy's left on the Bernadine's spur, and the main body of the division moved down into the ravine on the north side of the road. Both divisions covered themselves by skirmishers and supports pushed up the lower slopes of the spurs and along the Orthez main road, which soon became engaged with those of the French; but for the present no general forward movement was made. Whilst in these positions Picton's troops were, he says, "for nearly two hours exposed to the most continued and severe cannonade I ever witnessed, one of my 9-pounders had every man killed by round shot."[3]

Shortly after 11 a.m. Hill's corps began to move down from the Magret heights. One brigade of the Portuguese division was already in action in the Départ suburb against Harispe's troops holding the bridge with orders to, if possible, force their way across it. To distract the enemy's attention from the ford at Souars, where Hill had decided to pass the main body of his corps, the other brigade of this division moved down with orders to make a feigned attempt to cross at another ford, which

[1] Journal of a commissariat officer.
[2] Girod de l'Ain, vie militaire du Général Foy.
[3] Robinson, "Memoirs of Sir T. Picton," letter to Colonel Pleydell, 4th March, 1814.

WELLINGTON, THE CROSSING OF THE GAVES
had been discovered nearer the town, and afterwards to join the main column and cross at Souars. The route to this ford taken by the 2nd division and the cavalry brigade is uncertain. It is perhaps likely that Hill would as far as possible move behind the screen of the hills on the left bank in order to conceal his march; he could do so by increasing his direct distance from the ford by a little more than one mile, making it altogether three and a quarter miles.

The order to cross could not have been unexpected and, as it is reasonable to suppose that all the necessary preliminaries to the move had been made, the advanced guard of Barnes's brigade of the 2nd division, which led the column, could have moved off by 11.15 a.m. and reached the vicinity of the ford by 12.30 p.m.

Meanwhile on the allied left at St. Boes the state of impasse already described continued. The allies were unable to take the heights which Taupin's division held; and the French, despite several efforts, could not drive the 4th division from the houses they held on the edge of the plateau and about the church. "Things remained in this state for some time, and the battle seemed at a standstill, except that the French made several unsuccessful attempts to recover St. Boes," says Blakiston, adding that his "division (the Light) was in reserve on the heights opposite the enemy's centre and right, and of course had a good view of what was going on."[1]

In his despatch of 1st March[2] Wellington says

---

[1] Blakiston, "Military Adventures."
[2] Wellington to Bathurst, St. Sever, 1st March, 1814.

AND THE BATTLE OF ORTHEZ

that "Marshal Beresford carried the village of St. Boes with the 4th division under the command of Lieutenant-General L. Cole after an obstinate resistance by the enemy, but the ground was so narrow that the troops could not deploy to attack the heights. Notwithstanding the repeated attempts of Major-General Ross's and Brigadier-General Vasconcellos's Portuguese brigades, it was impossible to turn them by the enemy's right without an excessive extension of our line. I, therefore, so far altered the plan of the action as to order the immediate advance of the 3rd and 6th divisions to attack the left of the height on which the enemy's right stood."

There appears to be no record of the time when this order was sent, it was probably about noon, and that Wellington, who was then at the Roman camp, perhaps delayed giving it till then, as Blakiston suggests, so as to give Hill's corps time to cross the river.

Picton, having received Wellington's order, commenced his attack with his third brigade and the 6th division. Advancing up the narrow Lassoureille spur (393), they soon came under the fire of Foy's battery on the sandhill, and met with "a most obstinate resistance" from his infantry.[1] Pressing these back, however, the remaining four guns of Turner's battery were able to come into action about 400 yards to the west of point 393. Foy, seeing his advanced troops being driven back, and realizing how seriously he was being attacked, moved down from the hill to give orders to General Fririon; on his way he was badly wounded by a

[1] Picton to Colonel Pleydell, 4th March, 1814.

shrapnel bullet on the left shoulder and had to leave the field.¹ The casualty and departure of their commander caused what Lapène describes as "un découragement sensible." in the ranks of the right of the division. Under the allied pressure it began to give way and was gradually pushed back to and across the Dax road, whence it retreated in disorder over the rough and broken ground lying between the Dax and Sallespisse roads under the fire of the 3rd division guns, which were now able to advance and come into action on the rising ground about Escauriet.

Soult, seeing the retreat of Foy's division, sent a squadron of the 21st Chasseurs to charge down the road towards Orthez against the guns; riding over some of the 88th Regiment escort to the guns, the squadron got entangled in the narrow lane leading down the spur from Escauriet, and endeavouring to retreat were nearly all shot down or taken prisoners.

The remainder of the 3rd division had, meanwhile, commenced its attack on the centre in two columns, that on the right up the Lafaurie spur (points 528-558) and on the left up the Berge spur. Both were strongly opposed and progress was slow; a French counter-attack drove back the leading troops of Brisbane's brigade on the left, but rallying it again advanced.

Now about this time, probably in consequence of the route of Foy's division, Darmagnac's division —whether the order was given by Soult himself or

---

¹ Foy, with assistance, was able to walk up the Dax road to a house at the junction with that to Sallespisse, near where his monument now is, and there got a first dressing of his wound.

AND THE BATTLE OF ORTHEZ

by D'Erlon is uncertain[1]—was withdrawn from about Lafaurie and moved along the Sallespisse road to about Américain (565) where it took position across the road as a rallying point for Foy's division, now commanded by General Fririon. This movement opened more of the Dax road, and the ten guns of the 3rd and 6th divisions were able to move up to the high ground about the junction of the Dax and Sallespisse roads.

Whilst the fight was thus going on on the right bank of the gave, Hill's advanced guard had reached the river near Souars, held by a battalion of the 119th Regiment of Harispe's division. Henry thus describes the crossing of the river. " Immediately all was in motion, and we soon reached the ford, above which a thicket occupied by the enemy's tirailleurs, but not in much force nor did they make much resistance. A battery of horse artillery (Bean's troop) galloped in front of the column to the edge of the ford, and opening in beautiful style soon cleared them out. The corps then rushed into the ford and, in the course of an hour, 13,000 men and 20 guns had passed without the slightest accident."[2] General G. Bell says: " The ford was deep to our loins; we slung the cartridge boxes on top of the knapsacks, and the men linked arms to support each other in the strong current. Some cavalry formed above us so as to break the force of the stream, so we all passed over unmolested and marched on without halting

[1] Vidal de la Blache, " L'Invasion dans le Midi," p. 238: " As always, the greatest mystery exists regarding the action of Drouet D'Erlon, who commanded in this section. There are no traces of the orders given by him or any report of his."
[2] Dr. Henry, " Events of a Military Life."

WELLINGTON, THE CROSSING OF THE GAVES

for a moment." [1] The only casualties were a few in the advanced guard of Barnes's brigade.

The distance of the ford from the Orthez-Pau road is about a third of a mile. Having traversed this side road, the column, after moving a little way along the main road towards Orthez, wheeled to the right and moved up the long spur, which, springing from the main ridge near an ancient redoubt, runs in a south-westerly direction by points 572 and 597 down to the river. To the north of 572 this spur sends out an off-shoot—Motte de Tury, 585 and 393—which runs parallel to it and also to the main Orthez-Sault de Navailles road. Along this off-shoot moved a flank guard to cover the left of the main column. Fane's cavalry brigade moved towards Orthez, and were endeavouring to advance northwards by the main Sault de Navailles road; owing, however, to heavy artillery fire from the opposite heights[2] was obliged to abandon the road and join the rest of the corps.

Assuming Henry's estimate of the time taken to cross the river to be approximately correct, it would be about 1.45 p.m. when the whole of Hill's corps, less one Portuguese brigade, was over. This last brigade, being unable to force a passage across the Orthez bridge, did not cross until Harispe's troops had evacuated the town; the brigade then moved through the town and rejoined its division by the main road.

Now came the opportunity against the French right which Wellington had waited and hoped for as the result of his change of plan. Taupin's left

[1] Major-General Bell, " Rough Notes by an Old Soldier."
[2] Hamilton, " History of 14th Hussars."

AND THE BATTLE OF ORTHEZ

about 575 had been again pushed forward against Cole, Rouget's division had been mostly drawn towards its left to meet the attack of Picton's left column, and the connection between the two French divisions was almost severed. Wellington, on the Roman camp, seeing his opportunity, instantly seized it, and ordered the 52nd Light infantry, the only regiment of Barnard's brigade not then engaged, to cross the head of the ravine between the Roman camp and the main ridge and attack Rouget's right on the Lac spur.

The advance of the 52nd is thus described in the historical record of that regiment.[1] "The moment was instantly seized by Lord Wellington to thrust into this opening (as writes the historian of the Peninsular War) the veterans of the Light division—soldiers who had never yet met their match in the field—and with this view the left brigade of the Light division was ordered to attack on the left flank of the heights which had been occupied by the enemy's right. The 95th Rifle corps (2nd battalion and part of the 3rd battalion) remained on the knoll in support; the Portuguese Caçadores had been thrown out to the left front and were in the act of being driven back, when the 52nd Regiment moved along in column of threes to the front. The retrogression of the divisions both to the right and left placed the 52nd in a very critical situation, and the importance of the movement was known to every individual. The regiment moved up the road to St. Boes from the Roman camp till it arrived close to the ridge on which Major-General

---

[1] Captain W. S. Moorsom, "Historical Record of 52nd Regiment."

Cole was anxiously looking out for support. At this point the regiment deployed to the right across the low and marshy ground under the French position, and advanced in line, wading steadily through the marsh and accelerating the pace as it approached the hill occupied by the right of General Foy's (Rouget's) division. As soon as the crest was attained, the regiment halted and opened its fire on the force opposite, which at once gave way and retired with all its guns. Lord Wellington, who had directed the movement from the Roman camp, instantly sent a message to Colonel Colborne, not on any account to advance farther, and to remain in line; quickly the divisions on the left and right of the 52nd advanced against their disordered opponents, and the 52nd then occupied the prominent part of the position which had been abandoned by Foy (Rouget)."[1]

Whilst Rouget's right was assailed by the 52nd, Picton's columns were pressing hard on his left; thus taken on both flanks the division abandoned the Dax road at about 2.30 p.m., retreated in disorder down the northern slopes of the ridge, and was not rallied till it reached the Biega spur (441) about a mile and a half to the east. Meanwhile Wellington had ordered Beresford to again attack Taupin about point 575. The latter placing Anson's brigade, hitherto in support, in front again launched the 4th division, backed by the 7th and Vivian's cavalry across the neck against the heights.

A spectator, the commissariat officer already

[1] In the plan of the action given in Moorsom's History—a clear and good one—Foy's division is incorrectly placed in the position occupied by Rouget. In that in Napier's History the route taken by the 52nd is quite incorrectly shown.

THE LAC SPUR AND RAVINE FROM BELOW THE ROAD LEADING
TO THE ROMAN CAMP.

To face page 244

AND THE BATTLE OF ORTHEZ

quoted, thus describes what he saw of the action about this time. "The engagement now became general along the whole line. Our left column appeared to be rather losing ground and was suffering very much; the Light division was also severely engaged, and the English brigade of the 7th division moved down into the ravine to their support. A loud cheering, audible notwithstanding the roar of the cannon and rattling of musketry, drew general attention to the 3rd division, which was forcing its way to the enemy's main position enveloped in fire and smoke; the cavalry trumpets too were sounding near Orthez, and the French drums beating on the ridge above the town, which appeared completely darkened by their troops. Nothing decisive could be effected till the 3rd division should have finished its task of forcing the enemy's centre positions. All the eleven regiments forming the division were desperately engaged carrying hill after hill, until they were at length observed climbing the enemy's main position under a loud cheering and Light infantry bugles. A sharp struggle ensued on the ridge, the French cavalry charged, while their infantry fled over the vast track of level ground which lay in their rear."

Saved, owing to the capture of the Berge spur by the 52nd, from the previous devastating flanking fire of the guns there, the 4th division was at last able to reach the heights about 575, the 20th of Ross's brigade charged, driving back their opponents on to their guns, two of which were captured by the 20th. But now finding themselves isolated, cries began to be heard in the ranks of Taupin's division. "We are cut off, the enemy is on the road." A panic set in and the division abandoned its position, rushed down the narrow road from Plassotte to Laporte, and over the northern slopes of the ridge.[1] The defile at last open, Beresford pushed his troops[2] through, and forming a front beyond brought his three batteries of artillery into action on the Plassotte spur 575, pouring a heavy fire on Taupin's retreating troops. The whole of the line of the Dax road had now been gained, and doubtless all commanders were busy getting their commands in order after their advance and stiff fighting.[3]

According to Blakiston, it was whilst he was watching the advance of the 52nd that Wellington was wounded, a case shot bullet struck the hilt of his sword, driving it with much force against his hip, which was severely bruised and the skin

[1] Lapène, who commanded Taupin's artillery.
[2] The statement that it was the 4th division headed by Anson's brigade which eventually carried the 575 heights is made on the authority of Wellington's despatch of 1st March, 1814. In Volume VIII of the Supplementary despatches there is a report from Major-General Walker, then temporarily commanding the 7th division in Lord Dalhousie's absence, that the 7th division had replaced the 4th by Beresford's order, and that it finally carried the heights occupied by Taupin's division. Captain Vidal de la Blache in his account of the battle follows General Walker's report, as does also Mr. Fortescue in his " History of the British Army." In his report to Wellington, Beresford says that as the latter " was so immediately on the spot it is unnecessary for me to detail the district operations of the two divisions; but I will barely observe that the 7th was ordered and only took the lead of the 4th after that division under Lieutenant-General Hon. Sir L. Cole had in the most gallant manner resisted the attack of the enemy and driven him from his main position." In the plan in Napier's History, the 7th division and Vivian's cavalry are shown as advancing along the Dax road from the north against Taupin's right. It is not easy to reconcile all the various statements.
[3] Sir Harry Smith relates that after the battle he literally lost one battalion of his brigade, the 1st Caçadores, for two days, it having got mixed with the 6th division.

AND THE BATTLE OF ORTHEZ

broken. He was in considerable pain, could ride only with difficulty, and felt the effects for several days.

When Darmagnac's division had been withdrawn from the front after the retreat of Foy's division, it was placed by D'Erlon across the Sallespisse road about a mile east of its junction with that from Dax about Américain (565) as a rallying point. From Américain a long narrow spur runs out northwards to Biega and point 441. On this spur Paris's and Rouget's divisions had been rallied and prolonged Darmagnac's front to the right. Behind this line Taupin's division found shelter and continued its retreat towards Sault de Navailles.

Soult, whose position during most of the action had been about Lafaurie, hastened after Foy's retreat to the extreme left on the spur above Orthez, where Harispe was by now engaged with Hill's corps. In his report on the battle, he says: " The column of the enemy, which had passed by the ford at Souars, was in the meantime making progress on the left of the army, and also threatening our communication with Sallespisse. Clausel placed two battalions of conscripts, which had just arrived, in position on the Motte de Tury, and with the 10th Chasseurs à cheval and Baurot's brigade of Harispe's division was opposing the enemy's advance. At this moment I arrived on the left and saw that the army could not maintain its position without being compromised. I then ordered a retreat on Sault de Navailles. The movement of the right was carried out successively from one line to another. Darmagnac had been placed by D'Erlon so as to take the place in the line of Reille's corps, and when he retired was replaced in turn by Villatte's division." [1]

The whole of the Dax road from Orthez to St. Boes was now in possession of the Allies, and the time about 3 p.m., and the pursuit of the retreating French began on what was apparently the general principle that whenever the enemy made a stand in force, he was to be threatened in front and on both flanks. Accordingly, the 7th division, with Vivian's cavalry on its left flank, moved down the northern slopes of the main ridge so as to turn the Biega spur; the Light division against the centre of this spur, whilst the 3rd followed by the 4th moved by the Dax road and Sallespisse roads against Darmagnac about Américaine; and the 6th from the Dax road about Escauriet, moved across the southern slopes of the ridge against his left, having the Hussar brigade, which had now been able to move across from the Bayonne road, on its right.[2]

The movements of the flanking divisions necessarily took time, and the 3rd division, though aided by its guns and those of the 6th division in action on the rising ground to the east of the junction of the Dax and Sallespisse roads, was stoutly opposed by Darmagnac's skirmishers. On the flanking divisions coming up, the French retired; Paris and Rouget across country towards Sault de Navailles and Darmagnac along the ridge on to Villatte and part of Harispe's division, which

[1] Soult to Guerre, 6th March, 1814.
[2] The positions occupied by the retreating French, and the lines of advance of the allied divisions, are taken from the plan of the battle in Wyld's Atlas.

AND THE BATTLE OF ORTHEZ

Clausel had placed across the road to the west of Sallespisse. "In this manner the French yielded step by step without confusion, the Allies advancing with an incessant deafening musketry and cannonade, yet losing many men, especially on the right, where the 3rd division was very strongly opposed."[1]

Meanwhile, Hill's columns were pushing rapidly towards the main ridge. The Light companies of the 2nd division had gained the slopes west of 545, and opened fire on Sallespisse and the main road, whilst the main column farther east was heading down the gentle slopes to the north towards the road between Sallespisse and Sault de Navailles. Clausel, seeing he could no longer hold on to his position, sent off Villatte's division and followed with Harispe's as a rearguard.

Hitherto the French retreat had been conducted "in admirable order taking every advantage of the numerous good positions which the country afforded. The losses, which he sustained in the continued attacks of our troops, and the danger with which he was threatened by Lieutenant-General Sir R. Hill's movement, soon accelerated his movements, and the retreat at last became a flight, and the troops were in the utmost confusion."[2] Henry thus describes what he saw of

---

[1] Napier.
[2] Wellington to Bathurst, St. Sever, 1st March, 1814. All the accounts of eye witnesses corroborate this statement. Picton, in a letter to Colonel Pleydell, 4th March, says: "At this moment he began his retreat, which he protected with large solid masses of infantry successively taking up the most advantageous ground that offered, and this for some time was made in great order and regularity; but as evening approached and we pressed rather hard on his flanks, the disorder gradually increased and the different columns at length mixed and dispersed as at Vitoria."

WELLINGTON, THE CROSSING OF THE GAVES

the last phases of the French retreat. "At the village of Montbrun (Routun) we joined the cavalry and some of the leading infantry in pursuit. At this time the whole French army, despairing of effecting their escape across the Luy de Béarn at the bridge of Sault de Navailles if they kept to the St. Sever road, had broken irrecoverably, and the face of the country to a great extent was covered with a mass of fugitives, all arms were mingled, artillery without their guns, cavalry without their horses and infantry without their arms; were flying pell-mell, helter-skelter, whilst our guns were pouring shrapnel shells and round shot amongst them, increasing the general terror and confusion." [1]

Owing to the nature of the country over which the French were now flying, cut up as it was by enclosures, narrow lanes, much brushwood, marshy streams and deep ditches, the British cavalry had little opportunity of acting anywhere except on the high road. Thackwell gives the following account of the advance of the Hussar brigade: "As our centre began to close on the enemy's new position he (Villatte) gave way and commenced a precipitate retreat on Sault de Navailles. A squadron of the 7th Hussars was ordered to charge along the road leading to Salles; it succeeded in making some prisoners. Our brigade continued to advance and on reaching the hill in front of Salles, the French right wing was discovered retreating in the greatest confusion towards the Luy de Béarn. The 7th were ordered forward at the trot along the great road to St. Sever; about two miles from Sault de Navailles they turned to the left and

[1] Dr. Henry, " Events of a Military Life."

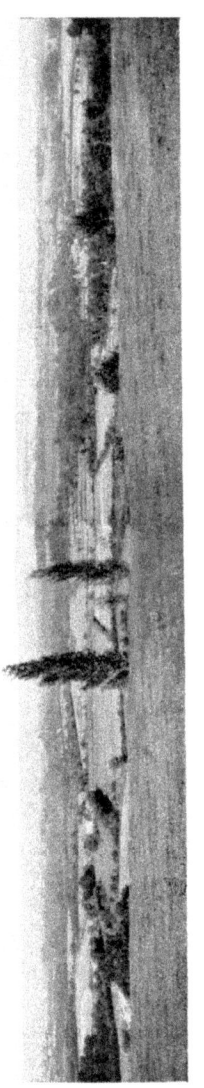

LOOKING TOWARDS SAULT DE NAVAILLES FROM NEAR SALLESPISSE.

AND THE BATTLE OF ORTHEZ

charged the enemy's rearguard. It scarcely made any resistance, and the 7th took 700 prisoners.[1] The 15th were ordered along the road to Sault de Navailles, but the 13th and 14th Light Dragoons got into the road before us from the right. When within three-quarters of a mile of Sault de Navailles, the 'enemy's centre and left were discovered passing the river by the flats and village of Sault de Navailles in the greatest confusion. These corps ought to have been charged, but an order was given against the measure. Had it taken place our reward would have been at least 3,000 *hors de combat*. The guns were now brought up and the enemy was cannonaded with some effect. The 10th Hussars took the outposts and the brigade was cantonned in the houses along the great road to Orthez."[2] On the allied left flank the opportunities for the cavalry were even less than on the right. Vivian thus describes it: "The ground was altogether unfavourable for cavalry. . . . I unfortunately all day could not get into action with my brigade, that is to say, I could not get among them. The country was completely intersected with deep ditches and enormous enclosures."[3]

When Soult determined to retreat, he sent General Tirlet, commanding the artillery of the army, post-haste to Sault de Navailles, whither the reserve artillery had already proceeded during

---
[1] Napier says: "About 2,000 threw down their arms, yet some confusion or misunderstanding occurring, the greater part recovered their weapons, escaped and the pursuit ceased at the Luy de Béarn."
[2] "History of 15th Hussars," Thackwell's Diary.
[3] Life of Lord Vivian," letter to his wife, Mont de Marsan, 2nd March, 1814.

WELLINGTON, THE CROSSING OF THE GAVES
the night of 26th/27th, to organize the defence of the passage over the Luy de Béarn. Tirlet posted the available twelve guns to the east of the village on a height on the right bank commanding the bridge and the main road, and taking some sapper companies which had not been engaged, set them to work on the defence of the high ground to the west of the village. The first of the retreating troops to arrive were sent to hold this ground. As others came in, they were reformed as far as possible and marched off towards Hagetmau. When Villatte's and Harispe's divisions arrived they were ordered to destroy the wooden bridge and defend the crossing until 10 p.m. and then rejoin the rest of the army. They arrived at Hagetmau at 2 a.m. on 28th, just as the other divisions were moving off for St. Sever. Berton and his cavalry and the 25th Light, who during the day had been watching the gave de Pau between Lescar and Orthez, being cut off by Hill's advance, retired by Mant and Samedet and rejoined the army at St. Sever, picking up on the way two battalions of conscripts marching to join the army.

Owing to the strength of the ground on the right bank of the Luy and the approach of night, Wellington decided to turn both flanks of the French position and not to attack it directly;[1] but the arrangements for doing so could not be completed before dark, and the troops went into bivouacs where they then stood, as follows:

[1] " Memorandum on Battle of Orthez ": " The great advantage of the ground on the right bank of the rivulet at Sault de Navailles enabled the enemy to make a short stand there, and the arrangements ordered to be made for turning the flanks of that very strong post could not be completed before the close of the day."

AND THE BATTLE OF ORTHEZ

On the left, the 7th and Light divisions with Vivian's cavalry brigade, on the left bank of the Luy opposite Bonnegarde between the road to Amou and the river.

In the centre, the 4th, 3rd and 6th divisions, across the main road about point 307, with Hussar brigade behind them.

On the right, Hill's corps and Fane's cavalry brigade to east of 6th division on the spur east of point 312.

The French casualties during the action amongst all ranks amounted to killed 529, wounded 2,037, and prisoners of war 1,358, making a total of 3,924.[1] But this was not the sum total of the reduction in Soult's army owing to the battle, for in addition some 3,000 stragglers, not all conscripts, "went their way straight on by Mont de Marsan to the Garonne, where they were intercepted. They were not seen again until the army arrived at Toulouse."[2]

The total casualties British and Portuguese in the allied army were 2,267 made up as follows:

```
 Officers killed  18, wounded  130, missing    1
 Other ranks  ,,  258,    ,,   1,761,    ,,   99
                 ───          ─────          ───
                 276          1,891          100
```

[1] Soult to Guerre, Grenade, 28th February, 1814. Casualty statement on 27th February, 1814:

	Officers.			Other Ranks.		
	Killed.	Wounded.	Prisoners.	Killed.	Wounded.	Prisoners.
Foy's division	4	20	—	40	272	13
Darmagnac's division	2	43	—	46	369	116
Taupin's division	8	19	5	69	444	46
Rouget's division	3	17	4	93	348	56
Villatte's division	—	5	5	35	96	198
Harispe's division	2	5	4	95	129	599
Paris's brigade	1	13	1	71	102	260
Cavalry	2	5	1	58	150	50
	22	127	20	507	1910	1338

[2] Vidal de la Blache, "L'Invasion dans le Midi," p. 382.

CHAPTER XVII

SOME OBSERVATIONS ON THE BATTLE OF ORTHEZ

ABOUT a month before the battle Colonel Bunbury,[1] who was on a mission from the Government to the allied headquarters, one day after dinner asked Wellington the question: Which of the French Generals opposed to him he considered the best General? "Lord Wellington went on playing with his dessert fork, looking thoughtful but smiling a little. 'Well,' he said slowly, 'well, I think Masséna was; at least I found him where I wanted him not to be. But '—after a short pause and smiling—' but, perhaps I did not then know so well what I was about as I do now.' I mentioned Marmont and Soult. 'Ah,' said Lord Wellington, 'Ah, Marmont was a great tactician, but he was too theatrical. It was Pas en avant! Pas en arrière! and while he was manœuvring I caught him. Soult is a very able man, excellent as an administrator; but, in the field, he is apt to doubt and hesitate and lose the proper moment for acting.'"

On the 25th February, Soult writing to the War

[1] " Memoirs of Sir H. E. Bunbury, Bart.," by his son, Sir C. Bunbury.

WELLINGTON

Minister says: "All the enemy's army, except that portion of it before Bayonne, is before me; it can by its numerical superiority continue to outflank me; but I hope that seeing me concentrated the General who commands it will hold it more concentrated, especially if he recognizes that I am determined to profit by any mistakes he makes, and attack him at the very moment a favourable opportunity occurs."

These extracts are given to show the opinion each of the opposing commanders had formed of his adversary. How true Wellington's estimate of Soult was is proved by the result of every fight since the allied troops had entered France. On the afternoon of 26th February Soult had one of those opportunities he was, according to his words, so eagerly looking for; he hesitated and lost it. Still undecided whether to give or receive a battle, he did not make up his mind till the evening, when he issued his orders.

"Of all the decisions to take it was the worst," says Foy, and most authorities seem agreed that Soult should not have fought at Orthez. Though the position occupied was a good one, the dangers lay behind it, to the north the two Luy rivers, a difficult country, and the River Adour, on the left flank the gave de Pau. But Soult's repeated assurances to the Minister that he only awaited a favourable opportunity to assume the offensive, and the fact that having so long delayed his dicision, "the two armies are so close together that neither side can avoid it,"[1] practically compelled him to fight.[2]

His resolution was, however, a half-hearted one,

[1] Soult to Guerre, Orthez, 26th February, 1814.
[2] Vidal de la Blache: "He dared not attack, he dared not order a retreat."

WELLINGTON, THE CROSSING OF THE GAVES

as his order shows; this is coloured throughout by the thought of retreat. The dispositions of his troops show he intended to fight a purely defensive battle without any manœuvring and then to retreat, pivoting on his right as soon as heavy losses had been inflicted on the attacking Allies. A dangerous proceeding in the face of a man so sharp sighted, so quick of decision and such a master in the handling of troops as he must have known Wellington to be.

There was little probability of Soult's hope being fulfilled that the presence of his concentrated army would impose caution or delay on his adversary. The victor of Assye was not to be intimidated by the sight of the French army in array on the heights about Orthez. Wellington had now obtained the objects of all his previous manœuvres; the junction of his two groups, Bayonne and its citadel closely invested, the possession of the Bayonne-Baigts road, communication with Hope's corps, the bridge over the Adour were all his. Now a complete defeat of Soult's army was his immediate objective, and he did not delay. After such reconnaissance as was possible, his orders were issued and the troops put in motion.[1]

In a previous chapter an attempt has been made to show what perhaps Wellington's aim was in his plan of attack. He rightly judged that the French right was the key of their position, for this gained,

---

[1] The statement in "L'Invasion dans le Midi," Vidal de la Blache, Vol. II, p. 229, based on Robinson's "Life of Picton," that *at daybreak* on the 27th February, Wellington reconnoitred the ground held by the French right from the Roman camp seems hardly correct, seeing that the French held the St. Boes plateau with cavalry and infantry, had pickets and reconnoitring parties out till driven back by the advance of the 4th division.

AND THE BATTLE OF ORTHEZ

their retreat northwards was immediately in jeopardy. To attack the French left and gain possession of Orthez presented no particular advantage; if the battle was won the town would be gained also, and an advance in this direction with the gave de Pau close on its right might be exceedingly dangerous. The enemy's centre was strong and strongly held, and again presented no advantage. There can be no doubt Wellington's decision was the correct one, and the fact that the plan had to be altered does not disprove it.

The failure to gain possession of the ground held by the extreme French right about St. Boes is generally attributed to the difficulties of the ground; but, as far as it is permissible to judge from its present aspect, these do not seem to fully account for it. Failure would appear to have been due less to the ground than to the superior power and judicious placing of the French artillery. The accounts of those present bear witness to its murderous effect on the repeated and gallant efforts of the 4th division to gain the heights.[1]

The 6-pounders of Ross' and Gardiner's horse artillery were unable to cope with the heavier French guns. These two troops had no casualties amongst men or horses,[2] whilst Sympher's battery of 9-pounders, in a more exposed position on the left, had heavy losses, Major Sympher being killed by a round shot very soon after the battery came into action. The lack of details in the information

---

[1] Autobiography of Sergeant Laurence: "We rushed up the formidable heights, but were again and again driven back by the fearful play of the enemy's artillery."

[2] "Letters of General Sir A. Frazer," letter from Major Jenkinson, "A" Troop, R.H.A., to Lieutenant-Colonel Frazer, R.H.A.

WELLINGTON, THE CROSSING OF THE GAVES

available and the conflicting statements made, especially as regards the movements of the 7th division, shown by Napier as advancing against Taupin's right by the road from Dax, make it difficult to form an opinion as regards the leading of both Beresford and Cole.

The failure of the attempts to gain point 575 and the Dax road as soon as had been expected caused Wellington to change his plan, or rather the orders he had issued. Is this to be put to his credit or discredit? When under ordinary circumstances a scheme or project for any particular enterprise has been drawn up by a man who can be expected to be conversant with the conditions under which the enterprise will be carried out and worked, and that those conditions are reasonably stable, it is not unreasonable, if things go wrong from some defect inherent in the scheme, that the author should be accused of want of knowledge, of foresight or of want of appreciation of some factor in the case. But problems in war are not of this nature; there will generally be little knowledge, and that always doubtful, on which to base them, and conditions are never likely to be stable. " It is not just to reproach a General for a mere change of purpose. War, by its ever varying nature, demands that a leader should adapt himself and his plans to the pressure of circumstances, however variable, and he merits our highest praise by acting with decision and rapidity in the face of discouraging and unexpected changes. Napoleon, in the campaign of 1796, when placed in a similar position, changed his resolutions according to the requirements of each day, and made it apparent that a general should possess sufficient

AND THE BATTLE OF ORTHEZ

mental versatility not to confine himself to one plan only. To the man of ordinary ability, the thoughtful evolution of a definite course of action requires such mental effort that he clings tenaciously to his scheme and dreads any alterations in his projects."[1]

Though Soult was a man of considerably more than ordinary ability, this latter was one of his conspicuous failings as a general. A soldier critic of his own nation thus expresses it: "Il semblait que le plan conçu et ordonné dans le cabinet etait un décret du ciel, auquel on ne pouvait rien changer."[2]

Though possessed of a lively strategic imagination, which led him to favour vigorous operations, when it came to put them into action in the field he failed from lack of determination and that lightning glance which tells a commander during an action that the decisive moment has arrived when his attack must be pushed home.

Wellington's mind was of quite a different type; it was full of expedients; when he found he could not act in one way, without hesitation he tried something else.[3] When his plans, which he likened to a set of rope harness, did not appear to work out as he wished and the harness broke, he did not stand still, but tied a knot in it, and did what he considered the next best thing. That he was so readily able

---

[1] Count Yorck von Wartenburg, " Napoleon as a General " (Wolseley Series).
[2] General M. Larmarque, quoted in " L'Invasion dans le Midi," Vol. I, p. 149.
[3] Sir Harry Smith records that at the battle of Toulouse about 2 p.m., when things were not going well, Wellington exclaimed, " Ha—by Gad, this won't do, I must try something else."

WELLINGTON, THE CROSSING OF THE GAVES

to do so is probably connected with the power he had of dismissing at will any particular subject from his mind. Blakiston, who had served under him in India and knew him well, says: "He had the power, I have rarely seen, of dismissing a subject from his mind whenever he chose, so that in the most difficult situations he could converse on familiar terms, or, while ordinary minds were fretted to death, he could lie down and sleep soundly under the most trying circumstances."[1] As an instance of the first, he remarks that during the battle of Orthez, "while we were amusing ourselves with conjectures of what was next to be done, Lord Wellington was walking his horse, quietly chatting with some of his staff just as if nothing of consequence was going on, although it was clear his principal attack was partially repulsed."

In his observations on the battle Napier says: "For two hours the 3rd division and the Hussars remained close to him (Soult), covering the march of the 6th and Light divisions through the narrow ways leading from the bridge of Berenx up to the main road; the infantry had no defined position, the cavalry had no room to extend, and there were no troops between them and Beresford who was then in march by the heights of Baigts to the Dax road. If the French General had pushed a column across the marsh to seize the Roman camp, he would have

[1] "Military Adventures," Vol. II. Major Blakiston was an officer of the Indian army at home on leave in 1813. Being desirous of seeing service in the Peninsula and knowing Wellington personally, he wrote to him, receiving a favourable reply, and obtaining permission proceeded to headquarters at Frenada in March, 1813, where he was "graciously received, and was shortly afterwards appointed to a Caçadore regiment in Kempt's brigade of the Light division."

AND THE BATTLE OF ORTHEZ

separated the wings of the Allies; then pouring down the Peyrehorade road with Foy's, Darmagnac's and Villatte's divisions he would probably have overwhelmed the 3rd division before the other two could have extracted themselves from the defiles. Picton therefore had grounds for uneasiness."

The charge brought against Wellington in the above statement is that for two hours he left Picton unsupported whilst open to an attack by at least three divisions of the French army. The two hours mentioned are not specified, but are evidently meant to be those taken by the 6th and Light divisions to join Picton from the left bank of the gave, say between 6.30 a.m. to 8.30 a.m. on 27th February. The criticism also implies that the whole of Beresford's column marched away from the assembly point near Baigts about 6.30 a.m. or soon after. In Chapter XV an attempt has been made to ascertain the approximate times of the startings of the various divisions and of their arrivals at their positions prior to the commencement of the engagement. If these are in any way correct, the premises on which Napier founds his criticism are false.

Assuming, as appears justified from the memorandum quoted, that all the troops were assembled under arms at daybreak, 6.30 a.m., we may endeavour to establish what the force about Baigts was during these two hours. Taking the first, 6.30 to 7.30 a.m.—from 6.30 to 7.10 a.m. there were present the 3rd, 4th and 7th divisions. At 7.10 a.m. the 4th division started, by 7.30 a.m. more than half of the division would still be on the ground and the head of the 6th division would be

WELLINGTON, THE CROSSING OF THE GAVES

arriving. Second hour, 7.30 to 8.30 a.m.—3rd division, 7th division, a gradually diminishing portion of 4th division, the whole of it within reach of recall, the greater part of the 6th division and all the cavalry, with the head of the Light division approaching. This statement shows there must be grave doubts as to the justice of the criticism. There are other reasons also. It seems unreasonable to believe that a general of Wellington's experience, his tactical skill and insight into his opponent's possible movements would for no apparent reason put a considerable part of his force into such danger. The very change in Soult's attitude, a stand instead of a continuous retreat, would be enough to induce caution on his part. It must also be remembered that he himself had crossed the pontoon bridge that morning and knew how the crossing was going on. It may be said, therefore, that during these two hours there were at least three divisions and two brigades of cavalry about or in close proximity to Baigts, which could be used to meet any French force thrown against them. All the three French divisions, which Napier considers could have been used to attack the 3rd, had moved during the night or very early morning from their positions on the previous afternoon, and were now at a greater distance from Baigts. Villatte's division on the heights above Rontun was about four miles from the allied assembly point. Napier too appears to neglect the influence of Hill's force, the actual strength of which was then unknown to Soult.

Wellington and others who were present have paid generous tributes to the skill with which Soult

AND THE BATTLE OF ORTHEZ

and his officers conducted the retreat of the French army. Taking advantage of all suitable ground, they opposed the advancing Allies "with solid masses of infantry," which in their turn "with great order and regularity,"[1] fell back on similar bodies. For a time all went well and in text-book style. But at length heavy casualties, fatigue and the ever increasing menace to their line of retreat by Hill's troops had their effects on diminishing moral, till the retreat became a flight, and the army was saved only by the nature of the country and the wound Wellington had received. Had he been able to ride as he usually did, it is unlikely there would have been cause for Thackwell's complaint of unenterprising cavalry leading. That the retreat was to a certain extent an already prepared one, does not materially lessen the fine performance of the French soldiers.

Though Wellington in this battle did not attain all he had perhaps hoped for, he was certainly not dissatisfied with the result.[2] Nor could he be otherwise than satisfied with what had so far been achieved during this campaign; all his immediate objects had been obtained, his opponent had been fairly beaten in a stand-up fight, and the French army having suffered heavily in men and moral, was now retreating northwards and away from Suchet. The situation now offered interesting possibilities. If Soult could be closely followed and pushed on to Bordeaux, a city lying on the left bank of the Garonne and not easily defended,

---
[1] Picton to Colonel Pleydell, 4th March, 1814.
[2] Wellington to Hope, Orthez, 28th February, 1814: "I have the pleasure to inform you that we completely beat Marshal Soult yesterday."

WELLINGTON, THE CROSSING OF THE GAVES

his whole army might again be caught there whilst attempting to cross the great river. Even if this could not be attained, the possession of the city and its great port seemed assured, which, with the waterways of both the Adour[1] and the Garonne, would greatly facilitate the supply of the allied army.

Perhaps no better evidence of the soundness of Wellington's strategy during this period of the campaign can be produced than his opponent's apologia for his conduct of it. Writing on the 4th March to the Minister of War in reply to the Emperor's strictures on his action, Soult states: "Your Excellency has told me that in order to prevent Bayonne being besieged I should never have moved to a distance from that place. I believe I carried out this instruction by keeping in proximity to Bayonne until the last moment possible, that is to say as long as I could do so without endangering the safety of the army. But the enemy's manœuvres obliged me to move to a distance, and I changed direction when I saw I was being pushed towards Bordeaux, where probably I should not have had time to cross the river in any order. Some months ago I thought of securing for myself a supporting second line by repairing the enceinte of Dax and forming an entrenched camp there, but I found I had not the means to do so and had to give up the idea. I doubt if I could have maintained myself there, because the enemy, owing to his great numerical superiority, could by repeating his outflanking

---

[1] The Adour was navigable by boats and barges carrying 15 to 20 tons from St. Sever to Bayonne.

AND THE BATTLE OF ORTHEZ

manœuvres have put the army in peril and obliged me to retire precipitately on Bordeaux by the Grandes Landes." [1]

[1] Soult to Guerre, Rabastens, 4th March, 1814.

APPENDIX A

ORDER OF BATTLE OF THE ANGLO-PORTUGUESE ARMY AND OF THE SPANISH TROOPS UNDER THE COMMAND OF FIELD-MARSHAL THE MARQUIS OF WELLINGTON

ANGLO-PORTUGUESE ARMY

Staff

Commanding the Forces: Field-Marshal the MARQUIS OF WELLINGTON, K.G., K.B.
Military Secretary: Lieutenant-Colonel Lord FITZROY SOMERSET.
Quartermaster-General: Major-General. Sir GEORGE MURRAY, K.B.
Adjutant-General: Major-General Hon. E. PAKENHAM.
Commanding Royal Artillery: Lieutenant-Colonel A. DICKSON, R.A.
Chief Engineer: Lieutenant-Colonel ELPHINSTONE, R.E.

Civil Staff

Commissary-General: Sir R. KENNEDY.
Principal Medical Officer: Inspector-General J. McGRIGOR, M.D.
Purveyor-General: Mr. JAMES.
Judge Advocate: Mr. F. LARPENT, Barrister-at-Law.

Composition of Divisions and Brigades

Lieutenant-General Sir STAPLETON COTTON, K.B., commanding the Cavalry

Brigades

Major-General O'Loghlin (Household brigade): 1st and

WELLINGTON

2nd Life Guards, Royal Horse Guards (2 squadrons of each).
Major-General W. Ponsonby (Lieutenant-Colonel Lord Charles Manners in temporary command): 5th Dragoon Guards, 3rd and 4th Dragoons.
Major-General Fane (Lieutenant-Commander Clifton in temporary command): 3rd Dragoon Guards, 1st Royal Dragoons.
Major-General Bock (Lieutenant-Colonel von Bulow in temporary command[1]): 1st and 2nd King's German Legion Dragoons.
Major-General Vandeleur: 12th and 16th Light Dragoons.
Colonel Vivian: 18th Hussars, 1st King's German Legion Hussars.
Major-General Fane (B.): 13th and 14th Light Dragoons.
Major-General Lord Edward Somerset (Hussar brigade): 7th, 10th and 15th Hussars.

Portuguese Cavalry

Brigadier-General D'Urbau: 1st, 6th, 11th and 12th Portuguese cavalry.
Colonel Campbell: 4th Portuguese cavalry (not brigaded).

The cavalry brigades were not numbered; in orders, etc., they were always designated by the names of their permanent commanders.
All the heavy cavalry and the Portuguese cavalry were in Spain. The only brigades with the army at this time were those commanded by Generals Fane (B.), Lord Edward Somerset, Vandeleur and Colonel Vivian.

Royal Artillery

Lieutenant-Colonel A. DICKSON commanding

Royal Horse Artillery

Lieutenant-Colonel A. S. FRAZER commanding

Troop
A The Chestnut Troop: Lieutenant-Colonel H. D. Ross, Brevet-Major Jenkinson in command, with Light division.

[1] General Bock was drowned in February, whilst on passage to England.

WELLINGTON, THE CROSSING OF THE GAVES

Troop
D   Captain G. Bean with Fane's cavalry brigade.
E   Major R. W. Gardiner with Hussar brigade.
F   Lieutenant-Colonel J. Webber Smith: Reserve artillery with Hope's corps.
I   Captain R. M. Cairnes: Reserve artillery with Hope's corps.

Field Artillery

Captain C. Dansey's brigade: 1st division.
Captain S. Maxwell's brigade: 2nd division.
Captain G. Turner's brigade: 3rd division.
Captain C. Mosse's brigade: 5th division.
Captain J. Michell's brigade: 6th division.
Major J. B. Parker's brigade: 7th division.
Captain T. A. Brandreth's Reserve artillery with Hope's corps.
King's German Legion artillery.
Major Sympher's brigade with 4th division.

Portuguese Artillery

Major Cunha's brigade with Portuguese division.
Major Arriaga's brigade: Reserve artillery with Hope's corps.
Captain C. Michell's brigade: Reserve artillery with Hope's corps.

Heavy Artillery

Captain W. Morrison's 18-pounder brigade with Hope's corps.
Mountain artillery, 1 brigade of 8 3-pounder guns.
Rocket detachment, Captain H. B. Lane, arrived in December, 1813, 50 men.

Ammunition Supply
1st division gun ammunition: Captain T. Hutchesson's company R.A.
2nd division gun ammunition: Captain Cleeves', R. German artillery, company.
3rd division gun ammunition: Captain W. Bentham's company R.A.
4th division gun ammunition: Captain Thompson's company R.A.

AND THE BATTLE OF ORTHEZ

1st division small arms ammunition: Lieutenant Preusser's, R. German artillery, company.
2nd division small arms ammunition: Captain P. Faddy's company R.A.

Each troop and brigade had five guns, 9 or 6-pounders, and one 5½-inch howitzer. The horse artillery troops had generally two 9-pounders and three 6-pounders; their establishment of horses, draft and riding, was from 175 to 183. The British and German field brigades had 9-pounder guns; the Portuguese artillery with 2nd division were 6-pounders. The mountain artillery guns were 3-pounders, some captured from the French and some brought from Portugal; they were carried on mules.

Engineers

5th, 6th, 7th and 8th companies: Royal Sappers and Miners

Infantry Divisions—First Division

Lieutenant-General the Hon. Sir JOHN HOPE, K.B., commanding a corps
Major-General HOWARD commanding

Brigades
1st, Colonel Maitland: 1/1st and 3/1st Guards and 1 company 5/60th Rifles.
2nd, Major-General Stoppard: 1st Coldstream Guards, 1/3rd Guards, 1 company 5/60th Rifles.
Major-General Hinuber: 1st, 2nd and 5th Line battalions K.G. Legion.
Colonel Busch: 1st and 2nd Light battalions K.G. Legion.
Major-General Lord Aylmer: 2/62nd, 76th, 77th and 85th Foot. This originally independent brigade was now attached to 1st division.

Second Division

Lieutenant-General Sir ROWLAND HILL, K.B., commanding a corps
Lieutenant-General Hon. W. STEWART, K.B.

Brigades
Major-General Barnes: 1/50th Foot, 1/71st Highland

WELLINGTON, THE CROSSING OF THE GAVES

Light Infantry, 1/92nd Highlanders, 1 company 5/60th Rifles.

Major-General Byng: 1/3rd (Buffs) and 1/57th Foot, 1st provisional battalion 2/31st and 2/66th Foot, 1 company 5/60th Rifles.

Major-General Pringle (Pringle was wounded at Garris, 15th February, and Colonel Hon. R. O'Callaghan, 39th Regiment, took command of the brigade): 1/28th, 2/34th and 1/39th Foot, 1 company 5/60th Rifles.

Colonel Harding: 6th and 18th Portuguese, 6th Caçadores.

Portuguese Division

Major-General LE COR commanding

Brigadier-General Da Costa: 2nd and 14th Portuguese.
Brigadier-General Buchan: 4th and 10th Portuguese, 10th Caçadores.

Third Division

Lieutenant-General Sir THOMAS PICTON, K.B.

Major-General Brisbane: 1/45th Foot, 74th Highlanders, 1/88th Connaught Rangers, headquarters and 3 companies 5/60th Rifles.

Colonel Keane: 1/5th Fusiliers, 2/83rd, 2/87th and 94th Foot.

Major-General Power: 9th and 21st Portuguese, 11th Caçadores.

Fourth Division

Lieutenant-General Hon. Sir G. LOWRY COLE, K.B.

Major-General W. Anson: 3/27th, 1/40th and 1/48th Foot, 2nd provisional battalion 2nd Queen's and 2/53rd Foot, 1 company 5/60th Rifles.

Major-General Ross: 1/7th Royal Fusiliers, 1/20th Foot, 1/23rd Royal Welsh Fusiliers, 1 company Brunswick Oels.

Colonel Vasconcellos: 11th and 23rd Portuguese, 7th Caçadores.

AND THE BATTLE OF ORTHEZ

Fifth Division

Major-General Hon. C. COLVILLE

Major-General Hay: 3/1st Royals, 1/9th, 1/38th and 2/47th Foot, 1 company Brunswick Oels.
Major-General Robinson: 1/4th, 2/59th and 2/84th Foot, 1 company Brunswick Oels.
Colonel de Regoa: 3rd and 15th Portuguese, 8th Caçadores.

Sixth Division

Lieutenant-General Sir H. CLINTON, K.B.

Major-General Pack: 1/42nd Black Watch, 1/79th and 1/91st Highlanders, 1 company 5/60th Rifles.
Major-General Lambert: 1/11th, 1/32nd, 1/36th and 1/61st Foot.
Colonel Douglas: 8th and 12th Portuguese, 9th Caçadores.

Seventh Division

Lieutenant-General the EARL OF DALHOUSIE, K.B.
Major-General WALKER in temporary command.

Colonel Gardiner: 1/6th Foot, 3rd provisional battalion 2/24th and 2/38th Foot, headquarters Brunswick Oels.

Major-General Inglis: 51st Light Infantry, 68th and 1/82nd Foot, Chasseurs Britanniques.
Colonel Doyle: 7th and 19th Portuguese, 2nd Caçadores.

Light Division

Major-General Baron CHARLES ALTEN

Major-General Kempt: 1/43rd Light Infantry, 2/95th and 3/95th Rifles, 1st Caçadores.
Colonel Barnard: 1/52nd Light Infantry, 1/95th Rifles, 17th Portuguese, 3rd Caçadores.

Unattached Portuguese Brigades

Major-General Bradford: 13th and 24th Portuguese, 5th Caçadores.

WELLINGTON, THE CROSSING OF THE GAVES

Brigadier-General A. Campbell: 1st and 16th Portuguese, 4th Caçadores.

ROYAL STAFF CORPS

Corps of Guides

According to the weekly state of 17th February, 1814, the strength of the Anglo-Portuguese army (exclusive of officers)[1] present in the ranks and fit for duty was as follows:

Cavalry	9,303
Infantry	53,524
Horse artillery (state of 25th February)	822
Foot (state of 25th February)	3,419
Engineers (state of 25th February)	420
Staff corps	144
Total fighting strength	67,632

In addition to the above there were on this date:

Sick and wounded	19,034
On command (includes 1,169 artillerymen)	6,847
Missing and prisoners of war still on strength of units	3,070
Brought forward	67,632
Total	96,583

The following table gives the strength of the cavalry and infantry divisions of the army on 30th December, 1813. As the differences in the fighting strength between the two states only amounts to 21 for the cavalry and 419 for the infantry divisions, the figures given may be taken as the approximate strength of the divisions when the campaign opened.

[1] As the regimental returns were probably sent in several days previous to 17th, this state practically represents the strength when the campaign opened.

AND THE BATTLE OF ORTHEZ

On 30th December, 1813, the strength present under arms and fit for duty (British, German Legion and Portuguese) of the divisions of the Anglo-Portuguese army was as follows:

	Officers.	Sergeants.	Trump'ters and Drum'ers.	Rank and File.	Total, exclusive of Officers.	Remarks.
British cavalry division	459	541	103	7,351	7,995	
Portuguese cavalry	159	74	42	1,213	1,331	
Total cavalry	618	615	145	8,564	9,327	
Infantry Divisions						Artillery not included.
1st division	259	385	140	5,948	6,473	
2nd division	325	435	189	6,193	6,817	
Portuguese division	180	208	71	3,670	3,949	
3rd division	327	400	194	5,343	5,937	
4th division	337	358	141	5,345	5,844	
5th division	246	307	128	3,616	4,051[1]	[1] Had suffered heavy losses at S. Sebastian and Bayonne, and had at this time 3200 wounded and sick.
6th division	317	360	143	5,219	5,722	
7th division	321	296	122	4,621	5,041	
Light division	208	265	121	3,773	4,159	
Aylmer's brigade	117	115	53	1,613	1,781	
Bradford's Portuguese brigade	72	124	63	1,529	1,716	
Campbell's Portuguese brigade	110	122	30	1,463	1,615	
Total Infantry	2,819	3,377	1,395	48,333	53,105	

SPANISH TROOPS

In January, 1813, Wellington had been appointed by the Spanish Regency Generalissimo of the Spanish armies. Though he had already tendered his resignation he still continued to exercise the command through a small Spanish staff at his headquarters under General L. Wimpffen, the Chief of the Staff. To Wellington personally was attached General Don M. de Alava.

At this time the Spanish troops serving directly under Wellington were:

4th Spanish army (Gallicians), commanded by Lieutenant-General Don M. Freyre, eight so-called divisions, one of which was besieging Santona and one, that of Longa, sent behind the Ebro for misconduct (murder and pillage) after the battle of the Nivelle.

The reserve army of Andalusia, commanded by General P. Giron, two divisions.

3rd Spanish army, commanded by the Prince of Anglona, three divisions.

It is difficult to give, even approximately, what the fighting strength of these troops was. Wellington, in a letter to Hope on 23rd December, 1813, estimated the strength of a Spanish division brought up to St. Jean de Luz as " about 4,000." If this figure be taken as a basis, the strengths may be put approximately as follows:[1]

4th Army, 5 regular divisions	20,000
Mina's division, formed from partisan bands operating in Navarre and Aragon	6,000
Andalusian reserve	8,000
3rd Army	12,000
	46,000

When the campaign opened three divisions of the 4th Army were with the Anglo-Portuguese army on French territory. Part of Mina's troops were investing Jaca; and the remainder in the Baztan valley. The rest of the 4th Army was cantoned beyond the Bidassoa about Irun and Oyarzun. The Andalusian reserve was in the Baztan valley, and the 3rd Army about Pamplona.

Two more divisions of the 4th Army were subsequently brought up into France, and joined Hope's corps at the time of the crossing of the Adour.

[1] A state of the allied army, dated 10th November, 1813, dropped at Passages by a British staff officer, which found its way to General Thouvenot, Governor of Bayonne, gives the following figures : 4th Army, 21,000; Mina, 7,000; Andalusians, 10,000.

APPENDIX B

ORDER OF BATTLE OF THE ARMY OF THE PYRENEES AFTER THE DEPARTURE OF THE REINFORCEMENTS SENT TO THE GRANDE ARMÉE IN JANUARY, 1814, AND THE INCLUSION OF ABBÉ'S DIVISION IN THE GARRISON OF BAYONNE

Commanding in Chief: Maréchal Soult Duc de Dalmatie.
Chief of Staff: Lieutenant-Général Count Gazan.
Commanding artillery: Général de division, Tirlet.
Commanding engineers: Général de division, Lévy.
Commissary-General: M. Faviers.
Surgeon-in-Chief: Rapatel.
Lieutenant-Generals commanding corps: Baron Clausel, Counts d'Erlon and Reille.
Commanding the cavalry: General Baron P. Soult.
1st brigade, General of brigade: Berton, 7 squadrons (present and fit for duty) 1,497
2nd brigade, General of brigade: Viall, 10 squadrons (present and fit for duty) 1,469

Total (cavalry) 2,966

Infantry

1st division: General Foy; Generals of brigade—
Fririon, Berlier (present and fit for duty) . 4,767[1]

[1] The strength of the infantry divisions is taken from the state of 15th January, 1814, as given by Vidal de la Blache in footnote to page 212, "L'Invasion dans le Midi," Vol. II. The total is stated to be 32,234, but as the figures stand it should be 34,234. After this date two divisions of infantry and three brigades of cavalry left to join Napoleon, and before doing so, there were certain transfers of men between certain divisions which might be reckoned to reduce the strength of those remaining by about 1,000 men. But against this may be placed the strength of national guards, not included in state, serving in Harispe's division, which was not less than 1,500 when the campaign opened. The figures for 15th January have, therefore, been retained as the divisional strengths.

WELLINGTON, THE CROSSING OF THE GAVES

2nd division: General Darmagnac; Generals of brigade—Chassé, Gruardet	5,642
4th division: General Taupin; Generals of brigade—Rey, Béchaud	6,428
5th division: General Marinsin[1] (Rouget, in temporary command); Generals of brigade—Rouget, Barbot	5,157
6th division: General Darricau[1] (Villatte, in temporary command); Generals of brigade—Saint Pol, Lamorandière	5,388
8th division: General Harispe; Generals of brigade—Dature, Paris, Baurot	6,852
Total (infantry)	34,234
Troops not in divisions, i.e., artillery and its train, sappers and miners, pontoon train, gendarmerie and military train (45 guns)	5,953[2]
Grand total of field army	43,153

Garrisons

Bayonne, General Thouvenot, Governor (of whom 11,183 were on duty under arms) (state 24th February)	13,667
Navarrenx (state 24th February)	991
St. Jean Pied-de-Port (state 24th February)	2,360
Lourdes (state 24th February)	61
Santona (state 24th February)	1,981
Total	19,060

[1] Marinsin was detached on 30th January to organize the national guards of the High Pyrenees, of which department he was a native. Darricau, a native of the Landes, was sent to that department for the same purpose on 20th January, and Villatte appointed to command his division temporarily.

[2] On 16th January, before departure of reinforcements for Grande Armée, total was 7,366.

APPENDIX C

TREATY OF VALENÇAY

THE principal articles of the treaty were as follows:

1. That from the date of ratification of this treaty there shall be peace and amity between H.M. Ferdinand VII. and his successors, and H.M. the Emperor and King and his successors.
2. That all hostilities between the two nations, so far as their continental possessions are concerned, shall cease from the date of ratification—with later dates as regards extra European possessions.
3. That the Emperor recognizes Don Ferdinand and his successors as King of Spain and the Indies, according to the hereditary rights established by the laws of Spain.
4. That the Emperor recognizes the integrity of Spanish territory as it existed prior to the present war.
5. That the provinces and fortresses occupied by French troops shall be evacuated in their present condition to governors and troops sent by the King of Spain.
6. That King Ferdinand engages on his part to maintain the integrity of Spanish territory, its islands and fortresses, especially Matron and Ceuta, and engages to cause all provinces, fortresses and places occupied by the British army to be evacuated by them.

Then follows provisions regarding prisoners of war, the rights of Spaniards who have served and followed King Joseph into France, that the evacuation of Spain by French and British troops shall be simultaneous, and the allowances to be paid to ex-King Charles IV. and his Consort from Spanish funds, and that ratification of the treaty should take place within one month or sooner, if practicable. By an additional article signed on 11th March, 1814, the ratification term was extended to 105 days from that date.

APPENDIX D

ORDER ISSUED BY SOULT ON THE EVENING OF 26TH FEBRUARY FOR THE OCCUPATION OF A POSITION ABOUT ORTHEZ BY THE ARMY OF THE PYRENEES

LIEUTENANT-GENERAL COUNT REILLE will take command of the 4th division (Taupin) and the 5th (Rouget). He will also have temporarily that of the 9th (Paris). The 21st. Chasseurs à cheval will also be temporarily attached to his command.

To-morrow, at daybreak, he will extend his line to St. Boes, keeping always to the crest of the high ground. He will also reconnoitre the Tihl (Dax) road, and must watch with the greatest care the movements of the enemy in front of St. Boes, and on the slopes which descend towards Baigts and Ramous.

The Count d'Erlon will change the front of the 1st. and 2nd divisions (Foy and Darmagnac), and will place them in the position which the 2nd division occupied this morning, having the ravine in front of them. Posts only are to be left on the spur crossed by the grande route (Point du Jour) where these two divisions were this evening. He will move his artillery to the plateau in rear, and place it towards the junction of the roads to Dax and Sallespisse. So placed Count d'Erlon will be in a position to support, if necessary, the right wing under Count Reille. The 15th Chasseurs is temporarily attached to his command.

Lieutenant-General Clausel will move the 6th division (Villatte) in rear of Orthez, and place it so as to be able to support the 8th division (Harispe), or move it rapidly to the plateau in rear of St. Boes to join the rest of the army, should an order to do so be received. The 8th division (Harispe) will leave in Orthez only an outpost to defend the bridge. It will have posts supported by one battalion in advance of the suburb on the

WELLINGTON

Peyrehorade road. The remainder of the division will be posted in echelons behind the town from the old château (Tour de Moncade) as far as the positions beyond it, which are almost parallel to the Dax road. The 8th division will therefore form the extreme left of the line, and will be in a position to defend Orthez if the enemy makes a frontal attack on it. If the division is forced to retire, it can manœuvre on the same crest, and command by its fire the grande route to Sallespisse, of which General Harispe must always keep command.

If the 6th division (Villatte) has to be moved to the plateau behind St. Boes, Lieutenant-General Clausel will move with it, and, when it joins the line, the 9th division (Paris) will once again come under his command; and he will give to General Harispe the necessary orders required by the change of position.

General P. Soult will order the Legion of the Hautes-Pyrénées, which is at Larom (three miles west of Pau), to retire at daybreak to-morrow on Pau to defend the town. He will give similar orders to the 22nd Chasseurs à cheval and direct the officer commanding that unit to send constant patrols on the roads leading to Oloron and Monein. These patrols are to advance until they come into contact with the enemy. He will also instruct Colonel Dessfossé to post a strong detachment at Lescar to reconnoitre the road to Orthez so that he may have constant information as to what is going on there. Moreover, the 22nd Chasseurs and the Legion of the Hautes-Pyrénées will be at the disposal of General Coutard for the defence of Pau. General Coutard must be so informed, and be directed to send his reports to the Chief of the Staff, at the same time informing the Generals in the line, and especially General Harispe, of all that takes place in the direction of Pau.

General P. Soult will leave two regiments of Light cavalry as well as the 25th Light infantry at General Berton's disposal, giving him instructions to watch the course of the gave from Lescar to Orthez, guarding the fords and defending them as far as he possibly can. If the enemy forces a crossing, and General Berton is obliged to retire, he will do so in the direction of Sault de Navailles, defending the ground foot by foot, and retarding the enemy's advance. In this case General Berton will report his movements to General Harispe and, if necessary, take his orders. General Berton must take every care not to allow himself to be forestalled by the enemy at Sault de Navailles, and, if he is obliged to

WELLINGTON, THE CROSSING OF THE GAVES

fall back there, he will take up a position so as to be able to protect the movement of the army.

Having given these instructions to General Berton, General P. Soult, with the two other regiments now with him on the left, will move over the hills to Sallespisse so as to arrive there at daybreak.

If it is necessary for the army to retire to-morrow, it will do so on Sault de Navailles. Count Reille will so manœuvre as to have a division at Amou to defend that point.

The reserve artillery will be at Sault de Navailles.

The headquarter ambulance at Sallespisse.

All the trains of the army will move this night to Sault de Navailles.

Engineer troops to be moved by the Dax road to its junction with that to Sallespisse, and will immediately proceed to repair the latter.

(*Signed*) Maréchal Duc de Dalmatie.

P.C.C.

Le Lieutenant-Général Comte Gazan,
Chef de l'état-Major Général.

INDEX

Abbé, General, 94, 107, 108, 109
Adour, River, 91, 92, 93, 97, 110, 114, 117, 126, 145, 194, 264
  crossing of, 118, 119, 120, 123, 161, 162, 165, 172, 173, 180, 185, 186, 193, 202
Aire, 118
Alliance, Grand, of Powers, acts and policies, 19-28, 102, 104
America, war with, 39, 74
Anglona, Prince of, 195, 275
Army, Anglo-Portuguese—
  bases and depôts of, 73, 74, 75
  casualties, 214, 253
  confidence in its commander, 138
  distribution on opening of campaign, 80, 81, 82
  general headquarters of, 125, 129, 147, 148, 161, 164, 194
  health, medical and hospitals, 33, 79, 80
  moral of, 33, 68, 213
  movements of. *See* divisions
  organization and strength of 204, 205 and Appendix A, 267 *et seq.*
  postal communication, 75, 76
  Staff, 267
  Staff, work of, 213
  supply of, 75, 77, 78
  transport, sea, 74, 75; land, 76, 77

Army, British, 10, 33, 38-43, 68
Army, French, of Pyrenees—
  after Vitoria, 83
  call of the Emperor for reinforcements, 102-106
  casualties, 139, 253
  communications of, 123, 209
  discipline of, 84
  distribution of, January, 1814, 93-97
  distribution when campaign opened, 110, 111, 121
  funds for, 84, 85, 87
  general headquarters, 93, 109, 132, 145, 149, 156, 178, 200
  medical and hospitals, 86
  moral of, 84, 85
  movements prior to opening of campaign, 92-101
  movements after opening. *See* divisions
  retreat from Orthez, 249, 262, 263
  strength of, 203, 204 and Appendix B
  supply of, 83, 85, 86, 87, 91
Army, Portuguese, 69, 70 and Appendix A
Army, Spanish, 71, 72, 73 and Appendix A
Arriverete, 144, 151, 171
Artillery, allied, 268, 269, 270
Ascain, 81
Ayherre, 97, 100, 110

INDEX

BAÏGORRY, ST. ETIENNE DE, 129, 143
Baigts, 189, 192, 197, 216, 223, 226, 231
Baltazar, Major, 84
Bardos, 92, 97, 101, 110
Barnard, Colonel, 228, 272
Barnes, Major-General, 242, 270
Barraute, 170
Bathurst, Earl, Secretary of State for War. *See* Wellington letters
Batty, Captain, "Campaign of Western Pyrenees," 117, 130, 182
Bayonne, 37, 80, 93, 94, 95, 96, 107, 110, 118, 119, 120, 121, 193, 203
Baztan Valley, 73
Bechaud, General, 236
Bell, General, "Rough Notes;" 241
Beresford, Marshal Sir W.; 69, 71, 125-29, 132, 157, 164, 187, 188, 190, 191, 210, 212, 223, 229, 232, 246, 258
Berenx, 157, 183, 187, 193, 196, 197, 223
Berlier, General, 236
Bernadotte, Crown Prince of Sweden, 19, 28
Biaudos, 94, 194
Bidache, 92, 97, 101, 110, 144, 171
Bidarray, 129, 143
Bidassoa, crossing of, 29, 208
Bidouze, River, 92, 97, 143, 144, 145
Bilbao, 74
Blakiston, Major, "Military Adventures," 238, 246, 260
Blücher, Marshal, Prince, 18, 102
Bonloc, 81, 98, 128, 133, 141
Bordeaux, 37, 113, 117, 118, 130, 156, 263
Boucau, 131, 173, 186
Boyer, General, 94, 95, 106
Brisbane, General, 236, 240, 271
Briscous, 97, 129

Buchan, General, 97, 271
Bunbury, Colonel, 36, 43, 76, 80, 254
Burghersh, Lord, 25, 26
Byng, General, 137, 270

CADELL, "Campaigns of 28th Regiment," 133
Cadiz, 38, 55, 56
Cambo, 99
Came, 92, 97, 101, 110, 155
Campbell, Brigadier-General A., 186
Caresse, 185, 187
Carlos, Duke of San, 64, 65
Carlos, General Don, 162, 172, 186
Castaños, General, 51, 52, 54
Casualties. *See* Army, Anglo-Portuguese and French
Cauneille, 187, 188
Clarke, General, Duke de Feltre, French Minister of War. *See* Soult despatches
Clausel, Lieutenant-General, Baron, 92, 96, 101, 110, 157, 182, 197, 199, 221
Clerc, Commandant, "Campagne du Maréchal Soult," 158
Cole, Lieutenant-General Sir L., 239, 246, 258, 271
Commissariat Officer's Journal, 153, 172, 244
Convoy, Naval, 77
Cooper, Sergeant, "Rough Notes of Seven Campaigns," 185, 234
Cope, "History of Rifle Brigade," 146
Copons, General, 65
Cortes, Spanish, 49 *et seq.*
Cotton, Lieutenant-General Sir S., 99, 125-29, 170, 171, 179, 263
Curtis, Dr., 55

DARMAGNAC, GENERAL, 94, 97, 248
Darricau, General, 92, 97

INDEX

De Lancey, Colonel, 133, 194
Départ, 182, 184
D'Erlon, Lieutenant-General Count, 94, 110, 133, 156, 171, 179, 220, 241, 248
Dickson, Colonel, C.R.A., 268
Divisions and cavalry brigades, allied, movements of—
1st division, 162, 173, 180, 181, 185, 186
2nd division, 126, 128, 129, 132, 133, 136, 147, 148, 150, 152, 155, 170, 171, 177, 183, 223, 237, 238, 241, 249, 253
3rd division, 100, 128, 130, 133, 140, 146, 153, 155, 164, 170, 177, 180, 187, 222, 235, 236, 237, 239, 244, 245, 248, 253
4th division, 99, 100, 146, 148, 153, 171, 185, 188, 189, 190, 222, 226, 227, 235, 237, 239, 244, 245, 248, 253
5th division, 99, 162
6th division, 99, 100, 163, 170, 177, 192, 193, 222, 225, 234, 236, 237, 241, 248, 253
7th division, 99, 100, 126-29, 146, 148, 163, 171, 175, 185, 189, 222, 226, 227, 237, 244, 248, 249, 253
Light division, 99, 146, 148, 153, 163, 164, 167, 175, 177, 191, 193, 223, 225, 228, 229, 238, 243, 248, 253
Portuguese division, 126, 129, 136, 169, 223, 237, 241, 242, 248, 253
Bradford's Portuguese brigade, 162, 193
Campbell's Portuguese brigade, 162, 180, 186
Cavalry brigades, Vandeleur, 81, 163; Fane, 100, 127, 128, 130, 136, 144, 148, 155, 159, 169, 237, 238, 240, 242, 253; Vivian, 99, 100, 129, 130, 146, 148, 155, 170, 171, 182, 183, 187, 222, 228, 237, 248, 251, 253; Hussar, 99, 100, 129, 130, 144, 148, 155, 177, 178, 185, 189, 190, 228, 248, 250, 253
Artillery, 127, 128, 151, 169, 170, 184, 222, 223, 228, 236, 237, 239, 240, 241, 246, 257
Mina's division, 129, 147, 155, 163, 169, 170
Morillo's division, 100, 128, 129, 133, 136, 146, 150, 176, 180
Divisions, French—
I Foy, 92, 93, 100, 110, 143, 150, 153, 156, 157, 171, 183, 195, 198, 220, 221, 234, 236, 237, 239, 240
II Darmagnac, 94, 110, 150, 154, 157, 183, 195, 198, 236, 240, 247, 248
III Abbé, 94, 107
IV Taupin, 94, 96-98, 144, 150, 183, 196, 219, 234, 242, 245
V Rouget (late Marinsin), 94, 110, 133, 149, 157, 183, 196, 219, 242, 247
VI Villatte (late Darricau), 92, 97, 144, 150, 157, 178, 179, 182, 184, 196, 199, 221, 248
VIII Harispe, 97, 98, 111, 144, 150, 157, 182, 199, 221, 237, 247, 248, 251
Cavalry, P. Soult, 98, 111, 160, 164, 196, 199, 240, 252
Dognen, 169
Domezain, 144, 147, 151
Dumas, General, " Neuf mois de Campagnes," 211, 213, 216
Dumouriez, General, 30, 89, 117
Dyer, Major, R.A., 228

FANE, MAJOR-GENERAL. See Divisions, allied
Faverot, Colonel, 196, 197, 211
Favier, M., Commissary-General, 132, 206
Ferdinand VII, King of Spain, 61, 62 *et seq.*

INDEX

Fifty-second Regiment, 242
Foy, General, 196, 197, 239, and Divisions, French
France, public feeling in Southern, 87, 88-90, 165
Frazer, General Sir A., Letters of, 187, 190, 257
Freyre, General, 51, 52, 71, 153, 194, 273
Fririon, General, 236
Fuenterrabia, 74

GARONNE, RIVER, 113
Garris, 135-50, 141
Gave de Mauleon. See Saison, River
Gave d'Oloron, 152, 153, 154, 159, 166
Gave d'Oloron, crossing of, 166-71, 175-80
Gave de Pau, 110, 156, 171
Gazan, Lieutenant-General Count, 275, 280
Geneva, 102
Gestas, 150, 152, 170, 177
Giron, General, 51, 195, 274
Gneisenau, General, 19
Greenhill Gardyne, "Life of a Regiment," 139
Guinarthe, 152, 158
Guards, National, French, 96, 161, 200, 201

HABAS, 188, 218
Halsou, 81
Hamilton, "History of 14th Hussars," 147, 151
Hamley, "Operations of War," 167
Harbours, 73, 74
Harispe, General Count, 95, 96, 109, 133, and see Divisions, French
Hasparren, 81, 99, 126, 129, 133
Hastinques, 101, 155, 171
Helette, 97, 101, 111, 128-33, 136
Henderson, Colonel, 12, 119, 123, 208
Henry, Surgeon, "Events of a Military Life," 139, 230, 231, 241, 242, 249

Hill, Lieutenant-General Sir R., 81, 91, 125-29, 131, 155-59, 163, 164, 193, 195, 222, 231, 233, 237, 241, 249, 263
Hope, Lieutenant-General Hon. Sir J., 120, 162, 172, 173, 184, 185, 194

IRISSARY, 97
Irun, 73, 117
Isturitz, 142

JACA, 111, 129, 134, 136
Jenkinson, Major, 187, 189, 190
"Journal of a Commissariat Officer," 153, 172, 244
Joyeuse River, 96, 99, 110, 122, 128
Joyeuse River, II, 135

KEANE, COLONEL J., 179, 236
Kennedy, Sir J., Commissary-General, 76, 194, 267

LAAS, 160, 166
La Bastide-Clairence, 92, 97, 110, 143, 146, 163
La Bastide de Béarn, 145
La Costa heights, 128, 129, 143
Landes, the, 90, 117, 118, 161
Lapène, Lieutenant-Colonel, 154, 196, 240
Larpent, F. S., Judge-Advocate, his diary, 33, 76, 78, 112, 138, 161, 173, 224
Lawrence, Sergeant, "Autobiography," 257
Lescar, 199, 200, 210
Leval, General, 94
Lisbon, 37, 73, 74
Loubieng, 177
Louhossoa, 81, 129
Luy de Béarn River, 215, 252

MAGRET, HEIGHTS OF, 182, 184, 186, 211, 213, 231, 237
Masparraute, 141, 153
Mauleon, 164, 178, 196, 199, 209, 210, 211
McGrigor, Dr., P.M.O., 79, 80, 267
Meharin, 133, 135, 136

INDEX

Mendionde, 98
Metternich, Prince, 17, 67, 103
Mills, Major, 188
Mina, General, 88, 99, 109, 129, 185, and see Divisions, allied
Monein, I, 152, 155, 179
Monein, II, 178, 201
Mont de Marsan, 106, 118, 132
Montestrucq, 177
Montford, 177
Moorsom, "History of 52nd Regiment," 184
Motte de Tury, 242, 247
Murray, Major-General Sir G., Q.M.G., 115, 173, 193, 195, 224, and see Orders, movement

NABAS, 159, 169, 170
Napier, "History of Peninsular War," 138, 187, 189, 225, 249, 251, 260, 261, 262
Napoleon, Emperor, 16, 17, 18, 19, 20, 28, 102, 103, 104, 105, 205, 212, 258
Navarrenx, 145, 160, 163, 164, 168, 169, 178, 201, 203
Nive, River, crossing of, 29, 92, 130

O'CALLAGHAN, COLONEL HON. R., 138
O'Donoju, General, Spanish Minister of War, 51-60
Oeyregave, 153, 171
Oloron, 196, 199, 200, 210
Oporto, 73
Orders, movements, allied, 125-29, 162, 163, 169, 170, 171, 176, 177
Orègue, 141, 142
O'Reilly, Captain, R.N., 180, 181
Orion, 174, 175, 176, 177
Orthez, battlefield of, 161, 168, 173, 184, 188, 192, 195, 196, 198, 199, 210, 211, 213, 215 et seq.
Orthez, battle of, 219 et seq.
  orders for, 219-21, 229, 230, 231, Appendix D

Osserain, 151, 171, 172
PACKENHAM, MAJOR-GENERAL HON. E., Adjutant-General, 267
Palencia, 78
Paris, General, 96, 134, 198, 220, 247
Passages, 38, 74, 124
Pau, 106, 118, 178, 199, 200, 210
Penrose, Rear Admiral, 125, 161, 194
Pessarou, 97
Peyrehorade, 93, 96, 114, 155, 156, 157, 171, 180, 211
Picton, Lieutenant-General Sir T., 142, 178, 179, 185, 187, 210, 228, 229, 230, 249, 271
Plassotte, 220, 246
Pläswitz, armistice of, 17
Plymouth, depôt at, 75
Porte-de-Lanne, 94, 207, 208
Portuguese Army. See Army, Anglo-Portuguese
Prague, Congress of, 18
Pringle, Major-General, 137, 138
Prussia, 21
Puyoo, 184, 188, 190
Pyrenees foothills, 115

RAMOUS, 18
Reille, Lieutenant-General Count, 94, 95, 100, 107, 108, 109, 198, 219, 220
River crossings and defence, 167, 205
Rhine, allied crossing, 102
Roads and communications in area, 115-18, 153, 174, 175, 217, 219, 226, 227, 228, 242
Roquefort, 117
Roman camp, 218, 219, 223, 243
Ross, Major-General, 234, 235, 236, 239, 245
Ross Lewin, Major, "With 32nd in the Peninsula," 231
Russia, 22

INDEX

St. Boes, 198, 218, 223, 226, 228, 229, 234, 235, 238
St. Esteben, 141
St. Gladie, 152
St. Jean de Luz, 74, 81, 124, 165
St. Jean Pied-de-Port, 92, 117, 123, 147, 203
St. Palais, 135, 137, 139, 141, 145, 164, 185
St. Sever, 106, 108, 250, 252
St. Suzanne, 193, 197
Saison, River, 145, 148, 152, 155, 159, 160, 164
Salies, 174, 183, 185, 193, 197
Salles, 193
Sallespisse, 199, 200, 240, 241, 247, 248
San Sebastian, 28, 37, 74
Santander, 37, 44, 73
Sault de Navailles, 118, 200, 201, 250, 251, 252
Sauveterre, 149, 152, 159-60, 166, 168, 170, 174, 177, 178, 179, 185
Schwartzenburg, Prince, 19, 20, 25, 26, 28
Simmonds, Lieutenant G., his diary, 69, 175, 191, 192, 193
Smith, General Sir H., Autobiography of, 191, 217, 228, 234, 246, 259
Smythies, "History of 40th Regiment," 188
Spanish army, 71, 72, 73
Sorde, 171, 185
Souars, 237, 241
Soult, Marshal, Duke of Dalmatia—
  advance in January, 1814, and result, 98-101
  appointed to command army, 84
  army's lack of confidence in him, 84, 85
  asks for recall, 108, 109
  call from Napoleon for reinforcements, 102
  courses open to him at commencement of campaign and forecast of allied plans, 122, 123, 130, 131, 132
  decision to fight at Orthez, 198, 255
  decision to increase garrison of Bayonne and its command, 96, 97, 102, 106, 107, 108, 109
  despatches to Minister of War, 96, 101, 107, 109, 121, 132, 134, 145, 149, 156, 160, 161, 164, 172, 178, 200, 209, 247, 264
  difficulties as regards discipline and moral of army, money, supplies and transport, 84, 85, 86, 87, 91, 93
  dominated by Wellington, 110, 207, 264
  excessive entrenching about Bayonne and its effect, 96, 102, 207
  general headquarters, 93, 131, 132, 145, 147, 156, 161, 164
  military position after allies crossed Nive, 91-94
  reiteration of allied numerical superiority, 145, 202, 203, 204, 255, 264
  retreat from line of Bidouze, 144, 145
  retreat on Orthez, 160, 177, 178
  retreat to Bayonne after battle of Nivelle, 29
  stand on gave d'Oloron, 134, 145, 154, 165
  system of defence of country and river lines, 205-208
  weakness as a leader, 94, 95, 109, 110, 156, 197, 254, 255, 259
  working of his cavalry, 196, 199, 200, 210, 211
Stewart, Lieutenant-General Sir W., 147, 270
Suchet, Marshal, 84, 106, 263
Surtees, "Twenty-five Years in Rifle Brigade," 175, 178, 182

INDEX

TARBES, 210
Taupin, General. *See* Divisions, French
Thackwell, Lieutenant-General Sir J., diary, 133, 146, 186, 187, 219, 250, 251
Thouvenot, General, Governor of Bayonne, 93, 107
Toulouse, 113, 131, 156, 209, 259
Treilhard, General, 96, 97, 105

URCURAY, 81, 100, 126
Ursouia mountain, 131
Urt, 81, 93, 126, 164, 194
Ustarits, 100, 146

VALENÇAY, TREATY OF, 62-67, 103, Appendix C, 278
Vandeleur, Major-General, 81, 163, 193, 268
Vasconcellos, Brigadier-General, 235, 270
Vidal de la Blache, "L'Invasion dans le Midi," 73, 85, 106, 109, 165, 190, 203, 212, 241, 246, 256
Villatte, General. *See* Divisions, French
Vitoria, battle of, 16, 32, 73, 83
Vivian, C., "Life of Lord Vivian," 122, 146, 179, 235, 251, 268

WEATHER, 29-31, 72, 85, 100, 125, 146, 155, 164, 166, 173, 181, 182, 186, 219
Wellesley, Hon. Sir H., Minister to Spain, 46, 53, 54, 55, 57, 58, 63
Wellington, Field Marshal, Marquis of—
age and health, 32
at Garris, 137, 144, 145
command of Spanish armies, 47 *et seq.*
concealment of his troops, 160, 212, 213
confidence in his army, 232
crossing of the Adour, 118, 119, 120
daring, decision, coolness and promptness, 212, 232, 242, 259, 260

difficulties, some of, want of money, 34, 35, 36, 125; inadequate naval support, 37; the provisional battalions, 39; incident at Santander, 44; the Treaty of Valençay, 62 *et seq.*
doubts regarding plan of campaign of Northern Powers, 31
general headquarters, 125, 128, 129, 147, 148, 164, 169, 185, 194
influence over his army, 112, 138, 232
local policy and its results, 88, 89, 90
Napier's criticisms, battle of Orthez, 260, 261, 262
opinion of Soult as a leader, 254, 255
orders, battle of Orthez, and change of plan, 221, 222, 223, 229, 230, 231, 232, 239, 243, 258, 259
plan of campaign, considerations and reason regarding it, 112 *et seq.*
prestige, reputation and position as a commander, 32, 33, 138
relations with British Government, 32, 33; Great Powers, 32, 112; Portuguese Government, 70; Spanish Government. *See* Command, Spanish armies
strategy and measure of his generalship, 110, 214, 256, 259, 264
surprises, 119, 205, 208, 209, 210
wound, 246, 263
Wellington, letters, instructions and despatches to and from—
Bathurst, Earl, Secretary of State for War, 31, 33, 35, 36, 50, 56, 66, 68, 70, 75, 92, 100, 103, 113, 140, 144, 158, 213, 230, 249

287

INDEX

Beresford, Marshal, 48, 142, 143
Bunbury, Colonel, 43, 76
Burghersh, Lord, 72
Dumouriez, General, 30, 89, 194
Freyre, General, 71, 153, 194
Hill, Sir R., 99, 158, 159, 195
Hope, Sir J., 194, 263
Liverpool, Earl of, Prime Minister, 17, 75
O'Donoju, General, 52, 53, 54, 56, 72

Wellesley, Sir H., 51, 53, 54, 55, 57, 58, 60, 61, 72
Woodberry, Lieutenant, diary, 228
Woolright, " History of 57th Regiment," 133

YORCK VON WARTENBURG, COLONEL COUNT," Napoleon as a General," 258, 259
York, H.R.H. Duke of, Commander-in-Chief. *See* Provisional battalions, 39 *et seq.*